COMPLETE CREATIVE WRITING COURSE

Chris Sykes

Complete Creative Writing Course

Chris Sykes

First published in Great Britain in 2014 by John Murray Learning.
First published in the US in 2014 by The McGraw-Hill Companies, Inc.

This edition published by John Murray Learning in 2020
An imprint of John Murray Press, a division of Hodder & Stoughton Ltd,
An Hachette UK company

This paperback edition published in 2020

1

Database right Hodder & Stoughton (makers)
The *Teach Yourself* name is a registered trademark of Hachette UK.

A CIP catalogue record for this title is available from the British Library

Trade Paperback ISBN 9781529352467
eBook ISBN 9781529352450

Typeset by Cenveo® Publisher Services.

Printed and bound by CPI Group (UK) Ltd, Croydon, CR0 4YY

John Murray Press policy is to use papers that are natural, renewable and recyclable products and made from wood grown in sustainable forests. The logging and manufacturing processes are expected to conform to the environmental regulations of the country of origin.

John Murray Press
Carmelite House
50 Victoria Embankment
London EC4Y 0DZ

For Siobhan and Bertie

About the author

Chris Sykes has written poetry which has been published in the UK and USA. He has had three stage plays produced and has worked extensively on radio as a writer and, for a brief while, as a sports commentator. Over a period of 30 years he has taught creative writing in major UK universities such as Warwick, Oxford, City University London and the University of Sussex, as well as a variety of starting-to-write courses at the City Literary Institute, London. He has led writers' workshops at the Cheltenham Literary Festival and performed as a singer-songwriter at the Oxford Literary Festival. In 2008 he produced a CD of 12 songs entitled Walking on the Beach. He is the author of Your Evening Class: Creative Writing, The Writer's Source Book and How to Craft a Great Story, all for Hodder & Stoughton. He is well versed in helping people get started in writing, nurture the necessary skills to tell a story, create believable characters and develop narrative, and has had many pupils go on to publish their writing. He currently lives in Lewes, East Sussex.

Acknowledgements

I would like to thank all the writing students I have worked with in 30 years of teaching creative writing. I honed and developed many of the exercises in this book in writing classes in Warwick, Leamington Spa, Oxford, High Wycombe, London, Brighton and other places, including mid-Atlantic on the *QM2*. Thank you all.

Please note that Chapter 14: Character and viewpoint and Chapter 16: Conflict and genre are adapted, with amendments and additions, from my own *Writer's Source Book* (Hodder, 2012).

Contents

Introduction: how to use this book

'Writing a poem is discovering.'
Robert Frost

'Writing is an exploration. You start from nothing and learn as you go.'
E.L. Doctorow

'There are three rules for writing a novel. Unfortunately, no one knows what they are.'
Somerset Maugham

Fiction seeks to involve you in a story world of characters and events. The simple aim of any non-fiction book is to give you information, to tell you facts or present arguments. But *this* non-fiction book seeks to involve you, too. It is not going to be just a matter of reading. You are here to *do* as well as to read. You will be encouraged to think things out for yourself, to analyse and record your thoughts and ideas, as well as to produce creative writing. This book will be for you whether you:

- are starting out wanting to write or just thinking about it
- want to explore your creativity in a variety of ways
- are writing already
- want to learn about different genres
- have settled on a particular field of writing.

It aims to:

- be enjoyable, give you some fun and stimulate you
- give you ideas and tools
- unlock and develop your creativity
- instil a sense of confidence
- give you experience of different genres.

Key quotes

Writers are agreed: the only way to write is to write:

'The way to get started is to quit talking and begin doing.' **Walt Disney**

'If you want to be a good writer, write.' **Epictetus**

'You only learn to be a better writer by actually writing.' **Doris Lessing**

Using this coursebook together with a notebook will encourage you to take part, think for yourself and be an active learner. We will talk more about notebooks in Chapter 1. Your notebook will be your writing book; a place to complete the exercises in this book, to record your thoughts and observations, and to play around with ideas. For now, get yourself something to write on and something to write with. If you have got a notebook, use that. If you have not got a notebook, use anything for now, but promise yourself you will buy one.

Towards a definition

Snapshot

Write down what *you* understand by the term 'creative writing'.

When you have done that, write down six things that you think are important to creative writing. Write them down before you consider the answers given below. Do it now. Write.

If you consult a dictionary, creative writing is considered to be any writing, fiction or non-fiction that is not journalistic, academic or some other technical form of writing. It includes most novels and epics, as well as short stories and poems. But if you ask creative writing students this question, the answers you get are sometimes quite different. They believe creative writing is:

- 'The creation of characters, plots and styles of writing inspired from life and imagination …'
- 'Writing that is intended to be imaginative and personal rather than merely informational: stories, plays, poems and so on …'
- 'Writing about things, stories, plays, poetry, in a way that reflects the way an individual experiences and explains life in order to communicate …'
- 'Fiction following fanciful and less fanciful themes – exploring life, situations and emotions through characters and plot …'
- 'Self-expression using words as the medium …'
- 'Moving beyond the intellect to a place that connects to emotions, heart and soul, in an attempt to gain a deeper understanding of ourselves and the world around us …'
- 'Many things – free flow of the unconscious – or ability to delve into the mind – a structured way of expressing to others …'
- 'Writing fiction. It could be short stories novels or poems …'
- 'Using your imagination to create a work of fiction …'
- 'A fictional expression of ideas or stories through written language …'
- 'Writing. Any form of writing is a creation – from proposals and reports through to poetry …'
- 'Putting your thoughts, feelings and emotions into a pattern of words that convey them in an accurate, readable and interesting format.'

You can see that there is a range and diversity of views and expectations among people taking writing courses. But there are common themes in these suggestions. Creating a work of fiction comes up quite often, whether it is in the form of a story, a novel, a poem or a script. There are references to the imagination, to self-expression, to thoughts, feelings and emotions, to the free flow of the unconscious. For those students, creative writing is writing that moves beyond the intellect; writing that is personal and emotional and imaginative and that reflects life as the individual experiences it.

You will have your own view but it will probably coincide in some ways with the definitions given here. Another lesson we can learn from these definitions is that there is difficulty in taking a tight, all-encompassing view of this subject. Creative writing can mean many different things to different people and whatever it means to you, your view is as valid as anybody else's. You can take from the subject what you wish.

Snapshot

Has considering the other definitions of creative writing helped you revise your own? If so, write down your revised views. Do that now. Write.

Can creative writing really be learned or taught?

Despite the growing history of teaching creative writing in this country, this issue is still often raised, implying doubt that creative writing can be taught or learned at all. The argument is often put forward that creative writing is not a subject like art, history or physics, and that great writers from the past did not attend writing classes; they taught themselves, or they were born with the gift and they just wrote. But why should we think that only people with the 'gift' can write and that creative writing cannot be taught? You, presumably, must think you can learn something about it, else you would not be reading this book. Publishers must presumably think some things about writing can be taught, else why publish this book at all?

It is the case that there can be a tendency in teaching creative writing to dwell on the technical aspects. This is because it is, in some ways, easier to teach these. You can say what a sonnet should be because there are rules to the form (or there used to be); you can lay down clear guidelines as to what a screenplay should look like because there are industry standard practices. That sort of thing is easy to get wrong and easy to correct and to teach. It is not so easy to teach whatever it is that makes one screenplay lift off the page where so many others sink beneath the surface. It is easy to teach the idea of writing good dialogue and some of the techniques involved, but not easy to teach someone to write the crackling dialogue of a great theatre piece or a terrific screenplay. This is the challenge and the issue at the heart of teaching creative writing.

As teachers, we know we can teach many of the craft elements, the technical aspects of writing, like layout and viewpoint and sonnet form. We can help people take short cuts to discover techniques and approaches they would have taken years to discover, through trial and error, on their own. We cannot teach the magical, inspirational element that separates a great piece of writing from the merely accomplished. Who would pretend otherwise? Most scientists were taught; many scientists learn how to test ideas; not all scientists are geniuses. And, as in any subject, good teachers can teach good students and inspiring teachers can inspire. Creative writing is no different from any subject in that regard. In fact, it is not unlike a great many other disciplines in which people excel. Sport, for instance.

 ## Donald Bradman, *The Art of Cricket*

'*The greatest of players can improve by means of concentration and practice, but the natural athlete must start with a great advantage.*'

Creative writing is not easy; it would be doing a great disservice to claim that it was and some people, as with sport, will have the advantage of greater natural talent than others. That does not mean that all people can't learn something and improve.

 ## Thomas Mann

'*A writer is someone for whom writing is more difficult than it is for other people.*'

 ## Focus point

Writing is not easy. It can be hard and it can be painful, but if you persevere it can also be personally very rewarding. If there is one secret to writing it is to enjoy it! So please enjoy your course – even the agony.

Why have you chosen to do this course?

 ## First thoughts ...

Believing that you can learn about creative writing must connect with your reasons for doing the course. What *are* your reasons? Think about your reasons and write them down.

It would be good if your reasons are clear to you at this point. But if they are not, then perhaps reasons other people have given for starting out on a creative writing course might help you clarify your thoughts. The reasons people have given are quite varied.

They range from specific ones …

- 'to develop my skills in writing short stories'
- 'to improve my writing and maybe move on to write a novel'

… to less specifically technical reasons such as:

- 'to improve my writing skills and to enjoy writing for pleasure [as it is part of my job]. I write for my job but I feel constricted by formula writing and fearful of truly expressing myself in a free way'
- 'to give myself permission to write. To take the first tiny step! Curiosity; I have been writing creatively for decades but have yet to attend a course'
- 'to have some discipline to my writing and to write without feeling overwhelmed'
- 'to overcome writer's block'
- 'because I enjoy writing but I've done little in the way of creative writing'
- 'to be more creative.'

There are as many reasons for doing a creative writing course as there are definitions of the subject. Does your reason for doing this course sit alongside any of the reasons just given? If so, that can be a help. You can see that you are not alone and that other people share some of the feelings you experience. Curiosity, fear, needing to give yourself permission to write; writing as part of the job, yet feeling trapped by that and needing to find self-expression, imagination, freedom. These reasons are felt by many people and are behind a lot of the motivation for writing and wanting to write.

We want to express ourselves, yet we are afraid to and need to give ourselves permission to be creative. These are very strong feelings, reinforced in a society which does not, on the whole, encourage creativity. You may feel this yourself. These feelings are not to be underestimated. But what goals do people have? Where do they want to end up? People's goals vary and can range from the quite specific to the quite general. Short-term goals stated by creative writing students can include wanting to:

- 'understand the structure of a short story, use of language, use of metaphor'
- 'write a short story, to understand more about writing characters'
- 'learn more about how creative writing helps people understand themselves and the world'
- 'start writing regularly, to enjoy writing, to gain some confidence'
- 'impose self-discipline, to write on a weekly basis, to finish the course, to enjoy the course'
- 'loosen up writing, to develop a new format of expression, to link thoughts and ideas'
- 'have confidence, to learn skills and techniques, to allow a free flow of thought onto paper'
- 'improve writing skills, to write short stories, to write a script'
- 'become less critical, to find it easier to write, to finish the work I start'
- 'have more confidence in my writing skills, to get enjoyment from expressing myself creatively'

- 'get back into writing, to begin to structure my book, to learn to write and put together a book'
- 'finish the first draft of my recent piece of writing, to improve my use of dialogue, to think about new ideas of writing.'

Note that these examples have yet to mention publication even though in their hearts a lot of people would seek publication. At the same time, people do realize that publication is not the main or only reason for wanting to write. Self-expression, curiosity, wanting to overcome fear, wanting to explore imagination, wanting to be more creative; these are the reasons why many people take a creative writing course. But many people, too, do want to be published. Understanding this should make you feel less alone and more confident as you undertake your course of study.

Students' long-term goals can be as varied:

- 'to finish my book, to continue to enjoy writing'
- 'to improve my writing skills, to create a collection of work, to help me to observe life slightly differently, to become a great observer'
- 'to get a short story published, to write some poetry, to plan a novel or novella'
- 'to write a novel, to publish my work'
- 'to delve deeper into my writing, to consolidate techniques and skills, to venture into further courses and write a novel or short story and get published'
- 'to feel as free in writing as I do in speaking'
- 'to open up the possibility of writing short stories'
- 'to write a children's book'
- 'to write a novella, book or short stories, to have the book published, to repeat the process repeatedly'
- 'to write a longer piece than I have written to date'
- 'to build a credible character'
- 'to write to the best of my ability and to gain enjoyment from doing so'
- 'to write stories that could be publishable, to write a novel is something longer to better understand myself and other people.'

 Snapshot

Now consider these two questions:

1 What do you want to get from this book? Give three immediate, short-term goals and three long-term goals.

2 How do you think this course will help you achieve these goals?

Take these thoughts, especially your goals, and write them down as a mission statement. Head it 'My mission statement'. Do it now. Write.

Has having done this helped you clarify your thoughts about the subject and what you hope to get out of your course? Keep this mission statement by you: it will help you stay on track with your work as you progress through the course.

The creative writing workshop

Where creative writing is different from some other subjects is that it has a high degree of participatory activity. The students in creative writing classes are asked to do things; they are asked to use their imaginations, their writing skills and their critical faculties. They are asked to write things down either on their own or in groups and to discuss their work in what are called Workshop settings. This can be a very challenging environment. The courage needed to present a poem wrenched awkwardly from somewhere deep within and written with a rudimentary grasp of form to a group of comparative strangers is not to be underestimated. The amount of courage needed to take criticism and comment on something created by one's own hand is very great.

A writer's workshop can take many forms, from a subject being introduced by a tutor and then discussed, from students simply being asked and answering questions, to writing, editing and revising new or existing pieces of work. They can be group led or facilitated by a chairperson or a tutor, usually a more experienced writer. But the key point is that students in creative writing classes are not passive receivers sitting listening to information as they are in some other subjects. They are active learners, wrestling physically with writing techniques and putting themselves on the literary line each time they submit work. This is probably one of the major reasons for the growth in creative writing as a subject over the recent decades: the learners are active and not passive and they are encouraged to draw on their own experiences and express what matters to them. In some institutions the study of English Literature has declined, even as the number of students taking creative writing has risen. Undoubtedly, the lure of fame and money, the idea of getting published plays a part, but the experience of speaking for oneself, or marshalling experience and ideas, of the excitement and pain of creating something from nothing, of using the imagination and of being fully active in the learning situation, rather than passively reading the works of others, also plays a huge part. In fairness, obviously reading is not a passive activity but there is a distinction between creating and reading one's work and reading and analysing the work of others.

Conversely, it must be admitted that in the teaching of creative writing there can be too much emphasis on getting students to write at the expense of looking at what other writers have done, at the expense of studying and learning from good models. One of the tenets of this complete creative writing book is that you cannot be a good writer without being a good reader. We will spend time looking at examples and models.

Focus point

This is a complete course in creative writing in which you will be expected to be actively engaged. You will be asked to read material and to do things; to try out ideas, to think, to write, to criticize, to understand as well as to create.

The book is designed to be as close to being in a classroom, in a workshop situation with a tutor as you can get. It is a complete course in creative writing and intends to tell you, show you and involve you in creative writing. Involvement will be high. You will spend a great deal of time doing and thinking about what you are doing. Thus, the 'lessons' are interactive and the materials are designed to give you things to

- read
- think about
- do
- reflect on.

This coursebook contains:

- advice on writing
- examples
- extracts from published work
- criticism, general points and discussion.

It will also have:

 short 'Snapshot' exercises to get you thinking about the processes of writing

 short practical 'Write' exercises to limber up your writing muscles and build your skills

 an exercise that asks you to revise a piece of work in the light of something new you have learned

 a series of longer reflective and/or writing exercises called 'Workshops'

 key quotes from a range of sources

 key ideas (essential concepts to grasp)

 focus points (key pieces of advice to carry forward).

Each chapter will end with a brief summary of what you have achieved and what the next steps are so that the chapters build on one another.

We cannot promise to make you a great writer, we do not intend to bring you fame and money; but we do promise you fun and enjoyment in an active, structured learning situation in which you will meet interesting concepts and ideas that will help you develop as a writer in a variety of forms and genres. Above all, you will be creative: being creative is at the heart of what we will do here. You will be challenged and introduced to new ideas that will help your creativity as well as teach you some of the fundamental tools and ideas of writing.

In such a short space, we cannot cover all areas in depth, but we will introduce you to key concepts in the areas of prose writing and scriptwriting and in submitting your work for publication or production. The course will also inform you as a reader of writing and a viewer of films. It will, as far as it can, mimic the experience of going to a creative writing Workshop. You will be set tasks; there will be discussion and reflection on your writing and the writing process.

The writing exercises

There will be a great number of writing, reading and comprehension exercises in the course. They will range from the small 'Snapshot' type exercises to the writing of large, more involved pieces. At the beginning of the course and in the first few chapters particularly, the exercises will start short and small. As we build on this beginning, they will get larger and more involved, achieving more and getting more in, as the course progresses.

You will be guided through the writing exercises and the writing process in general and in particular. As well as being given tips that could help transform your work, the exercises will seek to take you from the level of a beginner up to and beyond the intermediate stage so that you feel confident in editing and redrafting a manuscript to ready it for submission. The book will finish by focusing on publishing options and further steps you may take.

It is important that you do all the exercises as you will get the best out of your course this way. As well as being asked to write things, you will also be asked questions about the exercises, about a piece of writing or a quotation. One of the teaching techniques used will be to ask you to cover up the text immediately following the example so that you do not just read the answer suggested in the book but come up with your own. To that end provide yourself with a piece of card, A5 size or simply a bookmark, to cover up the text. Once you have written your response to the question, or said it verbally to yourself, have a look at the suggestion given for you in the coursebook. Try to do it in that order because it is intended as an aid to learning and a way of getting you started at thinking about these matters for yourself.

While we are not giving specific timings for all the individual exercises, except to say that some will be short and others longer, we suggest you take as long as you need with them. Probably you will spend

- one-third of your time reading the coursebook
- two-thirds working through the exercises.

Key idea

You will be expected to complete the exercises, respond to any questions and then to reflect on what you have come up with and the process you have gone through. This constant move between creativity and reflection is at the core of the creative process. Being creative is constantly a mix of doing and reflecting, and reflecting then doing.

Focus point

To get the most benefit from this course …

- Do it at your own pace
- Do not plough through the whole thing without stopping
- Take regular breaks.

What are the three most important things to do as a writer?

Snapshot

In your notebook, write down what you think are the three most important things you must do as a writer. Cover up the rest of this page with your bookmark or card and do not look at it until you have written down your thoughts. Do it now. Write

Now you have done that, you can look at what some students wrote when asked this question. One student wrote: 'Write, write, write.' Others said:

'Write every day, listen to what your readers say, enjoy your writing, communicate your ideas, engage your reader, develop your own style.'

'Use your imagination to the full, don't over criticize your work, write every day.'

'Keep writing every day, observe people, animals.'

'Learn skills and techniques, keep writing however difficult it feels.'

'Let go and trust the process.'

'Write every day, be a keen observer.'

'Believe in your ability to write, write down phrases and thoughts however random to encourage regular writing.'

'Think and express yourself freely without constraint.'

'Observe the world around you, practise writing, keep an open mind, observe, listen, create.'

'Believe in your ability, be confident, be disciplined, listen to criticism, use others as a sounding board.'

These are all great suggestions with a lot of truth in them.

But writing is not only about writing. Writing is necessary but not, as some people think, sufficient. We just wanted to make the point here that reading is equally paramount. How can you expect to write if you don't read? Surprisingly enough, there are people who believe they can, but in order to write you must read and read a lot.

H.E. Bates always said that he learned much of his craft through reading. In his book *On Writing* Stephen King stresses the importance of reading, too: 'If you want to be a writer, you just do two things above all others: read a lot and write a lot. There's no short cut' (p. 164).

James Friel

'Reading is the best source of inspiration, the best means to educate yourself and to witness the skills of others – and to witness their disasters. It is through reading that you learn to structure a tale, describe character, delineate action, judge what works and what, for you, does not.'

Key idea

There is much that is vital and essential to the whole engagement with writing but the three most important things you must do if you want to be a writer are:

1 read
2 read
3 read!

In some part of our minds, we would understand that we have to read in order to write but it is essential to flag it up in big letters at this point to make sure the balance of the creative process is understood. In a way, as one student once put it, reading is a given.

We can take it, then, that reading is important. But what sorts of things should you read? Books, obviously, but also newspapers, magazines, brochures, old copies of magazines at the doctor or dentist. Read the TV guide, car manuals, cereal packets, menus, signs, CD covers. Get into the habit of reading; read anything and everything. If you want to write scripts for radio, television or theatre then you should listen to radio, watch television or go to the theatre as much as you can. If your desire is to write screenplays, then go to films and read screenplays. In fact, whatever you want to write, you should do all of the above.

Snapshot

Reading is important – why?

Think about this question and in your notebook, write down three reasons why you think reading is important for writers. Write.

When you have done that see how your reasons compare with the answers below.

First of all, we read for pleasure: to enjoy the activity. But we also read to widen our vocabularies. As a writer you read to meet and familiarize yourself with different writing styles. To learn how other writers have done it and learn from them what 'works' – good writing, images, phrases, stories. Raymond Chandler rewrote stories from the *Black Mask* magazine in order to work out how other writers had told the sort of tales he wanted to tell. We read to learn what doesn't 'work' – what is confusing, boring, and dull; as well as to get information on place, setting and procedures. If you are writing something set in a hospital, a police force, a court of law then there will be procedures to be followed and researched. If you do not get them right you will lose your readers. We read to get ideas for story, plot development, character creation, dialogue. We read to get anything and everything. You never know when an idea is going to strike you. The more you read the more you will absorb and the better and more complex your work will become.

Key idea

If you don't read voraciously, you run the risk, among other things, of
- writing poorly
- writing things others have already written
- creating dull, uninteresting characters, situations or stories.

Stephen King, *On Writing*

'[Reading] offers you a constantly growing knowledge of what has been and what hasn't, what is trite and what is fresh, what works and what just lies there dying (or dead) on the page. The more you read, the less apt you are to make a fool of yourself with your pen or word processor.'

In Chapter 2 of *The Writer's Notebook*, James Friel has an exercise not unlike the following:

Workshop

What books and films can you remember reading or seeing in your life? Sit somewhere quietly with a paper and pen and let them come into your mind. Jot down why you think they have stayed with you and at least one thing that you remember about each one. Maybe you recollect some detail about a character or a particularly arresting image or memorable scene. Maybe it is the way the book or film opened or the way it ended. It might help to think of the books you read as a child; books, plays or poems you had to study at school; texts you studied at college or university, if you attended one. Is there a difference between the things you *had* to study and things you read or viewed for pleasure? Think about things you read or saw at significant times in your life. Perhaps these times are what make the piece of writing significant to you. Any songs that have stayed with you? Once you've made notes about one thing, another will probably suggest itself to you and another after that. Make notes about anything that comes into your mind; whether it is a television show, a song or a comic followed by *War and Peace*. Don't censor or edit something because you think it is too trivial to be included. Include it all and keep going until you have exhausted your search.

Do this exercise for at least 30 minutes, though it will probably take longer. This is not for anyone else to read. It is for you to understand, so just write brief notes. Write 750 words.

Now look over your list and see what sense you can make of it.

- Is there any pattern?
- Are there any common themes?
- Does it reveal any particular interests or obsessions?

Now, adopt the same procedure and make a second list (say, in 200 words) of the sorts of things you

- have written
- want to write
- or are writing.

Is there any correspondence between the two lists? Does anything surprise you? Is it as you expected or are there any glaring omissions? For instance:

- If you are trying to write a crime novel, have you read a lot of crime books? If not, you might want to remedy that.
- Do you want to write plays? If so, have you few or no memories of ever seeing anything in the theatre? Again, put that right.

Is your reading not very adventurous? Then branch out. Try to read something you have never read before. If you have never read a Mills & Boon romance, start with one. See what you can learn from it. What else do the two lists reveal about you and your reading and writing habits? Compare them and don't hurry over it; give it some thought. This will be useful information for you as a writer. Write down any observations you have.

A few years ago, the UK bookseller Waterstones did a promotion in which Sebastian Faulks listed 40 books that had inspired him to literary success. It was called the 'Writer's Table' and he listed the books that had shaped his career. Faulks wrote brief notes for each book on the list, explaining in 20 words or so why the books were important and why they mattered to him. They included classic novels like *David Copperfield* by Charles Dickens and *The Rainbow* by D.H. Lawrence, as well as poetry in the form of T.S. Eliot's *The Waste Land* and Philip Larkin's 'The Whitsun Weddings'. Faulks also had room for Ian Fleming's James Bond novel *Moonraker* as well as more contemporary novels. Look over the list of reading matter you have compiled and list six of them that have already inspired you or that you think could in some way inspire you with your writing. Write brief notes on why you think each piece of writing could inspire you. Write 200 words.

Finally – *how* do you read? This may seem an obvious question. We all know how to read, but how do you read as a writer? Write down five things you think it is important to look for when you are reading as a writer.

You will have your own answers, but one of the first things you can ask is do you like it? Whether you like the story or not; whether it grabs you is important. But even if you don't like it you can still learn from it. Sometimes you can learn even more from the stories that don't work for you. But the key thing is to try to find out why they don't. If you read a story that leaves you cold, ask why that is. Ask:

- What is missing?
- What could be left out?
- Is it the plot?
- Is it the characters?
- Is there a point to the story?
- Is it plausible?
- Is the language at fault? Too poor or too fancy? Does it show off too much?
- And if you read a story you love ask what is it about it that you like? Is it the plot, the characters, the setting, the atmosphere?

Summary

In this chapter you have learned about this course, considered what creative writing is, thought about the importance of reading, considered how you read, formulated your own personal goals and written your own mission statement.

From now on when you read, read with a purpose. Read to see if you can work out what a particular writer is doing with her or her writing. Ask yourself, are they stronger on plot than characters or vice versa? Do they evoke place well? If so, how? Read book reviews in the papers to see what other people are writing and what might be worth you reading. Make reading an important part of your life as a writer.

Next step

In the next chapter you will begin to think about the words that writers use and attune yourself to the tool of our trade – language. You will start to keep a notebook and a commonplace book (more on this later) and begin to look at things and think in different ways about what you see and therefore what you write.First published in Great Britain in 2014 by John Murray Learning. An Hachette UK company.

1

Organizing yourself as a writer

In this chapter you will learn some of the tools of a writer's trade. You will start to keep a notebook as well as a commonplace book; establish a writing routine, and consider other books and tools you will need.

Keeping a notebook

Starting out you will obviously need something to write *with* and something to write *on*. This might be paper, pens, pencil or a computer. One essential, as we have already said, is a notebook, *your* notebook, your *'writer's* notebook'.

Key idea

Many writers use notebooks; whether electronic or paper. Get yourself one.

There are some famous written notebooks that writers have kept which are well worth both aspiring and experienced writers looking at. Virginia Woolf and Katherine Mansfield kept diaries and journals that have been published and can therefore be studied by aspiring writers anxious to learn what the daily life of a writer is like. Samuel Butler's notebooks can be studied as can the notebooks of novelist Somerset Maugham. He kept a notebook all his working life and published excerpts from 1892 to 1949 in *A Writer's Notebook*.

W. Somerset Maugham

'I never made a note of anything that I did not think would be useful to me at one time or another in my work.'

Maugham goes on to refer to the notebooks as a 'storehouse of materials for future use'. This idea of a storehouse is a key concept for creative writing. The idea of harvesting and storing material to get you over lean months fits well the needs of the writer when the creative seasons are not always abundant.

BUILDING A STOREHOUSE

A storehouse is something to build up over time, to keep and to use to feed off through the lean months. And there are plenty of lean months in writing; plenty of times when you need to go to something for nourishment, sustenance and energy. Note also that Maugham does not say everything was used and was useful: only that he thought it might be useful. This itself is a useful attitude to adopt. To gather potential material you need to buy yourself a notebook.

Jack London, from 'Getting into Print'

'Keep a notebook. Travel with it, eat with it, sleep with it. Slap into it every stray thought that flutters up into your brain. Cheap paper is less perishable than gray matter, and lead pencil markings endure longer than memory.'

WHAT SORT OF NOTEBOOK SHOULD I GET?

Get one you like. Make it nice but not so nice that you are afraid to sully it. Some writers swear by old school type notebooks; others use hard-backed notebooks that are robust enough to withstand lots of opening and closing and thrusting into and out of jacket pockets or bags. These books can be kept and looked back on over the months and years to find phrases, half ideas jotted down, lines for a poem, or half ideas for a character or plot that might be developed now. They are also an interesting record of where you have been. They are places to record ideas that have caught your interest; scraps of dialogue you might overhear; images that come to you; snatches of songs. They are places to put down anything that grabs your interest. You should write without worrying about what anyone else will make of it, because no one else is going to see it. This is your notebook for your ideas and for your eyes only.

You might also want to try some kind of recording device to get down your immediate thoughts. The drawback of using, say, a digital voice recorder as a notebook is that you will then have to transcribe what you have recorded into a readable form, which could take endless hours of listening and typing, although these days you can get digital recorders which, with the aid of the right software, will do the transcribing for you. Recorders, digital or otherwise, do have their uses and you should make use of them, but choose what you want to use them for. They are no substitute for a good notebook and a favourite pen.

You could use an iPad; laptops and palmtops can also be a notebook. If you are skilled and proficient in using a laptop or some other portable computer device, then use it. Take your notes, record your visuals or your aural snippets. For ease here, we shall assume notebook means an old-fashioned written notebook. But please translate this into an electronic form if that suits you better.

WHAT SORT OF THINGS SHOULD I RECORD?

That is up to you. It would be easy to say record anything unusual that you see, read or hear, but each of us sees, reads and hears differently. The best advice is to gather what you think you may be able to use in your writing: what strikes you, what intrigues, what amuses you, what captures your interest. It might be something you overhear, or something you see someone doing or something you imagine. It could be something someone is wearing; a description of a room or building; a recording of the weather. It could be a strange sight. It could literally be anything; anything that somehow pricks your interest and which might generate work or that you might use in a piece of writing later. You don't always know how you are going to use it, that might only become clear days, months, years later, but that is not the issue here. Put it down because, then, you have it or at least you have a key to the memory of it.

It is amazing, too, how often we find what we are interested in. For instance, if you are working on a particular project or piece of writing about, for example, elephants, the mind and eye will quite likely pick out all sorts of sayings, images and references to elephants from the mass of confusing details and references that fill the world.

When taking notes, among the sorts of things you might note are:

- **People:** the way people look, act, dress and talk. People from real life will find their way into your writing, this is natural. Practise looking at people and listening to them as a writer would. Note details about them, colouring of skin and hair, colour of eyes, mannerisms they have, the way they dress and move.

 Key idea

People-watching is an essential habit to develop for a writer.

- **Dialogue:** Listen to the way people speak, what they say and how they say it. People interrupt themselves and each other; they trip over words, use the wrong words, repeat themselves, pronounce or mispronounce certain words interestingly. You should be listening wherever you are. If you hear something interesting, write it down. If you are not near your book, then remember it for a few moments, if you have to, but otherwise write it down, or you will lose that particular, individual flavour that attracted you in the first place. Sometimes the very phrase or word order is key and a paraphrase of it will not do.

- **Lists:** Making lists can be a way of trawling both experience and memory and the things that interest you. Writers often make lists of favourite books, favourite authors, favourite places, favourite foods, favourite films, and favourite music. Keep a section in your notebook for favourite words for favourite images.

- **Memories:** These are a great storehouse for writers. Memories are written indelibly in us. We draw on them when searching for situations, characters, emotions and they can often give us the basic idea of a character or a situation or a story. Often without realizing it we dig down deep into this storehouse and pull out experiences that provide the energy, the living sap for our writing. It can be productive to write down some of your memories; some of the earliest memories are rich with the power that we need in our writing. Learn to tap into this energy. Writing down, or writing out your memories in a creative way, putting them into a fictional form, can also be a way of healing yourself of traumas. This is often not just a side effect but a motivating factor for a lot of writers in their work.

- **Other writing:** When you come across a piece of writing that you like, make a note of it, write it down. Look at it, see why you like it, try to understand it. See what the writer has done; ask yourself what you can learn from it. Try to emulate it. It is a quite legitimate and age-old tradition to imitate. It has been one of the basic learning methods of artists in all forms and fields, to learn from a master; first to write in their style, to copy; and then to develop into finding your own voice and style.

> ## Key idea
>
> Decide who your masters are, who you love to read who inspires you and read their work again, not just for the pleasure, or for the story or the characters, but to see how they do it; to learn from them.

Before we go further with the topic of the notebook, it should be said that, as with everything, there is, of course, another school of thought on this. Some people think that if an idea is a good idea you do not need to write it down; if it is that good you will not forget it. Therefore you do not need a notebook. There is some sense to it but you must ask, is it a way of testing your memory or a way of testing an idea? You might think of something brilliant one day and if the idea is still with you next day then it might be a good idea, or it might contain the kernel of something useful. There again, it might not. There is no guarantee in either method that the idea you have is of any worth.

So, perhaps the best thing is to practise a combination of the two approaches. It is good to get into the habit of writing things down, but maybe you should not write down absolutely everything. As you progress, learn to discriminate between what has 'legs' and what doesn't. In the end, the best advice is to do what is right for you.

> ## Focus point
>
> Put this book down and go out and buy a notebook. It doesn't matter what type, but one you like and want to write in.

HOW DO I USE MY NOTEBOOK?

- Keep your notebook with you at all times.
- Be ready to jot down any good ideas. No – to jot down *any* ideas: you might only find out later whether an idea is useful or not.
- Get into the habit of carrying your notebook (or your digital recorder, iPad, camera or whatever) in your bag or pocket. Don't feel embarrassed. Don't wait until you are alone. If something strikes you and you are in a public place, get out your book and write things down.
- Be bold.
- It might be best if you use a pencil for writing in it and doing your exercises; then you can rub things out but otherwise do not be afraid to use your notebook freely.

Key idea

Your notebook is a place to try out ideas, to have fun with language, to enjoy language for its own sake. It is a safe place to play, to make mistakes, make discoveries and to explore. No one will see it but you.

WHAT SHOULD I WRITE IN MY NOTEBOOK?

Should your notes be full and detailed or short and cryptic? Should you write proper sentences or quick shorthand? Well, as with so many things, we are all different and we will take notes in ways that suit our differing abilities and temperaments. If you can write proper shorthand, then do that. If not, take notes in whatever style or quickness of hand suits you. These notes are not for anybody else to read, they are for you. They are not great literature, either; or not meant to be. They are working notes, sketches such as an artist might make while they are exploring a subject; while they are seeing what particular qualities it has and getting to know it. These notes are a way of you recording what you see, hear and react to and a way of building up a storehouse of material that you will be able to work from later.

Here's an example of a way of taking notes. This is a quick observation of a cup on a desk:

> *Shiny surface, covered in bouncing spots, spots like bouncing balls or floating balloons, red and blue and beige on its white surface. A spillage down the side like a pink smear or tear; blackcurrant. Handle like an ear. A circle at the top wider than the one beneath. The desk shines in its surface.*

It is not arty and it is not that good. 'Handle like an ear' sounds OK except it is a bit obvious and been done before. 'Bouncing spots' is more unusual and therefore more interesting. But it shows you that you have nothing to fear. You are going to write notes – not great art. It is all about looking; it is about observing and then putting things down on paper. That is all it is about.

Write exercise

Take an object that interests you. Sit down in front of it or set it down in front of you. Study it. Look at it for a while; note the following features:

- size
- shape
- contour
- colouring
- the way light strikes it
- whether it is shiny or matt
- anything else about it.

When you are ready, write down your observations in about 200 words. Try to be precise and write what you see. Sometimes it is helpful to try to keep your eyes on the object as you write and not on your paper (if you can read your own writing afterwards). If you can't do that, don't worry. It is just that sometimes this act connects you with the object better.

Edit

Now, read your notes over. Is there anything you want to:
- change
- improve
- make more accurate
- cut
- add or amplify?

If so, make some small changes but don't worry about rewriting and do not judge it. You've recorded your observations, now move on.

Write exercise

Take several objects, either objects that are already together or that you put together like a painter in a composed still life: maybe the clutter on your desk or the contents of the dining table. Repeat the same procedure: look first and when you are ready, start writing. 200 words.

Here is an example of notes taken in just this way:

> *Blue, black and brown piled on a chair; a shiny, waterproof coat and a cashmere scarf. A black hand of the Invisible Man; teeth a folded zip snaking beneath an empty headed hat. The clothes will stand up soon and walk away back into the cold.*

Edit

These are again just notes, though this time there is slightly more than observation in them. What more is there? Think about why this description is different from the previous one. Write down your thoughts before you look at the commentary below.

This description is different because a little more of the writer has crept in with things like the 'black hand of the Invisible Man' for the empty glove, and 'the clothes will stand up soon and walk away back into the cold'. If these have moved on from being just descriptions, what are they instead? What do you think?

The writer has introduced what are called images. These images are less factual, perhaps even poetic. We will study images later, but look at the notes you made. Are they factual or is there the hint of a potential image anywhere? Look carefully and see. If there is, note or underline it, you may use it later.

Workshop: writing outside

You will need to go outside for this workshop. You might be in a rural or urban environment; you might be surrounded by trees and fields, or streets and cars. Whatever the environment you are in, take this book and your notebook, go outside and start looking at the landscape around you, whether it is of fields or of buildings, with a view to recording some of it.

Place yourself somewhere comfortable; if you need to sit, find a park bench, or you might like to do it looking out of a café window.

But first, a word about writing in public. Some people have to overcome the difficulty of writing in front of others. It is true that writing is something that we generally do in secret, locked away, in small rooms. Partly that is in order to allow us to concentrate without distraction and without noise. But going out in public with a notebook and pen is as bad as going out with an easel and a paintbrush. If you have ever stood or seen someone stand in a field or street with an easel and a paintbrush or a drawing board you will have found that in very little time a crowd has gathered around to see what it is going on. And probably to pass judgement. In many ways writing is a less visible activity than painting to do outdoors but you may feel a wish to be invisible. Nevertheless this is something to be overcome. You will learn by doing it when you gain the confidence to write anywhere, anytime.

For this exercise, you can easily sit on the bench under a tree and make notes without catching the eye of anybody.

Observe, try to take in every detail from earth to sky and back again and when you are ready, write down every detail:

- the size and shape of any windows
- the brickwork
- the angles of buildings
- the colours of roofs, woodwork and drainpipes
- the colour of the sky. (Note – 'blue' will not do and it is not usually just one colour anyway.)
- Is there any grass? Describe it. (And grass is not just 'green'.)
- Are there any trees? Are they in leaf or not? Describe them.

Put in everything you see.

(*200 words*)

When you have done this, ask yourself if you have accurately put down what you saw. Can you add or change any detail to make it sharper or otherwise improve it? If so, edit your notes now.

While you are still outside, try the following shorter exercise as well. It will help you to hone in on what is really characteristic about something that captures your interest.

Find a bird or an animal that you can observe. Station yourself somewhere so that you don't frighten it away and simply look at it. When you are ready, start making notes about what you can observe. Include:

- physical size
- shape
- colour.

Also try to get down a sense of how it moves: are the movements smooth or jerky?

Next take notes about what you can infer. Is the bird or animal

- alert and lively
- anxious or sleepy?

(200 words)

Have you captured what is characteristic about this creature? If not, what would capture it? Write it down.

Now look over all your notes and review what you have done. Write down what you have discovered by doing these exercises.

(200 words)

Keeping a commonplace book

Having taken that these initial notes, the next thing we would do is take the process on a stage, take the raw notes and see if we can turn them into something else – this is what writers do. But before we do that there is something else most important that we must discuss – keeping a commonplace book. First of all we are going to understand what this is.

My commonplace book

What do you understand by the term commonplace book? Why is it

different from a notebook? Think about this and then answer these questions below:

- What is a commonplace book?
- What should my commonplace book contain?
- How do I organize my commonplace book?

Take your notebook, think about these questions and write down your answers to them before you look at the answers given below.

WHAT IS A COMMONPLACE BOOK?

A dictionary definition of a commonplace book is the 'collecting of material along a common theme by an individual'. Wikipedia, the free online encyclopaedia, says that:

commonplace books (or commonplaces) emerged in the fifteenth century with the availability of cheap paper for writing, mainly in England. They were a way to compile knowledge, usually by writing information into books. They were essentially scrapbooks filled with items of every kind: medical recipes, quotes, letters, poems, tables of weights and measures, proverbs, prayers, legal formulas. Commonplaces were used by readers, writers, students, and humanists as an aid for remembering useful concepts or facts they had learned. Each commonplace book was unique to its creator's particular interests.

They were once very popular books and are still popular under a new name. The popular name today for what is essentially a commonplace book is a blog. And what is a blog? We have all heard the name but maybe we do not understand what it means. A blog is a website. The word blog comes from the contraction of Web and log. It is keeping a log on the web, hence blog. Whereas logs were once kept by captains of ships they are now kept on the web by individuals who regularly put up commentary and descriptions of events for others to read. Blogs can also include material such as graphics or video. These commentaries on a particular subject of news are like personal online diaries. Blogs started as online diaries and they have grown in size and nature to combine text, image and links to other blogs and webpages. An important difference between a blog and a commonplace book is that blogs have an interactive capacity. Someone can leave comments on another person's blog. It is not common for other people to add to another person's commonplace book. You would not expect to have people adding things to your commonplace book. This will be something for you to keep but in many other ways it is similar to the more contemporary named blog.

Most blogs are word based but they also have photographs and images, some have music and videos, some have an audio element. These can form podcasts. This though, however interesting and up to date, is beyond the scope of our concerns. Although in passing it should be said there is quite a lot of scope for writing these days in these web-based forms. Some published writing has even started out in blog form.

You are recommended to keep a commonplace book; whether paper-based, digital or electronic, as in the form of a blog, it does not matter. The advantage of the old-fashioned paper-based commonplace book is that it leads you to develop a collection of material that you can handle physically and which can feed into your writing. The advantage of a blog is that other people can contribute *and* you might get published.

To maintain the physical form of commonplace book you will not require a website; you will require scissors and possibly glue and something to keep the collected material in. In practical terms this could be a book or folder or box file or desk drawer where you keep any visual or written material that you think will be useful to you in your writing. These could be

- cuttings from newspapers and magazines
- book reviews
- photographs
- tickets and programmes for events
- anything likely to be useable.

How do you organize your commonplace book? This will be up to you. It will be driven by your interests, what it is that catches your eye that you feel you would like to keep; a series of articles about a particular place or happening, current events. Whatever the supplementary material you need to help you create characters and places and stories in your writing you will need to find in other sources. You will need to be looking over time. As you read, a phrase might strike you and you might want to cut it out with the scissors and put it in your commonplace book. You might do the same with a photograph, an image, anything that relates to the work you are thinking about, planning or doing. The material itself will perhaps dictate the way you organize it but you might like to have general sections for:

- travel items
- interviews
- characters
- places
- newsworthy events
- crime or other stories
- poems you like
- book reviews
- photographs.

Your commonplace book might also resemble a scrapbook as you go on. It will be formed of a mixture of images, photographs and commentary. Once again there is a long history of keeping scrapbooks. This looking, this gathering of scraps from here and there and everywhere is an important element of writing.

The important thing is to get your mind used to it and to start collecting. Collecting is important also because it is a way of thinking about writing. You are gathering material for potential use in your writing and therefore developing ideas for characters, situations and plots. Thinking about writing is also a form of writing.

Writers at all times need to be on the lookout for things that are likely to be useful to them. They might be found in books, papers, or anywhere out in the world. Writers observe events and especially other people and store details about appearance, manners and description to be used later. Writers gather, collect and use the jewels and detritus of the world in their writing.

WHAT SHOULD MY COMMONPLACE BOOK CONTAIN?

The answer is whatever is pertinent to your writing:

- cuttings from newspapers and magazines
- book reviews
- photographs
- tickets and programmes for events
- maps and guidebooks
- anything likely to be useable.

HOW DO I ORGANIZE MY COMMONPLACE BOOK?

This will be up to you. Your material will dictate the way you organize it, but you might like to have general sections for:

- travel items
- interviews and photographs
- characters
- places
- newsworthy events
- crime, sports, royal or political stories.

It is important, too, that you gather material in your commonplace book regularly, as well as writing in your notebook. You must collect something every day and you must write something every day.

Key idea

Writing is not just about writing.

Do I need a routine to write?

The short answer is yes.

Key idea

Not only do you need to learn to write as a writer writes but to think as a writer thinks.

How do I establish a writing routine?

Think about this question and then answer these further questions below:

- Where do I write?
- When do I write?
- For how long should I write at any one time?
- How do I write? What is the process?
- What other items will I need to be able to write?

Write down your answers to these questions before you go on with this coursebook. Only when you have done that look it the suggestions given here.

WHERE DO I WRITE?

Anywhere; wherever you can.

Stephen King, *On Writing*

'The space can be humble, probably should be... and it really needs only one thing: a door which you are willing to shut.'

The use of the word 'willing' in this quote from Stephen King alludes to an important consideration for writers. How much of your time and yourself are you willing to give to the craft? How much of your time and yourself *can* you give given your personal circumstances? Are you prepared to shut out family, friends or paid work?

But where you actually write depends on the sort of space available to you. There are at least two crucial issues with finding a place to write: an issue of noise and an issue of privacy. Jane Austen used noise in a helpful way. According to legend she liked to write in a room where the door had a squeaky hinge. She would not let this be oiled because it gave her a warning of people approaching, allowing her time to hide her work away. Some writers listen to music when they are writing; obviously for them music is a stimulus where it would be a distracting noise to others. As for privacy and noise, Anthony Trollope wrote a great deal of his great work while travelling on a train between Dublin and Belfast. Other authors have written in many places as varied as hotel rooms, cafés and restaurants. Others have needed a cave-like space into which they have withdrawn, rather like the early cavemen who did their cave drawings back in the deepest recesses of their caves, as if that was the place where art came from and where it ultimately belonged. This may be what lies behind the sheds at the bottom of the garden that Virginia Woolf, George Bernard Shaw and Roald Dahl all worked in. Shaw had his desk on castors so that he could move it to follow the sun throughout the day and get the best light. There is something important about the creative process in that idea of art coming from the deep and into the light of day.

At the same time, though we may not need to write in literal caves, to create we need to focus the mind and energies on the work we are trying to conjure up. Magic cannot easily take place out in the glare of the public eye, with all the noise of the daily world going on around us. And yet, that said, magic does take place in public places. Actors can create magic before us in a packed theatre. David Mamet wrote a collection of essays called *Writing in Restaurants*. Novelist J.K. Rowling and poet Elizabeth Jennings both did a lot of their writing in cafés. Writing also takes place under the most enormous difficulties. Great works of literature have been written under conditions of great deprivation and duress. Solzhenitsyn wrote in the gulags. One thinks of other works written in prison or in concentration camps and smuggled out but the ideal must be somewhere comfortable that is conducive to being creative; somewhere quiet and private. No one is suggesting that you must pursue the rather romantic idea of the penniless author in the garret. The best thing would be for a separate room, though a quiet corner anywhere can work. A separate table in the corner of a room will do, but you might want it to be quiet and peaceful and away from the television. In summary, you may not be able to have your own shed or writer's room, but do what you can and find what works best for you.

WHEN DO I WRITE?

You should put aside some definite time, ideally at the same time each day or week. Take whatever time you can get; an hour a day ideally to start with, and then gradually build the time available to you for writing during the day and during the week.

 Focus point

Once you have chosen the time and set it aside, then keep the appointment; turn up and WRITE.

Do you write at dawn, at midday or at midnight? This depends on you and your personal circumstances. The best thing is to write when you are at your best and your circumstances allow; that might be in the morning, afternoon or late at night. Try to get the optimum conditions when you are liable to do your best work. Therefore you must try to organize your routine so that you can write at the same time of day, ideally at the best time of day for you and when you are at your most alert. It may not be possible for you to do it when you are at your best, but try to get the best out of what you can do. Try setting aside the same time and same amount of time each day. The rhythm gets into your bones. But if you can't manage that, then write when you can.

 W. Somerset Maugham

'Only a mediocre writer is always at his best.'

Anthony Trollope

'Three hours a day will produce as much as a man ought to write.'

Ideally, you should try to write for a couple of hours at a time because that way you will get through the limbering up phase and have the chance to get into some real writing. If you like to work late at night when all is still and quiet, then you might find you can do more – fatigue permitting. Early or late probably means you get the quiet time of the day and can do more, but do it at any time that suits you best.

Key idea

Write every day. Writing is like food and exercise: a little and often is better for you than a binge or a big fun run once a year.

Writing every day

Why do you think it is important to write every day? Consider the question and write your answers in your notebook.

Writing every day is important because you will produce material. Also you will establish the routine of writing. You will be keeping in touch with your writing life – you can't always manage to get to the piece of work you are working on, so, use your notebook. Jot down a scrap, or work over some lines of description or dialogue in any snatched moment. You can do it in a café or a restaurant or theatre or a cinema before the lights go down. Get into the habit of taking your notebook out when you see something that interests you, or when you have a free ten minutes. Look around, observe, and write things down. The more you do this the more material you will build up. And the more used you will get to doing it and therefore the less embarrassed about doing it. You should do this writing in a spontaneous manner, quickly and without trying to impress. You are trying to capture something vital and sparky that has caught your eye and that may be of importance to you as you develop your work. It is the sort of thing that great journal writers like Dorothy Wordsworth and Gerard Manley Hopkins have done over the centuries. Their journals are full of things which capture the moment and illustrate for us the writer's mind at work. But we are fortunate to share these journals. They were not written with that purpose in mind.

Focus point

As you work through this book progressively you should be doing these things progressively – reading, keeping up your notebook, collecting in your commonplace book anything that attracts you. You must also be writing. Write every day – it doesn't matter what it is but write something.

HOW DO I WRITE?

Just write.

There is nothing else that is going to get the marks down on the paper or screen than putting the hours in. Writers are peculiar. They can be as superstitious as sports people who will often make sure they wear the same clothes or equipment each time they play; or that they change in the same place in the changing room and dress in the same order. Keats needed to put on a clean shirt in order to write. Virginia Woolf could only write in the mornings. Schiller needed the smell of rotting apples in his desk to enable him to write. Develop the peculiarity in you, don't be afraid of it. Don't lock it away as society may well insist; it may well help you write.

Molière

'I always do the first line well, but have trouble with the others.'

Writing is also hard – anyone who thinks it is easy has never really tried. Making a piece of art work, and writing something is making a piece of art, is hard. Whether it is music, fine art or writing, doing it well is an achievement like no other. It can also become an obsession.

Key idea

When you are obsessed, you will know you are in danger of being a real writer.

We are not always at our best, for writing as for anything; that is fine. We are not always at our best in other things we do in life, much as we would like to be. Writing is no different from other activities we undertake and other tasks we set ourselves. But even when we are not at our best we need to get on with it. Only by doing it will we do it.

Key idea

Writing needs regularity to it. It is a habit that we need to form.

Though we probably don't think of it that way, believing it to be an imaginative or cerebral activity, writing is not solely something we do with our minds but is a very physical activity. The physical side is as importance as dance or sport. Dancers and sports people need to practise every day. So do writers. Though you might not believe it from the sorts of images we have of some famous writers or from what you think the activity of writing consists of, you have to be in good physical shape to write. You have to train as regularly as athletes, musicians or other performers. You have to keep in shape. The best way to do this is to do something every day. Like other obviously physical activities you have to loosen up, to limber up and to get the juices going.

The first part of your writing every day should consist of a limbering up. You might do an exercise, or read over what you did the day before in order to get into the right frame of mind. You will find there is a natural process of limbering up as you ease yourself back into the activity that you stopped doing the previous day only because you ran out of time or ground to a halt or were too exhausted to continue. You will also find that once you get through the limbering up phase and get into the actual writing that it starts to come better and faster. You are looser. You are back in the groove. This, if you are lucky, will continue for some hours until you are too exhausted to continue. Often towards the end of a session you can be on something of a roll; the ideas and the words to form them are coming thick and fast but you are fighting a losing battle against oncoming weariness. The brain starts to run down, you feel physically tired. You want to continue and don't really see why you should not be able to. If you were a sports person or an accountant this would be the time when you started to make mistakes. The only thing for it is to stop, rest and recover; to come back the next day and start the process all over again. Limber up, get yourself back into the place you were, and let the words, ideas and images come.

When you are starting out, you do not realize that they will come again, that you have to put yourself in the right place and in the right frame of mind to act as the conductor through which these ideas, through which the writing, comes. But with practice, patience and perseverance, it does come. When the body is used to putting itself in this place to create, the body goes there naturally. It wants to go there, because it has nowhere else it wants to be. The emotional high from writing is exactly like the high from playing sport at the highest level, or from performing. There is no substitute for it, and once you have had it you want to have it again and again. To do that you have to train and keep in shape. Your mind and body get used to being in that certain place at that same time every day. Your mental, emotional and physical muscles all get used to it and they expect to be there. If you expect to be there and you are there, then the likelihood is that you will regularly produce good work.

What other items will I need to be able to write?

- **A good dictionary:** if you have one, great. If not, get a good one. *The Concise Oxford Dictionary*, *Merriam-Webster's* or the *Chambers 21st-century Dictionary* are all fine.

- **A thesaurus:** This can be useful to help you find alternative words. *Roget's Thesaurus of English Words and Phrases* remains good.

- **A good guide to usage, punctuation and grammar** is essential, whatever standard of written English you have. *The Elements of Style*, by William Strunk and E.B. White is excellent and concise. *Fowler's Modern English Usage*, R.W. Burchfield, is also excellent – and bigger.

- Depending on what you are writing, a **good dictionary of slang** might be of use.

Summary

In this chapter you have learned some of the tools of a writer's trade. You have started to keep a notebook, started to keep a commonplace book, thought about establishing a writing routine of when and how you write and considered other books and tools you will need.

As you go through the coursebook, do not let the exercise stand in the way of writing. If writing begins to take over when you are engaged in one of these exercises, then let it: give it its head. It is hard enough to get started and get anything down on paper without worrying whether you are following the rules or not. The 'rules' are there to help you unlock not hinder your creativity. Do the exercises, but use them as a springboard for your writing.

Next step

In the next chapter we will look at a key part of the tools of the writer's trade – words. And to start that we will do a few small 'snapshot' exercises that build on the idea of note-taking. Building on the start you have made we will see how you can use anything as a starting point, even yourself, and continue to unlock your creativity. But for now, if you still have not done so already, go out and buy a notebook.

2

Starting to write

Because it is sometimes hard to get started on the actual writing, writers often start with finding something small to write about. It might be something outside themselves like one of the observations that we did in the previous chapter. They might see something in the street, observe an exchange between people; maybe they hear a snatch of dialogue or see an image that captures them. No writer really ever knows what is going to pique their interest and motivate them to invest time and energy in a piece of writing. Conversely the starting point might be something inside themselves, some small part of their own character, and emotional response to a person, place or situation. Or, it might be something based on a memory which they then try to move on from to make or create some new piece of writing. A writer might conjure up a character or a situation, place or an entire world from this small beginning.

We are now going to start with a series of deceptively simple exercises designed to begin small and see how you can make things grow and develop. What we will see is that ideas grow from small beginnings and they grow by asking questions of them.

🔑 **Key idea**

Ask questions of your ideas. Questions are like a fertilizer or a downpour of rain; they force an idea to develop and grow.

We are now going to do an exercise that would do as a start to generate writing, almost out of nothing and at any time. We will start with one of the simplest and oldest forms of writing: an acrostic. By the way, when you hear something described as simple don't think that that is the same as something being easy. The simple things can be the hardest. In this case, what we are going to write will be simple and, even better, fun. If you want to continue to do more later, of course, you could always stretch yourself.

What is an acrostic?

There are a number of alphabetical acrostics in the Bible; several of the psalms are acrostics. A good example is Psalm 119 where each group of eight verses is preceded by the Hebrew letters of the alphabet in order.

One of the oldest acrostics found is Roman and was discovered during excavations at Pompeii and also in England at the old Roman city of Cirencester. The writing of acrostics has an ancient heritage.

The following acrostic; written in Latin, it is quite famous. It is called the SATOR word square:

R	O	T	A	S
O	P	E	R	A
T	E	N	E	T
A	R	E	P	O
S	A	T	O	R

As you can see, an acrostic depends on visual patterning. Written down in the normal way we write prose – *rotas opera tenet arepo sator* – it loses a huge amount of its power and interest. But laid out in a square it is visually much more arresting. You have to see this poem to fully understand it because it is partly a visual piece of writing that has been ingeniously put together.

You sometimes see it printed in a grid, and included in books on word puzzles. Look at it again. Can you see that you can read it left to right, right to left and up and down? Check it out again; read it from bottom to top, top to bottom, left to right, and right to left. Quite amazing, isn't it? A rough translation from the Latin is:

The sower

Arepo

holds

with effort
the wheels.

Another translation is:

The creator
holds
the working
of the spheres
in his hands.

The earliest example of this square dates back to the first century CE and was found on a wall in Pompeii. It was also inscribed on many everyday Roman objects such as utensils and drinking vessels and found above doorways. It is believed the square was so prevalent because it had magical properties and was therefore used as a charm to protect homes and bring great blessings to people's lives. With this charm on the wall it was thought that no evil could enter a home. This is an early example of the link between writers and the spirit, magic, mystery and form in writing.

You are shortly going to write an acrostic, or three, about yourself. That may sound rather a challenge; acrostics can actually be quite complicated puzzles. Both simple and complex they can appeal to the puzzle-solving instinct in us. They were also used as a mnemonic device when books were not widely printed, to help people remember a piece of writing. The English poet John Davies made popular the celebration of people's names in acrostics. In 1599, he wrote a series of 'Hymns to Astroea' praising Queen Elizabeth I. Every poem in the sequence is an acrostic using the name Elizabetha Regina. Following this, acrostics became very popular and much criticized by poets who thought the writing of them was beneath them.

Joseph Addison

'The acrostic was probably invented about the same time with the anagram, tho' it is impossible to decide whether the inventor of the one or the other were the greater blockhead.'

But acrostics continued to be written. The mid-nineteenth century saw a host of acrostic books appear: 1855, for instance, saw the publication *of A Century of Acrostics on the most eminent names in Literature, Science, and Art, down to the present time: chronologically arranged.* The Prince Consort, Prince Albert, was celebrated acrostically in this tome. Queen Victoria is said to have been fond of the double acrostic, using it as a sort of puzzle to tease the readers. The double acrostic has the relevant name spelled out in both the first and last letters of each line. Famously, Lewis Carroll finished *Through the Looking-glass* with an acrostic poem praising the young female inspiration for Alice, Alice Pleasance Liddell.

But do not worry: you are not going to be asked to write an acrostic as complicated and complex as any of these. Though it *is* now time for you to do some writing.

Getting started

Write: animal acrostics

For our purposes, in the exercise an acrostic is a piece of writing in which the first (or last letter) of each line spell out a word or sentence. The letters make a pattern. The very word 'acrostic' seems to spell its own meaning if you listen to it: 'across – stick'. The sound it makes tells you that you write words *across* from a *'stick' of words*. We will start with some animal acrostics.

Here is a single word acrostic for cat:

Curly
Animated
Tail
– CAT

To make much more of the visual pattern aspect it could be written this as –

```
C
U
R
L      t
Y   n   a   ed    t    l
A     im        a i   l
                    l

            l l l l l
```

If we wrote an acrostic on the word 'dog', this time with the key letters d, o and g at the *ends* of the words, it could be:

Hound
Hello
Wagging

or

Hound
Hello
W   g   i   g
a   g   n

Observe an animal carefully. Hopefully, there will be one near you; if not, take a trip to the zoo or catch one on television in one of the many nature films. Observe, make notes and then describe the animal.

Look at some of the words you have used to describe an animal. Choose from those words to write an acrostic using a word that either describes the animal or its characteristic movements, or a mixture of both. Ask yourself:

Have you captured what is characteristic about this creature?

- Is there another word or two that would be more accurate?
- Is there anything else you could improve?

If so, make the changes.

Now write the acrostic and after you have done it try to lay it out on the page like the examples of the dog and cat, so that the form on the page mimics or relates in some way to the creature itself. For instance, a hedgehog might form a spiky ball, while a snake might wriggle over the page thus:

| Silent   arc -   - laaaastic |
| no   ing   eeee |
| -legs   kill - er |

This is a bit hard on snakes – they're not all dangerous killers – but you get the idea.

Focus point

Be accurate; say what you mean to say, but also revise if you need to, and then stop – put it away and come back to it again later.

Write about yourself

Write: self-portrait

The association between names and acrostics has proved fruitful in literature. Let us follow it a little further. It is often said in writing that you should write about what you know. Who in theory do you know better than yourself? Write your name down the page one letter beneath another, like this.

C
H
R
I
S

You are going to write a self-portrait in note form. Place yourself in front of a mirror. Full-length if that is possible. If not, then a head and shoulders will do. As before, first look, take as long as you need to look, before you make your notes. Note the obvious things first; your physical features:

- colour of hair
- colour of eyes
- shape of head
- shape of mouth

- size and shape of ears
- whether you are tall, short
- weight.

(*100 words*)

Now aim for a more internal observation. What can you say about your mood? Are you

- happy
- sad
- uncertain
- optimistic
- pessimistic
- exuberant
- resigned
- anything else?

(*100 words*)

As before, do not judge what you have written when you have finished.

From this exercise, choose an adjective (adjectives are 'describing words') to describe yourself. Use the letters of your name to start each new word. Using only one word for each letter, describe yourself honestly with simple, well-chosen adjectives. Be accurate and truthful. An example might be:

Christmassy

Happy

Rebellious

Intelligent

Smiling

If there are no words beginning with a certain letter in your notes – say there is a letter *y* or a letter *k* in your name and no word beginning with *y* or *k* in the notes – you wrote about yourself, then find a word that will work.

When you have finished writing, look at your acrostic and ask yourself if what you have said is accurate; try to see if there is an interesting choice of word or a potentially intriguing combination of adjectives; maybe the words reveal interesting hints or revelations about your character. (If so, the beauty of doing these exercises at home is that you can keep them to yourself!) In the example for my first name, you might think, I think a bit too much of myself; 'happy, reliable, sensitive and intelligent' are all good qualities. But in truth, of course, I'm not always like this. Sometimes I'm some of these qualities; other times I'm far from all of them, but often these do fit. I'm sure you'd probably say the same about what you've written down. But, if I look at the qualities by which I have described myself, the main thing I think about is not accuracy but that they are a little dull and I am more than a little full of myself. The picture is a pretty conventional one, isn't it; except for Christmassy? That is the interesting word or, at any rate, the one that stands out. Why did I use it? You could probably think of very good reasons why I might have used that. I bet you can imagine some good ones, but I will tell you. I put that down because I was born just after Christmas and my mother has said that was why she named me. You see, one truth in creative writing is that reality is often far more ordinary than the stories our imaginations can tell.

Edit

Go back to your writing and look at your name and see what you can make of the words you have chosen. Are they accurate to you, at least some of the time? If so, that is good because accuracy in creative writing is as important as it is in any other kind of writing. If you want to tell someone what a particular place or person is like you need to be accurate in your language otherwise you will not communicate what you wish to communicate. A reader might also want you to suggest colourful characters or atmospheres but to do so you still have to be accurate.

As you study your acrostic, ask yourself if it is, like mine, ordinary or conventional. But also ask yourself: is there a word or two that stands out? Is there any word that reveals something about you or evokes any memories? Look at that word. Write down why you used it and what it means for you.

In the next exercise on names, you are going to write more about your name.

Thomas Carlyle

'*Giving a name, indeed, is a poetic act.*'

Write: name acrostics

Answer these questions in your notebook:
- Why were you named?
- What you think of your name?
- What does it mean to you?
- Do you like it?
- Did you ever want a different name?
- Did you ever imagine yourself with a different name?
- What was it?
- Did you have a nick-name and did you like that?
- Do you have a middle name and do you like it?

Select three of these points and write for ten minutes about your name. At this stage, just let the writing come; it can just be notes and fragments, it does not need to be brilliant prose.

(*500 words*)

When you have done this, look at what you have written and see if you have learned anything about yourself. This writing could be developed into a piece of autobiography or could form the basis for an imaginative character in a piece of fiction – so keep it safe.

Different characters

Write: alternative selves

This time make up three different acrostics of your name. You do not need to tell the truth. Have fun; be inventive. This time Chris could be:

Charming

Handsome

Rich

Intelligent

Sophisticated.

That sounds good to me. All the things I would like to be. *If only.* You try.

When you have finished, ask yourself some questions about the characters you have sketched:

- Are they you or anything like you?
- What do you think of them?
- Do you like or dislike them?
- Are they alive, lively, dull?

I like him, the new Chris, but maybe he is a bit too smooth. What sort of a story might he appear in? If he was in a story like a Harlequin or Mills & Boon romance, say, he could be the male love interest. In another type of story, he might be set up for a fall, due to get his come-uppance. He is a bit too cosy and comfortable and smug, isn't he? He hasn't got enough light and dark; not enough wrong with him. If you are going to have a character like this, you need to put them in a situation that will challenge them.

In a different mood, Chris might be:

Childlike

Hurrying

Rash

Irritable

Sex-starved.

– a very different sort of character who would work differently in different stories.

Or, Chris could be:

Curious

Hungry

Randy

Insolvent

Showman

That's a cheat at the end, using a noun instead of an adjective, but who said you couldn't cheat?

Key idea

There are no rules in writing that can't be tested, if not completely broken.

Now we're going to repeat the acrostic exercise; this time with the name you always wanted. (Take your middle name or make up a name if you never wanted another name.) Again you do not need to tell the truth. You can have fun and be inventive.

Here are some examples of students having fun with their own names:

Brian	**Kate**	**Liz**
Brainy	Kinky	Lazy
Resourceful	Ambivalent	Insomniac
Insecure	Titled	Zzzzz ...
Annoying	Eccentric	
Nit-picker		

My middle name is Philip. I don't think I am, but I might be:

Piercing

Huge

Incisive

Long-winded

Insufferable

Pontificating

– Philip

This is, I hope, a very different character to me, but I'm not being accurate here. I'm having fun with language and with character. I'm taking part of me and creating someone I might be able to use in a story later.

Write: alternative selves

Try to create someone different from you in another six acrostics.

When you have finished, ask yourself:

- What have you come up with this time?
- Are any of the characters suggested by the words very different from last time?
- Are they more interesting persons than the first ones or are they less interesting?
- Ask yourself why.

Next, take the notes you have just made. Think of a fantasy name; maybe the name of an actor or actress, or superhero. How would you be different if you were this person instead? Write a character description of yourself in 200 words with this other name. Describe yourself doing something active, such as running, cooking or fighting. Feel free to imagine; have fun.

- What do you think of the character you have created?
- Is the character anything like you or is it very different?
- Could you imagine this character in a story?
- What genre of story would they appear in? (By 'genre', we mean a category of writing such as romantic fiction, science fiction, crime, thriller, fantasy or Western.)

Developing characters

Next, we are going to develop this material and learn something about how to:

- develop a piece of writing
- begin creating a character
- relate character to genre.

Write: character and genre

Pick a genre (romance, historical fiction, science fiction, murder mystery, spy story, Western, etc.) Take the character you have just created and write two short paragraphs, about 200 words in total, involving this character in an active scene in such a genre. (For example, put them into an argument in a science fiction story, or into a crime story or a romantic novel.) The main thing is to have fun writing this.

When you have finished you might feel there are the beginnings of a story there. Keep it.

Focus point

Keep everything you write: you never know when or how you are going to use it later.

These acrostics on names can be a handy way of summarizing characters. They form thumbnail sketches that can suggest character flaws and even potential stories. This can be an excellent way to both sketch out and hold on to character ideas.

Listen to a few more acrostic names, which are like thumbnail sketches of the characters:

Jack

Just

A

Cack-handed

Kleptomaniac

What sort of story would Jack appear in? It could be a comic story because he sounds a bit of a comic character and a cack-handed kleptomaniac has a comic, rather than a tragic sound and feel to it. Part of that comes from the meaning – being cack-handed is potentially funny. And though a kleptomaniac need not necessarily be funny, it could be. It could, of course, be a tragic story but the combination of kleptomaniac and cack-handed strongly pushes into comic territory. Part of this sense of the comic comes from the sound of the words: the *C*s and *K*s in cack-handed kleptomaniac, but it also comes from the very idea of a not very good compulsive stealer. This thumbnail sketch allows us to see quickly and clearly a comic character and gives us an intimation of some comic scenes that could take place. Such a small thing shows us a good deal.

Carol

Curious

Acquisitive

Regal

OTT

Lover

Carol's story might be dominated by such a character. She is curious and acquisitive. It makes one wonder whether she is curious in a general sense or more, curious about what she wants to acquire. On top of this she is regal. Is this something in her background: is she from a well-placed family or does she just bear a certain regality in her manner? A curious, acquisitive and regal character presents an interesting image of someone with good manners, cutting her way through a story and acquiring things as she goes. Perhaps she would appear in an historical pot boiler acquiring husbands, property or jewellery. She would be a colourful but perhaps destructive character in any story and if you add to this that she is an over-the-top lover we have quite a picture. But there is no doubt that she would be a strong character in whatever story she turned up in.

Leroy

Lovable

Egocentric

Rolling

Obvious

Yawner

If you were to pick out one word from this character sketch, it would have to be yawner. They key to Leroy's character is his yawning. He is lovable and eccentric; people like him, but the most interesting thing is that he is an obvious yawner. He does not do it in a secret or embarrassed way. He yawns in an open, obvious way. It is part of his character. He is either very tired all the time or extremely laid back. The picture is of an eccentric, engaging character yawning his way through life. You would need to put Leroy into a situation that challenged his yawning; in which he would have to stay awake to find and fight his way through. Then you could generate an interesting story.

Anna

Apologetic

Naughty

Nice

Agoraphobic

This is an interesting name – it has two As as brackets around two Ns in the middle. Anna. Quite often using names with two Ns in them, writers select the words naughty and nice. It is a potential rewarding combination given that they apparently conflict and having a conflict at the heart of a character is a good thing, but it is a bit obvious. The phrase 'naughty and nice' is very common. Hence, it may not be the most original couple of attributes to give to a character. But the idea of a naughty, nice apologetic agoraphobic is not common. This is quite unusual and so is a fresh take on a character. What is Anna apologetic about: her naughtiness, her niceness, or her agoraphobia? The very idea of an apologetic agoraphobic is a good one that has strong story potential.

Amy

Assertive (assured, asexual, artificial)

Manly (mannered, manic, mean?)

Young (yappy, yellow, yuppie?)

What sort of a story would assertive, manly, young Amy appear in? She would be in control of what she wants to do; she'd assert herself. In what way would she be manly: in looks or in attitude? That would be something for the writer to resolve, but it could be one or the other or both. We might pick up clues from the shape of her name too.

The short three letter name could suggest someone small, compact and strong. Who would you want to put in against Amy in a story to generate events? How would you challenge her?

Lena

Long-legged

Effortless

Nifty

Angelic

Perhaps you could put Amy and Lena together. The two of them contrast quite strongly in a physical sense; the short compact, manly and assertive Amy and the long-legged, effortless and angelic Lena. Lena is, of course, also nifty. What does this mean? What kind of attributes does a *nifty* character display? She is clever, adroit, smart and stylish. Lena might make a great contrast to Amy. From the contrast between, them a story could be generated.

We have potentially created six characters here, characters that could play a part in a novel or a number of different stories. You might want to consider putting some of these characters together in order to see what sort of story could be developed. We have already mentioned the idea of Amy and Lena coming together and causing a certain amount of colourful conflict. What would happen if curious, acquisitive, regal, over the top lover, Carol, got together with cack-handed kleptomaniac Jack? Or perhaps teaming regal Carol up with the obvious yawner, Leroy, might drive them both mad. This idea which might seem just like a bit of fun actually has the potential to produce stories rich in character and conflict.

You can see how these little thumbnails contain the core ideas for characters and even suggest potential stories and genres.

Character and conflict

Snapshot exercise

Write three acrostics for names you like and three for names you don't like. See whether you can get a tension, or contradiction in two of the qualities.

What ideas do they suggest about stories and genres?

(200 words)

The two Cs, character and conflict, are essential for good fiction. Give a character ambiguous or competing goals and you have the potential to create an interesting character and maybe to develop a plot.

Here are some examples:

Paul

Perfect

Articulate

Uncommon

Liar

This character could be comic or serious. The fact that Paul is perfect is a difficult notion for us to swallow. Anybody described as perfect we would probably be suspicious of, in our cynical age. We would want them to come unstuck in one way or another. But the combination of perfect and articulate is good. These are good, strong attributes for a character to have. Combine them with the fact that he is an uncommon liar and you have fantastic inner tension. Between good and bad. Characters with an inner tension are excellent for fiction. Paul would be a strong and potentially dangerous character in a story because he would be believed and his lies could do great damage. It would not be necessary and rather obvious to make him a politician, because we have a rather cynical view of politicians. Paul could play someone who is good on the surface but an uncommon liar underneath. Iago, in *Othello*, is certainly an uncommon liar, and he is articulate and quite perfect at it. He is, too, the engine of that play. He drives it with his perfect, imaginative and corrosive lies.

Gary

Gigantic

Articulate

Rowdy

Yob

This sketch of Gary is very strong and clear, and quite unambiguous. He is a gigantic man, either physically or in personality. He is a rowdy yob. One is not surprised to see large, rowdy yobs. They are a bit common and obvious. But Gary has the attribute of being articulate. This is interesting. Thinking in stereotypes we might expect Gary to be inarticulate given that he is a rowdy yob. How much more interesting it is to make this rowdy yob an articulate man. Perhaps he can argue his case. What if he is a rowdy, articulate yob lawyer who bullies and argues his way in court?

Zola

Zany

Outrageous

Laughing

Artistic

Zola is a lively character: zany, outrageous, laughing and artistic. These are all upbeat, lively characteristics and she would bring energy, wildness, a certain zany quality to any story.

Write: alternative selves

Look at the ones you have done and see if they suggest characters and potentially stories. Is there any way you can tweak them by changing the odd word? What difference was there between the ones you liked and the ones you didn't like? Which gave you most? Which ones could you take on furthest? Can you put any of them together to generate a story? If so, do so.

Write a short piece in which two or three of these characters come into conflict over something.

(200 words)

We are coming to the end of this chapter. We hope you have had fun and also have learned something on this stage of the journey. Whatever you have produced, it you will probably have moved a long way from you, your name and the letters with which you started. This really is what writers need to do; have fun and learn.

Key idea

Writing is like life. Have fun and try to learn something on the journey.

As we said at the beginning of the chapter, writers often start by finding something small, whether an observation or a feeling they have or a reaction to something inside themselves; but they take some small part of the world that intrigues and move on from it to make or create some new piece of writing; something larger, more intriguing and unrecognisable from the small beginning. This could be anything: an entire story, a character, a situation or a place. We hope this is what you will have started to do with these simple exercises, though on a much smaller scale.

Focus point

Keep the pieces you have written. We will return to this material again as it is something we will develop later in creating character.

Summary

In this chapter you have produced a few short pieces of creative writing. You have written several simple acrostic poems, begun to create characters and to think about genre. You have also made a start with creating characters and the connection with a story. You can see what a long way you have come. We hope that whatever you have produced, by the end of the exercises you will have moved your writing on a long way from the initial starting point. We hope you can see that the way to make it grow is through hard work and the application of technique. Keep trying these exercises for yourself. Keep trying to develop characters with conflicting qualities that would work well in stories as either heroes or villains.

Next step

In the next chapter you will practise tricking your mind into being creative. You will give yourself permission to write nonsense by freeing yourself from the idea that everything has to make sense and begin to explore the basic components of language and how these come together in writing.

3

The components of language – nouns and verbs

In this chapter we will look at the all-important components of language and do some exercises that seem to be nonsense but will hopefully stir up some of your creativity. You will learn to write an alphabet piece; challenge yourself by writing a piece based on a letter of the alphabet; look at the components of language – nouns and verbs; and write a short piece around a phrase or sentence.

Alphabet soup

Write

This exercise is to help you limber up and see how you can find a fresh image or idea. Write down all 26 letters of the alphabet in a random order in a single line across the page. Make sure you don't miss any letters out!

Check. You should end up with a line something like this:

M Z Y S T W A C Q D E R L F H G I K X P V N B J U O

Now write a piece of prose, or a poem, of 26 words in length taking these letters for the first letter of each word. Write it in the order as given; do not change the order of the words. That is part of the challenge. Do not add any other words, for example, any of the little words so useful to us such as 'the' and 'and' and 'it' and 'of', etc.

Don't worry about making sense or writing nonsense – just go with it.

(*26 words*)

Read through what you have written. Is it nonsense? Maybe, but is there also the semblance of sense in at least some part of it? Often the words suggest an image, or sometimes a story fragment. Perhaps a character is doing or saying something curious or interesting; something with potential to trigger an idea or place or a character to be developed. It is amazing how often something hangs together and amazing how much our minds want to make sense of things. For instance, here is just one example from the above letters –

'Maria's zodiac yielded several terrestrial wobbles, all clearly quickening despite earlier results. Losing force, her geometry increased kinetic X-ray power, very nearly bursting Julian's untidy overalls.'

This is crazy but it is also a very active piece. It has a setting; it seems to take place in some sort of laboratory. If not a laboratory perhaps the use of the word zodiac suggests some sort of astrological predictions which are causing terrestrial wobbles. There is trouble in the astrological universe. We have two characters, Maria and Julian, who are involved in some potentially comic scenario. We don't know what sort of scenario but Maria seems to have a spot of bother in that she is 'losing force'. Because of this her geometry increases kinetic x-ray power and very nearly has an effect on Julian's untidy overalls.

You can see her winding up the Doctor Frankenstein laboratory equipment in an old Hammer Horror movie. Or maybe not. Whatever, you do get quite a lot from 26 random words!

Write

Here is a second set of random letters:

S D C A U W T R K X G L Z F M P H N E J Q Y O B I V

Cover up the text below and using these letters, see what you can come up with.

(*26 words*)

Key idea

We often have to trick our conscious, logical and controlling mind into playing; it is from this play that great creativity can come.

Edit

Have a look at your piece.
- Is there an arresting image or comic idea or occurrence?
- Can you decide why it is striking or unusual?
- Can you make something of any small part of it?
- If so, keep it: you may want to use it later.

If there is nothing unusual or striking in any part of your words, try doing it again with the same set of letters or another random assortment and see what you get this time. The important thing is not to be too conscious and controlling about it in first draft, and not to worry if you are writing down nonsense. It is from nonsense that we sometimes get great sense.

You might also try changing the names in your piece, if there are any, or one or two of the words to make it more interesting or arresting.

Here is an example from the same letters. Look it over and ask yourself, what is the most interesting part of it? Is there anything in it with potential for an image, a character or situation?

> *Slowly Daniel caressed Agatha upstairs. Wilhelmina trampled Richard Keighley's X-rays. Gavin lusted zealously for Maud's pyjamas. Horace, not enjoying Julia's questioning, yielded. Oliver Bartholomew indiscriminately vomited.*

What is the most interesting part of this piece? What about:

> *Edgar lusted zealously for Maud's pyjamas?*

Why is that interesting? The idea of someone lusting after someone's pyjamas is unusual and therefore striking. It is fresh and not trite and it is funny as well. Why would someone lust for someone else's pyjamas? Presumably because they are lusting for the person who wears the pyjamas but are unable to do anything about it. Maybe Edgar is too shy, too inhibited to approach Maud properly. So he sees her pyjamas hanging on the line with the wind filling them out and he lusts for her. A discovery like this could spark off a situation, a character, any piece of writing or could be saved to be used elsewhere.

What about the names Agatha, Maud and Horace? They suggest a place and a period, do they not? Perhaps it could be some kind of weekend house party in the 1920s?

The context just came in the writing. There was no intention to set out and put this into the 1920s, but here is an idea: what if we change just the names?

> *Slowly Daniel caressed Alan upstairs. Wang trampled Ric Koln's X-rays. Erika lusted zealously for Mo's pyjamas. Hidalgo, not giving into Juanita's questioning, yielded. Ozzie Banderos vomited.*

The zippy pace is still there but just changing the names can make this piece seem from a different place and a different time. With Daniel caressing Alan and Erika lusting for Mo's pyjamas we are already in different territory. Wang, Ric Koln, Erika, Mo, Hidalgo, Juanita and Ozzie Banderos sound as though they are from a contemporary film; definitely not 1920s or '30s.

 Key idea

If you haven't thought about it before, think about how names carry a great deal of power in them and how they can also suggest period and place. It is not too fanciful to suggest that they carry a time and a place with them.

If you ever look at the names on old tombstones in a cemetery, note how common particular names are in particular periods, and how much less common they often are in your own time. Names like Maud and Arthur, Montgomery and Horace are not as fashionable now as they once were: presumably they were the Zaks and Sharons and Traceys of their day.

If you are writing a piece with certain sorts of names in, think about changing them. You might end up changing more than the names.

 Key idea

Changing the names of people and places in your work can give an old piece a new dimension and bring vague writing into focus.

Snapshot

What is the point of this game? Why suggest that you write this?

Write down three things that have come up for you in this exercise.

By putting words together in a way that you would not normally do they can suggest oddities of character, situation and place which may stimulate or feed into any piece of writing. It also limbers the mind and tests and develops your vocabulary.

If you are stuck with a piece of writing, try this word game, or another like it, and see what it unlocks.

Workshop: alphabet writing

This is an exercise that takes the challenge on a stage further. In this exercise, every word of a story or poem must begin with the same letter of the alphabet. If you want help before you start, look at the example below.

Poem in 'G'

George's gentrified Georgian
garden grows giant gladioli,
geraniums, gardenias, gloxinia.
Ghostly glistening grubs gather
going glob, glop, gloop
guzzling George's garden growth.

There is a lot of green in this piece; each and every stem seems to be full of sap and the green pigment found in plants, chlorophyll. Without using the word green the words that have been used, gladioli, geraniums, gardenias, gloxinia suggest the stems and green leaves that those glistening grubs are munching their way through. It is a paean to green and the thwarted ambitions of gardeners.

Now it's your turn to write:

- Choose a letter of the alphabet.
- Write a short poem of no more than 25 words in which every word begins with that letter.
- Don't worry about rhyming the poem.

For further practice, now try to write a piece in prose:

- Choose a letter of the alphabet.
- Write a short prose piece of no more than 50 words in which every word begins with that letter.

If you want help with this workshop exercise before you start, look at the example below.

Prose piece in 'D'

Doctor Deborah Dean denies Dennis Dougal dessert. Dennis demands Deborah delays doing dirty dishes. Deborah doesn't discuss demands denied. Desperate, Dennis, disconnects Deborah's dishwasher, dislodging dirty dishes. Deborah dislikes Dennis's disruptive distraction. Ditching Dennis, Deborah discusses divorce. Downcast Dennis doorsteps Deborah's Dormobile. Deborah devours doughnuts. Doomed Dennis dies. Deborah defoliates.

Here we have a complete story, the poor, troubled relationship between Deborah and Dennis, in exactly 50 words. The tone is sad-comic. We have characters, a situation, movement and development in the piece. These are concepts which we will look at as the course progresses, but getting all that into to such a short piece is an achievement. And doing it with the severe restriction of starting every word with the same letter is not easy. This kind of exercise is fun, if you approach it in the right spirit. It can also test your vocabulary.

What did you manage to come up with?

If you got stuck, try to finish this one:

Albert arranged azaleas angrily. After attaching and aligning an aspidistra alongside, Albert assisted Andrea at …

Snapshot

What is the point of this game? Write down three thoughts on its point and value.

The point of this game could be to warm you up, limbering as an athlete might, or to force you to dig deep for words. You have to avoid the most obvious and immediate word. In doing so, you further stretch your vocabulary.

At least one published work has been written in this style, 'Shadrach Stevens Speculations, Sally Sparkle's Serio-Comic Story', a piece originally printed in San Francisco in 1877 to 'describe the doings of, the then most conspicuous mining speculator, Shadrach S. Stevens'. It was a short story written only using words beginning with the letter S.

This exercise also shows you that you can create meaningful pieces while struggling with severe restrictions and form.

The building blocks of English

Ron Simpson, *Essential English Grammar*

'Nouns and verbs are the basic building blocks of the English language … understanding nouns and verbs is central to our knowledge of English grammar and many other parts of speech can only be explained in relation to nouns and verbs.'

We are now going to look at the basic components of language.

NOUNS

Snapshot

What is a noun? Write down what you think a noun is. Do this before you look at the definition below.

The *Oxford English Dictionary* tells us the origin of noun is Old French, from Latin *nomen* meaning 'name'.

A noun is the name of a person or thing. There are four kinds:

1 **common nouns** (the words for articles and creatures), for example, hat – the red hat was on the floor; the cat sat on the mat.

2 **proper nouns** (the names of people, places, ships, and institutions, which always begin with a capital letter); for example: Peter Pan, Paris, the Pompidou Centre.

3 **abstract nouns** (the words for qualities, things we cannot see or touch, and things which have no physical reality); for example: honesty, happiness, loss, poverty.

4 **collective nouns** (the words for groups of things); for example: committee, team, the clergy, the public, the Cabinet.

Another way to look at the difference between common and proper nouns is to consider common nouns as general (i.e. city) and proper nouns as specific (i.e. Paris).

There is a lot that is important here for creative writers – but first of all we need to look at the distinction that has been made between concrete and abstract nouns.

Snapshot

What is a concrete noun?

Write down your answer to this question in your notebook before you look at the definition below.

A concrete noun is not something made out of concrete. A concrete noun is something that we can apprehend with our senses – i.e. something we can see, touch, hear, taste or smell. Common nouns and proper nouns are concrete.

Snapshot

What, in contrast is an abstract noun?

Write down your answer to *this* question in your notebook before you look at the definition below.

An abstract noun is something we cannot apprehend with our senses – i.e. something we cannot see, touch, hear, taste or smell. We have already given examples of both:

- **Concrete nouns** The red hat was on the floor; the cat sat on the mat.
- The hat, the floor, the cat and the mat are all things we could see, touch, hear, taste or smell. (Though tasting the floor or the cat might not be that good an experience.)
- **Abstract nouns** Honesty, happiness, loss, poverty.
- None of these things can we see, touch, hear, taste or smell, but they are still the names of things.

This distinction between these two classes of things is important for creative writing in ways that we shall go on to see. But it is sufficient to say now that writing in a concrete way can give life and physicality to a piece so that when a reader says something like, 'I was there. I could see the whole scene,' it is almost certainly because the writing is concrete and physical. If someone is taken to a place or situation it is because the writer in their writing has taken them there. Also when a reader is not engaged by a piece of writing, when they feel a piece of writing is distant, general and vague, it is because the writer has failed to take them there. And they will have failed quite likely because of a lack of the tangible physicality and detail provided by concrete nouns.

We will explore this further but for now the aim is to draw attention to the parts of language essential to us as writers. We will be doing more of this as we work our way through the exercises.

C.S. Lewis, *Letters to Children*

'*Never use abstract nouns when concrete ones will do. If you mean "More people died" don't say "Mortality rose."*'

Snapshot

Make a list of ten concrete nouns (naming words – things we can experience through touch, taste, sound, sight and smell),

Make a list of ten abstract nouns (naming words – things we cannot experience through touch, taste, sound, sight and smell).

Here are two such lists of nouns.

Concrete nouns
- Pope
- chair
- car
- Prime Minister
- Queen
- telephone
- book
- tree
- dog
- window

Abstract nouns
- poverty
- happiness
- love
- grief
- jealousy
- popularity
- joy
- excitement
- prosperity
- misery

Keep your list. We will use these lists later.

VERBS

Using verbs well is another essential component of language.

Marianne Moore

'*Poetry is all nouns and verbs.*'

43

But what is a verb? Write down what you think it is before you look at the answer below.

A verb usually denotes an action, an occurrence, or a state of being. A verb says what a person or thing does, and can describe:

- an action, for example, walk, throw
- an event, for example, snow, happen
- a state, for example, be, have, seem
- a change, for example, become, grow.

Verbs occur in different forms, or *tenses*. The most common tenses are:

- the **simple present** tense: the girl swims in the sea
- the **continuous present** tense: the girl is swimming in the sea
- the **simple past** tense: the girl swam in the sea
- the **continuous past** tense: the girl was swimming in the sea
- the **perfect** tense: the girl has swum in the sea
- the **future** tense: the girl will swim in the sea

Each of these forms is a finite verb, which means that it is in a particular tense and that it changes according to the number and person of the subject, as in:

I am

we are

you swim

he swims

An infinitive is the form of a verb that usually appears with 'to', for example:

to walk

to shout

to swim

This may sound basic, even tedious and the sort of thing you did in school, but it does no harm to go over the basics. In fact, it is essential.

Key idea

In many ways all you need to write are nouns and verbs. You can certainly make yourself understood with them in a foreign language in a foreign country. And in a moment of danger, 'Fire! Jump!' or 'Snake! Run!' would certainly get the message across.

If we take one word from each of the lists we have made, the concrete nouns (Prime Minister) the verbs (desire) and the abstract nouns (popularity) we could make this sentence:

'The Prime Minister desires popularity.'

What is wrong with this sentence?

Apart from being a little obvious – as all prime Ministers probably desire popularity, certainly around election time – there is nothing wrong with it. In the right context, it is perfectly fine. It is a factual and ordinary bit of reporting such as you might find in any political sketch or news reporting, but to be more creative we need something different.

Let us go back to the lists. Changing the abstract noun 'popularity' to 'poverty' could give us:

'The Prime Minster desires poverty.'

Is this a more interesting sentence? Think about it: 'The Prime Minster desires poverty.'

Possible answers. It is more interesting because:

- It makes us think.
- It challenges our preconceptions of what a Prime Minster would and probably should want.
- It raises questions.
- It could all be a lie.
- It makes us ask, does he or she want poverty at a personal level or for the country at large? Or does he or she desire it in a rival for office?

This testifies to the value of an unexpected word in a sentence. Any time the expected happens in a sentence it is potentially dull. Even quiet surprise can make for a more interesting read than what is loud and obvious. 'The Prime Minster desires joy/love/excitement/jealousy', all offer other, interesting alternatives.

But what happens if we go back to the sentence 'The Prime Minister desires popularity' and take a different verb from our list of verbs? Choosing 'loves' as in, 'the Prime Minster loves popularity' gives us a little more. We could have a character driven by the love of popularity, but again that is not too unusual. Let's choose a verb that looks totally wrong; for instance the verb 'eats' as in:

'The Prime Minster eats popularity.'

Is there any sense to this and any context in which it could work? Keep it and write your thoughts down in your notebook.

Write

Write a short piece, prose, poem or dialogue in which you use this.

(*200 words*)

What did you come up with? Anything?

On first view this appears nonsense.

- How can anyone eat popularity?
- Does he or she literally eat the national newspapers?
- Is he or she always out giving speeches at rallies?
- Does he or she have a great hunger for it, a great appetite for the love of the people?
- In what way does this manifest itself?

We want to ask how could a sentence like this actually be used. Could a character in a story actually say, 'The Prime Minster eats popularity?' Well, yes, he could in a derogatory or approving way.

Compare it to the original sentence. This new sentence raises questions and also potentially creates a vivid, if puzzling picture.

It does this through the language, which is colourful and less literal; it has begun to take on an imaginative sense. Creative writing has imagery in its blood. Image making is something we shall go on to say more about but first let us see how swiftly an image can communicate.

Such a line, when used by a character, also tells us something about the character. What type of character in what sort of story would use the line, 'the Prime Minister eats popularity?' A political opponent? A journalist out to get him? A PR man hired to boost the PM's image?

Write

Write a short piece, prose, poem or dialogue in which you use the phrase 'The Pope loves misery.'

(100–200 words)

Here are some suggested ideas:

- He is personally unhappy.
- He loves requiem masses and dark vestments.
- It is something to do with the way he wants Catholics to practise the faith.

Write

What does 'The Pope loves grief' suggest? It creates the image of a man dressed in black in a dark Vatican full of requiem masses and sad prayers.

Write a short piece, prose, poem or dialogue in which you use this.

(200 words)

A good image instantaneously makes a good picture.

'The Pope loves happiness' and 'The Pope gives happiness' are also obvious and ordinary sentences. As statements they are not unexpected, but changing the noun as in 'The Pope loves misery' raises more interesting possibilities. In what way does he love misery? Think about this question. And then what about changing the verb from 'The Pope loves happiness' to 'The Pope burns happiness'?

This creates another image altogether; the image of a busy, energetic and very happy man giving everyone around him a buzz.

Being creative and asking questions

What can we learn about being creative, about being in a creative state of mind from this playing with words? Write down your thoughts.

We can learn that being creative is – partly an attitude of mind – an attitude of looking beyond the obvious, the factual, and the ordinary. We are not trying to *report* on things in creative writing in the way that a journalist reports on the world, factually.

We spend a lot of our time and energies trying to create images, pictures, characters, scenarios, trying to bring into being creations that never existed before. To do this we are:

- partly communicating differently
- partly using language differently to effect that communication – using words in new and odd combinations

- partly playing with words and expectations
- partly being unusual and surprising.

It will be very important for us to go on to look at the creation and use of images in writing; this we will do in a subsequent chapter. But first we will lay the groundwork for this by further exploring nouns and verbs. Here are some more examples of odd combinations from the word lists.

The tree buries grief.

The Queen inhales joy.

The window eats love.

The book desires prosperity.

The chair loves misery.

The car burns jealousy.

The telephone desires happiness.

Let us look at these odd sentences. In the second one on the list it says the queen inhales joy; how exactly does 'The queen inhale joy?' At first it makes no sense, but think about it. If we think about it, test it with questions, we will be able to start to establish a context and a meaning. How could the queen possibly inhale joy? If Joy was the name of one of her dogs and the queen absolutely loved her smell, then she could bend down or pick the dog up, bury her nose in its fur and inhale Joy. That might be an amusing way of doing it, but doing it this way also avoids the difficulty. How does anyone inhale joy? The problem is that it is an abstract noun, is it not? How can you touch, see, smell, taste an abstract notion like joy? We need to find concrete equivalents of abstracts notions to be able to write about them in that way. So, how do we make the idea of joy concrete and tangible? What event would be joyous for the queen?

What if she was standing at the open window of her palace, breathing in the cold country air and with it a sense of joy fills her. Or, what if on the wedding day of one of her children or grandchildren she looked on the spectacle and inhaled joy. That is better because it is less literal. We know that she is feeling great pleasure at the event and that is what the sentence tells us without actually saying it. It is the fact that it does not actually say it that gives it the effect it has.

What about the first sentence? How does 'the tree buries grief' work? The literal mind asks how a tree can bury anything. Trees are surely incapable of taking a spade and digging a hole to bury anything. But then remember this is creative writing. If you are to make sense of this sentence you have to approach it differently. You have to try to think of ways that a tree might be able to bury something. Let us ask it questions again. What do trees have, what are they made up of? They are made up of hard trunks, branches, roots and leaves. They often have thick, leafy heads in which something might easily get lost, or buried. A kite for instance, or an old plastic carrier bag could easily flip up into the big head of a tree and get buried. An old tree house, built years in the past could lie forgotten and buried in a tree. Imagine that some sad act had happened in that tree house and you can understand how the tree might bury grief. Some old trees have hollows in them. Some have quite large hollows in which things could be secreted or hidden; things large as people. Imagine a character in a story suffering a loss. A farmer, say, spends his time in an orchard where he spent happy times with his wife. It would not be difficult to imagine a scene in which by enfolding him in its thick, roof of leafy branches the 'tree buries grief', for *him*. Or maybe a mother, the farmer's wife, buries her stillborn child under the trees on the farm and 'The tree buries grief'. In such ways it is not only possible, but exciting for us to make sense of the seemingly nonsensical.

Let's look at another of the sentences. How can a chair love misery? We have the same initial response here. A chair is inanimate. It cannot love anything or anybody. But we need to think round that.

Key idea

To be creative we need to forget the literal mind as it is often the enemy of creative writing.

Think of the innumerable stories in existence of what happens if an inanimate object comes to life. There is a classic short story by D.H. Lawrence called 'The Rocking-Horse Winner' in which a boy secretly rides his rocking horse to pick the winning horses in various races. Here the writer has imagined the inanimate object of a rocking horse in a very different light. The films about Herbie, the lovable Volkswagen Beetle, and the 'Toy Story' and 'Cars' franchise from Pixar all have at their hearts this idea. Inanimate objects come to life and have a personality. This has become a staple of science fiction and of writers wanting to explore the idea of robots developing personalities and lives of their own.

So what can we do with a chair? In what ways can we imagine a chair loving? Imagine the chair, sitting in the corner of a dark room; an old chair, probably leather with a high back and worn arms. Generations of people have sat in this chair feeling sad and depressed, and somehow the chair has drawn out their misery. Maybe the chair even has a personality. We could be into some fantasy or gothic piece here were the chair has a life and is the sort of thing that enslaves happy people, into servitude of misery. Writers like Edgar Allen Poe or Stephen King might be very imaginative about this sort of thing.

Focus point

The possibilities are out there. The door to these possible worlds is the language; the words we use. We need to ask questions and imagine possibilities and then we need to be open enough to use them when they appear.

Write

Write a short piece (maximum 100 words) using one of these sentences. Use the image exactly as it is written here somewhere in the piece. Write it as prose or poetry.

(100 words)

Write

Look back at the list of concrete and abstract nouns you made earlier. Put a concrete noun from your list, a verb and an abstract noun in a sentence, in that order. Do not choose the ones that make sense. You must try not to do the obvious. Stick a pin in the lists if you want to, anything to make it less conscious and more accidental and random. Use only three words: add no more. Make up five to seven sentences along the lines of the examples given earlier.

What have you come up with? Do you have any potentially interesting or suggestive images? Try one word, then another; change them around and see if another one is more effective.

Write

Take one of your sentences and write a 200-word piece in which you use the sentence either as the opening words or the last words of the piece.

(200 words)

Key idea

The literal mind is the enemy of creative writing; confront, confuse, confound it.

Summary

Ernest Hemingway and John Steinbeck are often pointed to as writers who eschewed the use of both adjectives and adverbs. That is not entirely true but the lesson is a good one that you should certainly be careful about using these two elements of language. Read some Hemingway and some Steinbeck to see exactly how they do write.

Next step

However, they exist in our language so adjectives and adverbs must have a purpose and they do have a place in your writing. We will explore that place in the following chapter where we will continue our exploration of the components of language before moving on to further explore one of the key strengths of creative writing – images.

4

The components of language – adjectives and adverbs

'The road to hell is paved with adverbs,' wrote Mark Twain. And we might add adjectives, too. However, used sparingly and judiciously, they can be extremely powerful tools in the writer's toolkit. Use them freely first and then hone them down as you revise and edit. In this chapter you will learn to use adjectives and adverbs in your writing; use figures of speech such as metaphors and similes; consider the use of imagery in your writing; and start creating images

Adjectives and adverbs: what's the difference?

What is an adjective? Write down what you think it is before you look at the answer below.

What is an adverb? Write down what you think it is before you look at the answer below.

The adjective is to the noun what the adverb is to the verb. So, what is an adverb? The adverb is to the verb what the adjective is to the noun. The school definitions for these words were conventionally: an adjective describes a noun, and an adverb describes a verb. There are writers and writing books that will tell you that you should not use adjectives and adverbs at all; that you should strike them out.

But the very fact that they exist, that we have adjectives and adverbs, means that there must be a need for them, else why have them? The purpose of these words is to qualify nouns and verbs. The danger in using them is that they dilute the nouns and verbs, that they take away and reduce their power. First of all, let's take the adjective. An adjective is a word that describes something, for example: blue, clever, French, miserable, broken, dull.

Most can be used either before a noun – for example, the blue car, a clever dog – or after a verb like 'be', 'seem' or 'call' – for example, 'The car is blue'; 'I wouldn't call her dull'; 'He seems clever.'

Some adjectives can be used only before a noun – for example, the chief reason (you cannot say the reason is chief). Some can be used only after a verb – for example, the canoe is still afloat (you cannot say an afloat canoe). A few can be used only immediately after a noun – for example, the president elect (you cannot say either an elect president or the president is elect).

Let us consider the adverb. We have said that an adjective describes a noun, and an adverb describes a verb, but there is more to it than that. An adverb is used in several ways. Firstly, an adverb is used with a verb, to say:

- **how** something happens – for example, 'She runs quickly.'
- **where** something happens – for example, 'We live here.'
- **when** something happens – for example, 'She left work today.'
- **how often** something happens – for example, 'She always drinks gin.'

Secondly, an adverb is used to strengthen or weaken the meaning of:

- **a verb** – for example, 'She truly meant it'; 'I almost fell down.'
- **an adjective** – for example, 'He is very bright'; 'This is a slightly better result.'
- **another adverb** – for example, 'It comes out terribly easily'; 'The men nearly always get home on time.'

Thirdly, an adverb is used to add to the meaning of a whole sentence, for example: 'She is probably our worst member'; 'Luckily, no one was angry.'

In writing or formal speech, it is wrong to use an adjective instead of an adverb. For example, use 'Do it properly' and not 'Do it proper.'

And just to make it even more confusing, many words are both an adjective and an adverb, for example:

'A fast horse.'

is an adjective. But

'She ran fast.'

is an adverb.

'A long time.'

is an adjective. But

'Have you been here long?'

is an adverb.

We all use language freely in our everyday lives without bothering with these things and it can actually raise issues and even confuse by drawing attention to them, but, as writers, the more we know about the tools and components of language the better. So, with this theory lesson behind us and with the hope that this has helped and not further confused, we will practise some of these.

Key idea

Write, write, write; use adjectives and adverbs freely to keep the flow. Edit them down later.

Snapshot

Make two lists – a list of ten adjectives and a list of ten adverbs; see below for examples.

Adjectives	Adverbs
broken	terribly
worn	badly
light	hungrily
red	slowly
blue	greedily
clever	nearly
slow	guiltily
dark	awkwardly
fast	quickly
dull	carefully

Write

Take this sentence, 'The cat ate its supper.' Write three or four different versions of this sentence by adding an adjective and an adverb from the list you have compiled. Change the adjectives or adverbs to see what effect this has.

(100 words)

Using qualifiers

We are going to return to a sentence we used previously: 'The Prime Minister desires popularity.' Let us see what adding an adjective and an adverb from our lists can give us:

If we add 'clever' and 'hungrily' we might get:

'The clever Prime Minister hungrily desires popularity.'

Or using 'dull' instead of 'clever':

'The dull Prime Minister hungrily desires popularity.'

Or if we take 'dark' instead of 'dull':

'The dark Prime Minister hungrily desires popularity.'

Or instead, if we take two new words, 'broken' and 'slowly', from our lists we might get:

'The broken Prime Minister slowly desires popularity.'

They are all different sentences and 'The clever/dull/dark/broken prime ministers' are very different prime ministers. They all have different motivations too. In a story you might want to get this across in a different way, but have we added to our images here? The answer must be yes; a small proof of the value of adjectives and adverbs.

Let us take another sentence we used previously – 'The tree buries grief.' How can we develop it by adding the adjective 'broken' and the adverb 'slowly'?'

'The broken tree slowly buries grief.'

Is this an improvement? Has the addition of these two new words added anything at all? What do you note about the sentence 'The broken tree slowly buries grief', as compared to the sentence 'The tree buries grief'?

Possible answers:

- The adjective describes the tree.
- The adverb describes or adds meaning to the action.
- Both are economical.
- The rhythm of the shorter sentence is quicker.
- The rhythm of the longer sentence is slower.
- The word 'slowly' suggests a transformation that happens over time.
- The sentence might suggest that the grief is deeper and more significant.

It also raises questions such as:

• Why is the tree 'broken'?

• How does this broken tree relate to the grief?

By contrast, if we change the adverb to 'almost': 'The broken tree almost buries grief', suggests something different again. The grief here is more difficult to overcome, perhaps.

Returning to our sentence about the Pope – 'The Pope loves happiness' – and adding the adjective 'clever' and the adverb 'guiltily' could yield this:

'The clever Pope guiltily loves happiness.'

There is a feeling of one too many words here; maybe we could dispense with clever, but taking it as it stands, what sort of picture do we have?

• Why does the Pope guiltily love happiness?

• Does he feel he somehow should not love happiness?

• What has happened in his upbringing or early life to cause this belief?

These are interesting questions that the sentence points to. But the question we need to ask is: is there a point to these new words? Are the adverbs and adjectives mere decoration or have they added to the meaning?

Key idea

By careful use of adjectives and adverbs we can develop the pictures we write, adding colour, adding character, and adding complexity. But we can also clutter our sentences with too many words, so be warned.

As in all creative writing, judicious, thoughtful, imaginative use of the components of language is all paramount if you seek to write well. The real advice is to understand the components of language such as adjectives and adverbs: understand what their function is in language and use them where you need to.

A lot of beginning writers use too many adjectives and adverbs. It might be that they think they bring nouns and verbs to life by piling on adjectives and adverbs. That to describe a day as being 'cold, dark and icy grey' makes it more vivid. In some cases, piling on the words does work to good effect, but in most cases the opposite is almost always true. Less is more and more is a lot, lot less.

A string of adjectives like 'fresh-dug, earth-covered, knobbly, waxy pink potatoes' detract from each other. It is impossible for a reader to keep all those modifiers in his head by the time he comes to the noun or verb. They suck the power off the nouns or verbs, too.

Inexperienced writers also resort to using clichés or well-known and used word combinations, particularly in describing smells and tastes: 'a rich aroma', 'rather dreary winter vegetables', 'piping hot'.

A consequence of using too many adjectives can be that beginning writers fall into using dull and clichéd language in other places as well. But as a fault this is correctable. You can do something about it. With much reading to develop the vocabulary and much writing to write out all the clichés in yourself, you can steadily move on away from these afflictions. This point also touching on revision and rewriting but in actual fact when you are writing it is always better to put something down, because you can keep the flow of ideas going. It is always possible to go over it later. In many ways, editing is when the real writing comes.

 ## Key idea

Stage one in writing is to get something down on paper; anything, clichéd or otherwise. Stage two is to edit and revise.

But having done all this preparatory work we are now in good shape to tackle another key element in creative writing: images and imagery

Images and imagery

 ## Snapshot

The words 'image', 'imagery', 'simile' and 'metaphor' are central to creative writing and we need to explore them, so what are they? Write down what you think each of them means.

 ## John Fairfax and John Moat, *The Way to Write*

'The image is a device – in fact, of all those available to the writer it is the most powerful.'

SIMILES AND METAPHORS

Let us look at the simile. A simile is a figure of speech involving the comparison of one thing with another of a different kind using words such as 'as' or 'like' to link them, for example:

'The rain was as clear as a shower curtain.'

'Pear blossom lay like confetti on the lawn.'

Everyday language is rich in similes. We commonly say things like:

'like two peas in a pod'

'as strong as an ox'

'as poor as a church mouse'

'as rich as Croesus'.

We say that something can

'spread like wildfire'

'sell like hot cakes'

'run like the wind'

'be like a bull in a china shop'.

What is the difference between a simile and a metaphor?

A metaphor is a figure of speech that goes further than a simile. It says that something *is* something else that it could not normally be called, for example:

'The moon was a yacht floating upon calm seas.'

'Amsterdam, the Venice of the North'

Metaphors also work by suggesting that something appears, sounds, or behaves like something else, for example, 'burning ambition' or 'the long arm of the law'.

Examples of metaphor and simile

We will look again at similes and metaphors in the next chapter but we can note here that all language is capable of being metaphorical. We use metaphors freely when we say things like, 'He shot my argument down.' Or 'The Prime Minister is under attack.'

But a metaphor is a specific figure of speech, as is a simile. Let's look more at the differences:

Her hands are baseball mitts – *metaphor*.

Her hands are like baseball mitts – *simile*

Both similes and metaphors make connections between things that are unlike each other. A metaphor says something *is* something else; metaphor stamps one likeness on another. A simile says something is *like* something else. A simile is like a bridge between two riverbanks. The word 'bridge' that links the banks is *like* or *as* or *than* or *resembles*.

Raymond Chandler uses similes a good deal, such as: 'He entered a room not quite as big as the Yankee stadium.' Or a man sitting at a desk smoked 'a cigar not quite as big as an unfurled umbrella'.

Examples of similes

Here are some more examples.

On faces:

'A face like a squeezed orange' – Ben Jonson

'A face like the San Andreas Fault' – anonymous

'A face like a mixed grill' – Victoria Wood

On hands:

    'Fingers like fat maggots'

    'A hand clammy as a wet fish'

    'Hands podgy as old baseball mitts'

Examples of metaphors

    'He has the heart of a lion.'

This does not literally mean he has the heart of a lion, but it shows the courage, pride and ferocity that we associate with a lion; with being lionhearted.

    'It is raining cats and dogs.'

Again, not literally; though thinking of it literally raining cats and dogs conjures a funny and surreal image.

Shakespeare's work is full of metaphor. Here are two famous ones. The first is from *Romeo and Juliet*:

> *But soft, what light through yonder window breaks?*
> *It is the east, and Juliet is the sun.*

Juliet is not just *like* the sun, she *is* the sun.'

And an example from a Macbeth soliloquy as he contemplates the murder of Duncan …

> *Out, out, brief candle! Life's but a walking shadow …*

Life is not *like* a walking shadow but *is* a walking shadow.

In metaphor you can see that one thing is not being compared to another; one thing *is* another. This is why metaphors are thought of as stronger than similes. There is no bridge. Instead one meaning is stamped on another.

FIGURES OF SPEECH

You can extend metaphors; make them longer and more complicated. This can become hyperbole. We cannot go into that here, but you might like to look it up yourself. Personification is another figure of speech which you might like to look up, along with animism, paradox, allegory, analogy and symbols and symbolism.

But the real question with imagery for writers is not how to analyse it, it is how are we to come up with it in the first place. How do you create metaphors and similes? We will now turn to ways of making and using images.

Creating images

There are two ways to approach making images:

1 **to take an existing image and make it new or fresh**

2 **to make a new image.**

We will tackle both these ways, but first of all in preparation, and building on the last lesson, make a list of 15 concrete nouns.

Here are some examples:

- snowdrop
- racehorse
- treacle
- flower
- wind

- book
- window
- dustbin
- gun
- rain

- medicine
- door
- car
- shoe
- sky

WORKING WITH CLICHÉS

We will start by working with clichés.

A *cliché* is a French word for a phrase, expression, or idea that has been overused to the extent that it has lost any of its originality; where it could well once have been novel and forceful it has become tired and hackneyed. If you call something a cliché you are most likely being critical or negative about it. Clichés are to be avoided because being tired and hackneyed they make writing tired and hackneyed. Where there could and should be liveliness and freshness in a piece of writing there is instead a dull sensation as the dull image hits the page. Almost anything in a piece of writing can be clichéd. A situation in a story, any plot device, or character, or figure of speech can become a cliché; anything that has been overused and worn out and become commonplace. In the context in which we are considering it here any image which once was freshly minted but which is now old, worn and familiar is a cliché. We want to avoid clichés and write images with freshness and novelty. But to do that we can start with a cliché or two.

The idea behind this exercise is to take some existing clichés and see if we can make fresh images out of them. For example, here are some clichés:

- as cold as ice
- as wise as an owl
- as bold as brass
- as deaf as a post
- as soft as a baby's bottom

- as tall as a beanpole
- as green as grass
- as black as night
- as hard as ice
- as cool as a cucumber.

You can see that these images were once novel and fresh but, over time, have become over familiar, so that they are now commonplace and hackneyed. They are obvious, are they not? They do not give a lift to the writing; they are uninspired so offer no hope of inspiring. They are the first thoughts that might come into our minds while we are half awake following a rough night. We want more than that. How do we get more?

Snapshot

Make a list of ten clichés you can think of.

From your list of clichés, take away the thing the comparison is made with; for example, in 'as cold as ice', taking away the thing that the comparison is made with, in this case 'ice', leaves you ending up with half-sentences like this:

- as cold as …
- as wise as …
- as bold as …
- as deaf as …
- as soft as …

- as tall as a …
- as green as …
- as black as …
- as hard as …
- as cool as …

Write down the ones *you* thought of.

Key idea

Not everything we write is gold; but, equally, not everything we write is dross.

In a moment, you are going to be asked to take your list of concrete nouns and your list of potential comparisons and see if you can put them together in any new ways you can think of. I want to stress the point here that you must not be too conscious or deliberate about this. A lot of the emphasis of this book has been and will continue to be that we must try to use our conscious minds and out instincts as much as we can. Writing has a huge element of conscious control in it but it also has a vast amount of letting go and allowing other things to come through. 'Other things' sounds vague and deliberately so. How can we characterize something if we don't exactly know what it is?

Key idea

The history of creativity is littered with artists being surprised by their creations; by not being certain where an idea came from or how something developed. Accident plays a huge part in creativity.

So when you do this exercise, don't decide in advance whether something is going to 'fit' or not. Who knows what 'fit' is in this context anyway? Remember the nonsense creations you made in the last chapter; the nonsense sentences and the alphabet soup pieces and do this in the same spirit.

Snapshot

Now, taking your list of concrete nouns and your list of potential comparisons, see whether you can put them together in any new ways. For example:

'as cold as ... a snowdrop'

'as cold as ... a race horse'

'as cold as ... a gun', etc.

What do we have?

'as cold as ... a snowdrop'? (That is possible, but it is not there yet.)

'as cold as ... a race horse'? (That does not really work. It would need supplementing with other material to make it work.)

'as cold as ... a gun'? (It is a simple, obvious description but this could work. Guns are metallic and dangerous and in the right place in the right story it might have an effect.)

Write ten new images using the words from your list or the list at the start of this section.

Edit

What did you come up with? If any work really well, keep them. You may be able to use them in a piece of writing. But if any don't work well, see whether you can change any words over to make a better fit. But you should also ask why a particular image does not work.
- What do you think makes a *good* image?
- What do you think makes a *bad* image?
- Write an example of a *good* image from your list.
- Write an example of a *bad* image from your list.
- What is the difference?

Rewrite your images to make them work better. If they do not work, set them aside.

Focus point

Not all ideas are good ones. Not all ideas work. It will take you some time, but, through practise, try to develop the judgement of what works and what doesn't; it is an essential element in creative writing.

DO NOT FORCE IMAGES

A comparison can stand out in a piece of writing as being forced or fancy. Forcing an image to work is not going to help the writing. It is bad to twist and force the language into something that does not suit it. This is doing the language a disservice; it is going against the nature of the language. Our language has a wonderful facility for allowing us to create all sorts of new things out of it; all sorts of new inventions. It will take us into directions that we had never dreamed of going, but we must not twist and force and compel it into shapes it does not want to make. We must learn to work with the language and not against it. It is as bad to be over fancy with language as it is to force it. A certain style is a necessity in writing, but style that creates meaning, not style at the expense of meaning.

Maybe a certain comparison doesn't work because the two ideas are so dissimilar. It might be that the context could begin to make it work, though even then it might not be enough. But it is important that we do not 'beat ourselves up' over this, to lapse into vernacular for a moment. It is a very important thing to take on board in writing that not everything we write is gold; but equally, not everything we write is dross. The truth, as ever, is somewhere in the middle. Sometimes we can rescue a piece of work and make it quite good. Other times, something is just not going to work and we should take what we can from it and move on.

 ## Snapshot

When you get a chance, read through five or six of your favourite authors. See if they use similes and metaphors and, if they do, what sort of images they come up with. Make notes on them, write them down in your notebook and see what sorts of images they are. Do they draw on things like the sea, or nature, or animals or people? What oddly, unconnected things do they connect and how do they connect them? Write them down and study them; that is a really good way to learn.

If you find an image or images you like, think about what you like about the images. If your favourite authors use few such figures of speech, note that too. That may be important to your reading and even more important to your writing. We must give a note of caution here. It is important to note that not all writers use such figures of speech. Jean Rhys seems to be a writer not drawn to use them with the same abundance as P.G. Wodehouse, H.E. Bates or Raymond Chandler. So we should sound a note (metaphorically) of caution. For all geniuses like Wodehouse who dazzle with their imagery, many others either see no need for it, or try and fail.

 ## William Strunk, Jr. and E.B. White, *The Elements of Style*

'The simile is a common device and a useful one, but similes coming in rapid fire, one right on top of another, are more distracting than illuminating. The reader needs time to catch his breath: he can't be expected to compare everything with something else, and no relief in sight. When you use a metaphor, do not mix it up. That is, don't start by calling something a swordfish and end by calling it an hourglass.'

Key idea

Use figures of speech like metaphors and similes sparingly and well.

Good and bad images

Before we move on to the next exercise, let us examine some other examples from the lists we have compiled:

'as wise as … cough medicine.'

Is this a good or bad image? Write down what you think. Include why.

It seems hard to make this image work. Why is that? Is it because the ideas are too dissimilar? Is there some context in which you could make this work? If you were trying to make this work you would have to provide a context to begin to make it stretch.

How about the image 'as wise as … treacle?' Does this have something to it? Think about it; write down why you think it works or does not work.

'He's as wise as treacle.' This might mean he is not very wise. Or that things stick to him. But it is not altogether a flattering view of his wisdom. The idea maybe that things stick to him willy-nilly without much thought or sifting. 'As wise as cough medicine' might also be saying not very wise.

What do you think of the image 'as wise as … the wind?' This is potentially an interesting, poetic image – 'He's as wise as the wind', which makes one think of a mystic or a medicine man from a Native American Indian tribe.

- 'As deaf as a shoe?' (This could be used in the right story.)
- 'As soft as the sky?' (This again is possible.)

Other suggestions that have something about them:

- 'as hard as a flower' (Try it in 'Jack is as hard as a flower.' Not very hard then.)
- 'as hard as rain' (How does that work? Rain is said to fall hard, but this is merely descriptive. If the image has to do with texture, somehow it needs more work or it needs to be discarded.)
- 'as green as treacle' (making a comment on a character's environmental credentials – not very green then)
- 'as black as a gun' (menacing).

Write

Take all the images you have come up with in this chapter (and any from the given examples that you like) and write a piece that uses them all. Use the images one after the other to guide the writing. Get in as many as you can and do not worry whether it is making sense or not, just have fun.

(750 words)

Edit

The piece you have just written might have gone in any direction because of the nature of the images you are using. When you have finished see if there is anything in the piece that you can edit to make coherent. Try to come up with a piece that hangs together. Large parts of it might be nonsense but see if any sentences, paragraphs or parts of the writing work. If they do, either make them into a coherent piece by writing some new parts to link them, or keep the sentences/parts that work for use in another piece.

Summary

The point of the last few chapters has been to get you to think about the components of language; the tools of our trade. Words are what we use to form and communicate our ideas to others. As writers we need to know our tools and use them well. We have also been looking at new combinations of words, trying to give us new and striking images. In your reading, see if you can spot striking images used by writers. Make a note of some in your notebook. Note any that you think strain for an effect too.

Next step

In the next chapter we will continue working with metaphors and similes to make some new images. We will start the chapter by doing some revision on our understanding of similes and metaphors and by trying to then move on to write some new images.

5

Writing poetry using similes and metaphors

In this chapter you are going to learn more about similes and metaphors; to make new images; to write a simile or two based on hands and feet; and to create metaphors. We are going to play and have fun and see what can come out of that approach.

Derek Walcott

'If you know what you are going to write when you're writing a poem, it's going to be average.'

 ## Robert Frost

'Writing a poem is discovering.'

Similes

REVISION: WHAT IS A SIMILE?

Look at these examples:

'as like as two peas in a pod'

'as black as coal'

'as cold as ice'

'as brave as a lion'

'as cunning as a fox'

'as deaf as a post'

'as slippery as an eel'

What do these examples have in common? Your first answer might be that they are clichés. As we have already said, a cliché is something tired, something familiar, something overused and worn out. As such, you may well have heard all of these before. But the over familiarity of these examples aside, what else do they have in common? Answer: they all make a comparison and similes are all about comparison. They all say one thing is like something else. Some writers find the simile an invaluable part of their armoury; it gives colour and verve to their writing and they also have fun with it. Such a writer is Raymond Chandler whose crime novels are full of striking similes.

 ## Raymond Chandler, *Farewell My Lovely*

'Even on Central Avenue, not the quietest dressed street in the world, he looked about as inconspicuous as a tarantula on a slice of angel food.'

Workshop: similes on hands

Find some hands to write about. It is better if you do not try to write about remembered hands but about hands that you can see. They may be your own or someone else's. Look at them. Just simply look at them. Do not rush this. Take in the physical nature of the hands. Do what you should, at this stage, be quite accustomed to: ask questions.

- What sort of hands are they?
- Male? Female?
- Are they smooth or rough and gnarled? (Hands that have worked or soft, office hands)
- What condition are the nails in? Well-manicured or chewed?
- Is there a ring or rings or marks of a ring?
- Do they have any scars, marks, tattoos?

Now try to think what these hands remind you of. It does not matter how odd it is. Make a list of things – the obvious things like forks and sausages; the less obvious things like …. Well, you say …

When you are ready, write down five comparisons – for example: 1 Hands like knives … 2 Hands like shovels … etc.

Here are some examples of images on fingers:

1 **'Fingers like fat maggots'** The comparison is between fingers and maggots. It is a visual comparison between things not dissimilar in appearance. The simile makes visible the plump, shiny, wriggly digits. But as well as the visual sense the simile carries with it a sense of the physical feel of the fingers; it also conveys a judgement that they are probably not very nice. Who would honestly like to be touched by a hand with fingers like fat maggots? This is another important point to make about creative writing.

Key idea

Our choice of comparison can carry with it a judgement or a strong suggestion to the reader how we want them to both visualize and judge a piece of writing such as a character in a story. An image such as 'fingers like fat maggots' would not endear us to this character but would signal to us what the writer wants us to think of the character.

2 'A hand clammy as a wet fish' is also not very nice and would do the same job of directing the judgement readers would form of the character. Though we can see the fish, this is an image strongly based on the *feel* of the hand; damp and cold and clammy, more than the visual look of it.

3 'Hands podgy as old baseball mitts' Here we have a sense both of how they feel and how big they are. It is a combination of the feel and look of the subject. It again shows us the magic and speed of thought that an image contains. It hooks into character creation and even a situation; do we have a sporty character here or a character in a sports story? Imagine a character in a story with hands podgy as old baseball mitts. What sort of situations and scenarios would this character get involved in? This simple image does begin to convey quite a bit beyond itself. The word 'podgy' is doing some descriptive and judgemental work too. It is guiding our judgement of the writing and the characterization of the character.

Another visual comparison could be:

4 'Hands like tea cups'. This image is built around the shape that hands can make when cupped. Maybe these hands could even have things poured into their cup-like shape. This will probably be small (they are not mugs). Maybe they are made of bone china and suggest a delicacy of situation and character.

These examples show the interconnectedness of things. In discussion, we treat a lot of concepts such as images, character and story in separation when, in fact, they belong together. They work together in our writing and can only be fully understood in relation to other concepts. Separating them out is a way of getting to know and practising them, but they will only fully be understood when they are working together. That is when they take on their multiplicity of meanings and layers. The more you study, the more of the connections you will see. Seeing the connectedness of things is an important mark of learning in any subject.

Workshop: similes on feet

Repeat the same approach and try writing some images with feet. For example, 'Feet like ...'. Follow the same procedure; let your mind wander, jot down any ideas that come into your head and then write down five comparisons: 1 Feet like flippers ... 2 Feet like tree roots ... 3 Feet like bricks, etc.

Snapshot

In your notebook make a random list of 20 everyday objects that have nothing to do with each other (e.g. egg, armchair, teapot, book).

When you have written down 20, find two of the objects in your lists that do not usually have a relationship with each other and yoke them together into a simile. From this list of 20, do three to six similes.

Here are some suggestions for images based on eggs and armchairs:

'She sank into the chair like ... a knife into a shell.'

'She sank into the chair like ... teeth into a shell.'

'She sank into the chair like ... a soldier into a soft-boiled egg.'

What do you think works well here, and what do you think works less well?

With the last example you can almost hear her sigh as she sinks into the deep yellow cushions. Perhaps the chair is yellow and a little egg-like in shape itself.

Or another suggestion:

'Years of sitting by the window had poached the professor's chair arms.'

And maybe the professor, too. Or how about this?

'The armchair was white, with cushions brown as freshly laid eggs.'

These are nice images that would go well in a piece of writing. They would sharpen the eye and bring pleasure to the reader. Nor would they necessarily stand out as being forced or fancy, which, as we have said, can be a danger with images. Notice the use of the word *as* instead of *like*. This is another way to make the comparison on which similes depend.

Snapshot

Write three similes comparing a thistle and a hedgehog. Follow the same procedure: let your mind wander, jot down any ideas that come into your head and then write down the comparisons, using 'like' or 'as'.

Here are some suggestions for images based on thistles and hedgehogs:

'The thistles closed its prickles like a hedgehog under attack.'

This is OK, but not so surprising. The following is better:

'The thistle cut into her hands like a startled hedgehog.'

You might think the thistle and hedgehog are too similarly prickly but given this task in class, a writing student came up with an amusing picture:

'Bob's thistle-trimmed, army issue haircut, changed his usually placid face into that of a slightly demented hedgehog.'

This is a nice comic picture and the image sits well within it. It is neither forced nor strained. It sits nicely in the writing and allows the image to come easily to the mind.

Key idea

Bringing the image easily to the mind is something that all good images should do. Once an image is or seems forced, it is failing.

Snapshot

Write three similes comparing alcohol and eyes. Follow the same procedure: let your mind wander, jot down any ideas that come into your head and then write down the comparisons.

Snapshot

Take two things unrelated and unlike each other and make a comparison between them. For example:

> house compared with peach
>
> fruitcake compared with pillow
>
> shoe compared with flower
>
> cat compared with kettle
>
> suitcase compared with old photograph.

You try writing some more similes using the same method.

Here are some examples: some good, some not quite there yet:

> The fruitcake chewed like a soft pillow.
>
> The house glowed like a peach in the sun.
>
> The suitcase glided like a sepia image.
>
> The shoe burst like a flower in spring.
>
> The cat stood like a hissing kettle.

Focus point

When you first come to use similes you may enjoy the experience so much that you overuse them. Good. Carry on; overuse them to your hearts content. When you have done so you will begin to mine the words for better similes, harder ones, similes that are original, imaginative and alive.

Making images

So far, we have covered different ways of creating images; now we will try adding to our images.

The images we have created so far have been in many ways the most focused. We have concentrated on a simple comparison, one thing for another without allowing anything else to intervene. We are now going to see if we can unite the other parts of language that we looked at in the previous lesson: the adjective and adverb.

What can adjectives and adverbs bring to an image? We have printed out a grid for you below. You can copy it in your notebook or use a piece of paper and draw the columns on the paper. You would either need to cover up the various columns as we go through the exercise, or fold the paper in an origami-like way. Whichever way you do it, try to follow the instructions carefully. They may seem complicated at first but they can help produce interesting results.

Workshop: making images (1)

Look at the template provided below and draw one like it for your own use.

1 Adjective	2 Noun	3 Adverb	4 Verb	5 Adjective	6 Noun

With your card, bookmark or spare hand (or fold the paper), cover up the entire grid except for column 1. In this column write five adjectives, one in each box, and each beneath the other. Try to write quickly and without thinking about it too much. You should get something like this:

1 Adjective	2 Noun	3 Adverb	4 Verb	5 Adjective	6 Noun
red					
bleak					
big					
fresh					
large					

Then cover up the entire grid except for column 4. In this column write five verbs, one in each box, and each beneath the other. It is especially important that you try to write quickly and without thinking about what you wrote last time. Do not try to find words to fit. Just write. It is important to cover up all the other columns too so that you are not reminded about what you have written.

At this second attempt you should have something like this:

1 Adjective	2 Noun	3 Adverb	4 Verb	5 Adjective	6 Noun
			runs		
			swims		
			sucks		
			sweats		
			rumbles		

Now cover up the entire grid except for column 2. In this column write five nouns, one in each box, and each beneath the other. Once again, when you have written the words try to forget about them and clear your mind for the next column.

After that cover up the entire grid except for column 5. In this column write five adjectives, one in each box, and each beneath the other.

After that cover up the entire grid except for column 6. In this column write five nouns, one in each box, and each beneath the other.

After that cover up the entire grid except for column 3. In this column write five adverbs, one in each box, and each beneath the other.

If you have followed the instructions you should end up with something like this:

1 Adjective	2 Noun	3 Adverb	4 Verb	5 Adjective	6 Noun
red	dog	quickly	runs	pink	pig
bleak	car	guiltily	swims	swollen	flower
big	star	angrily	sucks	round	shoe
fresh	jelly	smoothly	sweats	blue	paunch
large	horse	carelessly	rumbles	happy	barrel

Reading across the page, you will have five sentences as in the finished example above. What sense do any of them make? The first one reads:

'Red dog quickly runs pink pig.'

Can we make anything of that image? On the surface it is gobbledygook. But let us spend some time with it. Say it over, out loud. 'Red dog quickly runs pink pig.' 'Red dog quickly runs pink pig.' It is a bit of a tongue-twister but does it have any potential in our writing at all? It has an interesting shape in the mouth. It starts and ends with short, quick words. Red and dog and are both three lettered monosyllabic words. 'Runs pink pig' is quite quick forms of words to end the sentence. Again they are monosyllabic. Because it ends this way we somehow get a sense of the pink pig running off the sentence and on into something else. Into another part of our story, perhaps. This gives the line movement. The different word is the word 'quickly' in the middle of the sentence. What does this do? Oddly enough, it slows it up by tripping us up with the extra syllable. 'Red dog quickly runs pink pig.' There is a built-in hitch here which affects the rhythm. This may or may not be interesting, but can we do anything with it? Is there any context in which this sentence could work? Yes. Imagine a red dog in a children's story chasing or snapping at the heels of a very pink pig. That context seems to fit.

 Key idea

The stranger the initial images we create are, the more chance we have of mining some gold.

How about number two?

'Bleak car guiltily swims swollen flower.'

This is a strange one. (Aren't they all? Yes, luckily.)

Maybe this image has an underwater quality to it, given by the word swims. Can we imagine a car swimming? Yes, given the sorts of images we see in films and on TV, we would have no problem imagining a car swimming on the sea or underwater.

This is also a bleak car. Why is it bleak? What is it about this car that makes it bleak? Has something happened to it to make it bleak? Does it look bleak or does it feel bleak? Your conscious mind might tell you that a car can neither feel bleak nor un-bleak. It has no feelings. But this car is bleak and guilty. This is a troubled car. It can feel. It may look or feel bleak but it certainly feels guilty. We have a car with feelings. There is what is called personification in this image.

Write

Take one of the images you have created, or use one from this chapter, and write a short poem. The poem need not rhyme (but can if you wish). You must include the image you have chosen as part or all of one line. Pick an image which is striking and which has a sense of rhythm to it and use that rhythm to guide you as you come up with the other lines. The poem should be 4–10 lines long.

Personification is yet another figure of speech, and once much used in poetry. We have already looked at simile and metaphor, but personification is a figure of speech that gives an inanimate object, such as this car or an abstract idea, human traits and qualities, such as emotions, desires, sensations, physical gestures and speech. Examples are 'the dogs were *suffering* from the cold.' 'The doll sat in the pram, looking *sadly* at its owner.' 'This motorway really *loves* to jam.' In these sentences we have projected our human feelings onto something that does not feel. How does it work in this context? – 'Bleak car guiltily swims swollen flower.'

Even if it is bleak and guilty how can it swim a swollen flower? Can you let your minds play with that image in order to make sense of it? It has a surreal quality that might work in the right piece.

Number three is:

'Big star angrily sucks round shoe.'

Is this something in outer space or a sulky film star driven to sucking her own shoe; or perhaps someone trying to get on in the industry by sucking someone else's round shoe?

'Fresh jelly smoothly sweats blue paunch.'

An uncomfortable image which, if we add the explicit comparison could read 'Fresh jelly smoothly sweats like a blue paunch.' Not much nicer but vivid, which is what we are after.

'Large horse carelessly rumbles (like a) happy barrel.'

This has a pleasant comedic feel to it.

These images are not bad for a quick bit of word jotting.

Some other sentences that have come from this exercise are:

'Green sun briskly pricks small ball.'

The story is not clear but the green sun has potential.

'Tired cat lazily eats brave footballer.'

A tired lion having its lunch.

'Magic cheese furiously kisses grey bed.'

Well, if it's magic cheese, it can do anything.

Workshop: making images (2)

Repeat this exercise but focusing it on food and the theme of the senses. See what results you get. Try to come up with ten images. When you have done so, choose the best five and put them together in whatever order you like to make a poem. Do it now. Write.

You might have got some results like these:

'Sweating cheese blistered like fresh tarmac.'

'Dying pigs exploding like soufflés.'

'Grey sewage fizzled like popcorn.'

'Quick eels rebounded like rubber bands.'

'The fitted nylon sheets flapping on the line like burnt omelettes'. (Very yellow but without using the word.)

With a bit of work tidying up the images (focusing them) and finding a suitable title you could end up with something like this:

Hot summer city

Bed sheets flapping like burnt omelettes.

Sweating cheese blistering like tarmac.

Grey sewage fizzling like popcorn.

Dying pigs exploding like soufflés.

Workshop: making images (3)

In your notebook or on a separate piece of paper, draw yourself another grid. This should have five columns along the page and eight rows down, so that it looks like the example given below. In each of the boxes along the top write to the following, in box 1 adjective; in box 2 adjective; in box 3 and 4 write noun; in the final box 5 write verb.

1 Adjective	2 Adjective	3 Noun	4 Noun	5 Verb

When you have done that, use the grid to make lists *down* not across the page. Do not try to match anything up either across or down the page. In fact, try all you can to avoid doing so. Try to grab words randomly from anywhere. Just write seven adjectives then another seven followed by seven nouns, seven more nouns and finally seven verbs.

For example:

1 Adjective	2 Adjective	3 Noun	4 Noun	5 Verb
broken	bitter	duvet	child	trembles
falling	old	shoe	blossom	eats
rainy	lost	piano	bird	dances
dusty	winter	tutor	dandruff	swings
happy	worried	Sunday	brain	flies
worn	burning	storms	student	sleeps
raw	yellow	cat	eggs	runs

From the grid that you have made for yourself, pick and choose words to try and make some images. The images need to be six words long and in the form of the following – Adjective followed by Noun followed by Verb followed by comparison ('as' or 'like') followed by Adjective followed by Noun. This might seem complicated, and it actually might help you to make another grid, but to make it clear, here are a couple of examples taken from the grid above:

Worn (adjective) shoe (noun) dances (verb) like (comparison) a lost (adjective) child (noun)

worried bird trembles like falling blossom

old tutor sleeps like a dusty piano

The comparison in these images is achieved by using the word 'like'. As in 'Worn shoe dances *like* a lost child;' 'old tutor sleeps *like* a dusty piano'

Now *you* try and make half a dozen images in the same manner. To remind you, the sentence should start with an adjective and be followed by a noun, then a verb then the word 'like' followed by another adjective and another noun.

See what you can come up with.

We began this exercise wondering what adjectives and adverbs could bring to an image. In some cases, they have developed the images in really quite interesting ways. Some of these images need more effort to make them work, but some of them are quite close to being workable. This first one has an interesting quality to it:

'Old tutor sleeps like a dusty piano.'

Could this work as an affectionate picture of an old music teacher? Could you write a story starting with this beginning? 'The old tutor slept like a dusty piano.' But imagine his head, full of those notes!

A poem or a piece of fiction that started this way would be intriguing. A lot of readers would be caught by the mystery in the words and would want to continue reading.

 Key idea

Getting a reader to continue reading is one of the essentials of writing creatively.

How about this second image we created?

'Worn shoe dances like a lost child.'

Again, it is strange but this is an image with a real visual quality to it. Could you write a piece with this as its beginning?

'The worn shoe danced like a lost child.'

or

'The worn shoes danced like lost children.'

This is intriguing. It makes sense and doesn't quite make sense. It holds the interest. Again, this would intrigue and as a reader you would wait for the development of the image.

Here is a third one:

'Worried bird trembles like falling blossom.'

This would also work in the right context. It has the imagist sense of a Chinese or Japanese poem to it. There is also a quality of touch and sound, however faint, coming across in the trembling as you can almost see the soft, downy feathers coming out of the bird as it shakes, and drifting like blossom.

This is not a bad haul. What did you come up with? Can you tinker with any to make them work? See whether you can get a poem or two out of them.

 Edit

Read your images over to see if they are fresh, or original. Keep those that are; try to work on the others to get them to the same level. Can you use any parts of the others to make them work? Sometimes taking part of an image or a sentence and adding it to another can make something that was not working successful. Try it now and see what you can come up with.

If you are interested in doing any further reading on this, try Chapter 2 and Chapters 4–6 of *The Way to Write,* by J. Fairfax and J. Moat, published by Elm Tree Books in 1981 and reprinted fairly often since then.

Metaphors

As we have said, metaphors do not make a comparison. Or rather the comparison is of a different sort; it is, in a way, more compressed and condensed, more direct. Metaphors do not use the comparison of 'a' or 'like'; they just go straight ahead and stamp one thing on another by saying that something *is* something else. A metaphor may, for example, talk about the sofa not being like an egg, but as if it *was* an egg.

Metaphors can be stunningly original and make such an impact they communicate directly with the reader.

Orson Scott Card, *Alvin Journeyman*

'Metaphors have a way of holding the most truth in the least space.'

They can also, like many similes, become clichéd, hackneyed and dead.

John Singleton and Mark Luckhurst, *The Creative Writing Handbook*

'Overuse has turned many a good metaphor into a dead metaphor or a cliché. But every cliché began as a freshening and imaginative idea, only for the rest of us to ruin it for the creator.'

Well-known examples are:

'Religion is the opiate of the masses' (Karl Marx)

and:

- stone cold
- armed to the teeth
- back in the saddle
- to touch base
- blow a fuse
- elbow grease
- ice cold
- difficult to swallow
- red hot
- mending fences
- in the firing line.

All of these metaphors were probably 'red hot' when they were first invented, but through over use and over familiarity, they have lost their heat and therefore any power.

Key idea

Be on the lookout for dead metaphors. They have the sound of a dead language.

On the other hand, you could take some dead metaphors and have fun with them.

'As an actor he was 'red hot' at that moment in time. You just had to go near him to feel the glow coming off his skin. The fire in his belly melted even the stone-hearted critic.'

Or:

'The truth was difficult to swallow. It kept him retching all night.'

 ## Write

Find as many clichéd metaphors as you can. Write them down in your notebook

Write a short poem, a few lines, interpreting them literally. For example:

He was hard-hearted.

The clear porcelain of her emotion

slammed up against his chest,

shattered and smashed to the floor.

 ## Snapshot

- Choose something ordinary (e.g. a chair, a fire-extinguisher or a dustbin).
- Think of qualities the object has or is like (e.g. a chair like a toadstool; a dustbin like a mouth; a fire-extinguisher red as blood.
- Try and turn these into metaphors (don't use 'as' or 'like').

For example:

'The dustbin is a hungry mouth.'

'The dustbin is an armchair.'

'The chairs are toadstools.'

You try.

 ## Snapshot

You can also make metaphors in stages:

1. Make a simile – e.g. 'the dustbin like a hungry mouth'
2. Cut out the word 'like' – e.g. 'the dustbin, a hungry mouth'
3. Move the image in front of the noun – e.g. 'the hungry mouthed dustbin.'

This gives us the sense of a voracious, animal-like, hungry mouthed dustbin devouring everything.

Another example:

1. 'fire-extinguisher red as blood'
2. 'fire-extinguisher red blood'
3. 'blood-red fire-extinguisher'

You try. Make up six metaphors in this way, built around ordinary everyday things. Put them together to get a poem. You will need to play around with them, adjust the odd word, focus an image or two, but do your best and see whether you can make them fit.

Snapshot

You can extend the metaphor. This is easy and can be great fun. Take one of your metaphors and 'extend' it into a poem – that is, instead of settling for one idea, keep adding to it, as in:

Hungry mouthed dustbin
wide jaws open, licking
the garbage, crunching
broken glass ripping
wet cardboard, crushing
plastic bottles, gulping
rotted fruit, meat
and two veg. Stuffed
and contended
it slumbered, belching
its aromas
up into the night.

You try. Take one of your metaphors and extend it into a poem in this way.

Snapshot

Take six of the similes you have created in your notebook, or find six in the last two chapters of this book, and turn them into metaphors.

For example:

'The bird was falling blossom (as the gunshot echoed)'

'The child was a worn shoe (lost in a puddle)'

'The tutor was a dusty piano (dark, big-shouldered with a wide, ivory-white grin)'

See, once again, if you can develop any of them into a short poem.

Workshop: the 'Furniture Game'

Consider this list of 'things':

a musical instrument	a tree	a relative
car	a country	an animal
fruit	a time of day	a colour
vegetable	the weather	a flower
item of clothing	a season	a hat.
jewellery	a drink	
a desert	a genre of film or a novel	

Add to this list yourself, if you wish, in your notebook.

Now, using this list as a guide we are going to create the picture of a person. For example:

He is a slug of whiskey from a hip flask
A thick tweed suit and Donegal cap
Shamrock on a rainy day
A body swerve in a phone box
And a mountain in an avalanche.

Who is he?

Answer: a big, athletic Irish rugby union player fortified, probably, despite the whiskey, with many pints of Guinness.

You try.

Think of someone you know, either in person, or someone famous, and describe them in terms of items on the list in this book or your own list.

Firstly, use questions in the following form and select categories from those listed above:

If this person was a musical instrument, what instrument would they be?

If this person was a time of day, what time would they be?

If this person was an animal, what animal would they be?

If this person was a car, what car would they be? (Remember, not what car would they own or drive, but what car would they *be*.)

When you have answered 10–12 questions in this manner, choose the best and put them into a poem in the style of the example above. You will want to spend some time putting them into the right order so that they create the best effect. Your aim is to create a sense of the person without saying they are who they are – for example, write about the Queen or the US President without saying that is who you are writing about.

(For more on this game, check out *Does it Have to Rhyme?*, by Sandy Brownjohn.)

Summary

In this chapter you have worked on similes and metaphors. You have made new images, written a simile or two based on hands and feet, and you have been shown ways to create metaphors. You have been encouraged to have fun with the language in making new images and in writing brief, imagist poems. To take this further, read some poetry centred around images; English poet Craig Raine has many striking images in his poems. The imagist poetry of William Carlos Williams would also be good in this context. Even if poetry is not your thing, doing this would be useful to you. For, although metaphors and similes are at the heart of poetry, they do not only exist there and are equally much used in prose.

Focus point

Keep taking risks and new challenges. You would never be able to come up with anything new if you were not prepared to have fun and to take risks and try something different.

Next step

In the next chapter you will build on the work done so far and begin to explore the senses and understand what it is to look at the world of senses as a writer.

6

The five senses (1)

In this chapter you will begin to explore the senses; consider the range of senses; explore the sense of sight; and look as a writer, not just as a citizen. We will consider what is the most popularly used of the senses in writing and how knowing and developing facility with the senses can bring your writing to life.

Exploring the senses

In the previous section we searched for ways to describe what we saw – images that would conjure pictures in our writing and in our (and our readers') minds. In doing this we were working with writing that was visual. The fact that we can see images in our minds and can help readers to see images is connected with our sense of sight. Creating visual images is fundamental to good creative writing, something known to many great writers.

 ## Joseph Conrad

'My task … is by the power of the written word to make you hear, to make you feel – it is, before all, to make you see. That – and no more – and it is everything.'

We will shortly do some exercises based on observation and sight but it is important to say at the outset that, as well as sight, we should keep all the other senses in mind. Pictures are not only visual; when we see things we quite often hear or imagine sounds as well as receiving information from the other senses.

 ## Key idea

Strong writing is equally full of other sensory material; not only visual.

 ## Rebecca McClanahan, *Word Painting*

' … ignoring the other senses in your writing is like sitting in a gourmet restaurant wearing earplugs, work gloves, and a surgical mask over your nose and mouth.'

Though some of this other sense material is not always accessed by writers, it can and should be used in as much of your writing as possible. Practising writing from the senses will enable you to build on your learning so that you can begin to develop the writing of full and quite complex scenes containing a lot of good, sensory detail.

 ## Key idea

Practising writing from our sense of sight is a very important thing to do in creative writing. Writing what you see helps the development of your writing descriptively but so does practising writing from all the senses.

Workshop: the senses

We are going to start small; we will separate out the senses and consider them one by one. But first of all we are going to start with some questions.

- How many senses are there? Make a list of your senses in your notebook.
- Now make a new list, of your senses in order of importance to *you*.
- Now, think as a writer – which senses do you think a writer would most want?
- Is there any difference between these lists? What is that difference and why? Think about it and make notes in your notebook.

Write

Think of a situation in which you might be in danger if you lacked one of your senses. Write 100 words for each sense.

Think of a time when it would be an advantage not to have one of your senses. Write 100 words for each sense.

Write down five pleasant reasons for having each of your senses – one reason for each sense.

What order do you think the senses are used in writing? That is to say what sense is most prevalent and what least used? Before you look at the answer below, think about this question and write your answers in your notebook.

The order of the senses usually used in writing is:

1 **sight – the number-one sense**
2 **sound – good second**
3 **touch – strong third**
4 **taste**
5 **smell – for the last two it is a toss-up between them.**

To see whether this is true, have a look at some of your favourite writers.

There are exceptions to this; and you are probably immediately trying to think of them.

Patrick Suskind's *Perfume* is a book built around the sense of smell. Such books stand out because they are unusual. Many of the examples given in this book have been visual, particularly in the previous chapters where we were talking about making and developing images. The sense of hearing, the use of sound, comes a strong second in writing. The sense of touch comes third. If you look at any writing you like you will probably find that there will be a lot of visual material; quite a lot about the sounds of things and a degree of writing about the touch and feel of things, but you will probably have to hunt much more to find examples of things that taste and smell. For these last two senses, taste and smell, it is very much a toss-up between them which is used more or which is used less in writing. They are perhaps used about the same. This is not surprising since they are by their nature linked.

Taking all this on board it is obvious that writers need to use their eyes and be good observers of people and situations. They also need to be good listeners; they need to develop a good ear for dialogue. But writers also need to access their other senses because these senses are sometimes forgotten or overlooked. Taste and smell do not get as much attention as they warrant but they are important and excellent areas for making writing evocative and come alive.

In this chapter and the next, as we have said, we will explore all the senses and look at ways of accessing and using the entire range of sensory material in writing. But first, as it is the most dominant, we are going to continue to concentrate on exercises on the sense of sight.

 Write

You will need to go outside for this exercise. Go to a place and look intently. It could be a busy or a quiet place: a train station, a market, a supermarket or a shopping precinct. Concentrate on taking in as much as you can. As you did in the observation exercise in an earlier chapter, let your eye rove over the scene and then write down what you see. Write quickly, as if you were an artist making a sketch of the place. Concentrate on things like buildings, market stalls, seats, windows, rather than people. Do this for no more than five minutes.

(350 words)

Take a short break, then begin to concentrate on one thing: a piece of a wall, a picture, a floorboard, a hole in a floorboard, a flower, a window, a door, someone's face. While you are there in front of it, write down a description.

Be meticulous; write in absolute detail.

(400 words)

Compare the two pieces. Note any differences.

 Edit

Take these two sets of notes and rewrite them as a piece of description. Use what you believe the most significant or telling details of the place that you have written down. You don't have to use all your notes; just the details that say most about the place or bring it to life. Be selective in what details you choose. Choose the most telling and appropriate

In your first draft you might well have come up with something all inclusive, suggestive, sketchy, and atmospheric. It may also have the energy that comes from speed. These are all good things in writing. Working it over could well produce something detailed, analytical and very focused. This might be slower and have less pace. Both approaches are equally valid and equally useful in writing. One has a little more focus than the other, that is all.

Focus point

It is not accidental that sight is the most used of all our senses. In order to describe an object or situation clearly you need to see it. If you as writer can't see it, then it is more than likely that you will struggle to help your reader to see it. In your writing you need to put down on paper words that will allow the reader to get a clear mental picture of what you want them to see. This takes a good deal of research, accuracy and observation.

Key idea

Observation is key to seeing; and to writing.

If you wanted to break sight down into different ways of seeing, observation would have to be one of them: looking at and studying things, objects, and people. To look at, to observe, is one of the fundamental skills of any artist. Consider how carefully painters must look at the subject or object they are painting. How they must train their eyes and hands to work together. It is not so dissimilar with writers. Writers must learn to look; they must learn to see and record what they see. One of the earliest exercises you did in this book was to look at something and to write down what you had observed.

Write

Find a tree; look at it closely. Answer some questions:
- What type of tree is it?
- Name it. If you don't know the name, find out.
- Describe the leaves; are they different on the underside and on the top?
- Any fruit or nuts?
- Any caterpillars on them?
- Describe the bark, the roots.
- Has anything been carved on the trunk?
- Put in anything you observe, anything you can find to say.

(200 words)

Next describe a car.

- Is it new, old, deserted, rusty, shiny or dull?
- What is the bodywork like?
- Are there any dents?
- Is it well looked after or a neglected old jalopy?
- What is on the back seat?
- What is on the floor?
- Is it driven by a man or a woman?
- Is it driven by someone older or younger?
- How can you tell?
- What are the details that enable you to make this judgement?

(200 words)

When you get the chance, choose some things yourself; practise looking at a succession of things and make notes in more and more detail.

 ## Focus point

The more you look, the more you see. Practise looking at things and making notes.

 ## Write

Make a list of things that you don't like, things that are ugly or repulsive to you in some way. Everyone's taste is different but it might be graffiti, tattoos, body piercing, sickness or maggots in a fisherman's basket. It might be the sight of famine in Africa, it might be television pictures of a war-torn land. It might be a slaughterhouse, it might be barbed wire. Whatever it is, make a list.

(750 words)

Now take one of these things and write a passage where you describe it as beautiful. The piece of writing should transform the ugliness of the thing into something beautiful.

(350 words)

Make a list of things you find beautiful: someone's face, a flower, a view of hills, a portrait, a beautiful city, a beautiful baby. Now take one of these things and write a passage in which you make it ugly. Transform this beautiful thing into something ugly and nasty.

(400 words)

This exercise has hopefully helped you to look at things in a different and unexpected way. Part of the problem we have with seeing is that we do it all the time, naturally. It is so familiar to us that we don't think we need to practise it. We see all the time, every waking second, so we think we do not need to make any special effort to see. But we can get lazy in this. We can see in accepted and lazy ways so that we don't properly look at what is before us. And we are certainly not seeing it as a creative writer could and should be seeing it.

Key idea

Just because your eyes are open it does not mean that you see.

While an ordinary member of the public could look at something and not see anything special, a writer should be looking for detail; for that concrete piece of detail that will be most telling in the picture they want to create.

W.H. Auden

'A man has his distinctive personal scent which is wife, his children and his dog can recognise. A crowd has a generalised stink. The public is odourless.'

W.H. Auden's comment on the dangers of being too general and the importance of detail that evokes another of the senses, smell, could equally apply to *all* the senses.

Transformation

A writer might also be looking for atmosphere and for the detail that would evoke that. A writer, any creative artist, can also transform something from what is conventionally ugly, to something beautiful, and vice versa. This is what nature has the power to do.

Think of some of the natural disasters that occur; volcanoes that erupt, or mud slides that engulf towns and cities. The Roman city of Pompeii was destroyed and completely buried under ash and pumice when Mount Vesuvius erupted in 79 ce. Pompeii was lost for nearly 1,700 years before it was rediscovered by accident in 1748. Since then, its excavation has provided a wonderful insight into the life of a city of the Roman Empire. It has become one of the most popular tourist attractions of Italy and a UNESCO World Heritage Site.

There are other examples in nature of absolute devastation occurring and within a shorter span than Pompeii a thing of strange beauty is created in its place. Sometimes within a few years, at least within a generation, flowers have grown and crops have returned to devastated land; nature has made beautiful what was broken, devastated and ugly. Another example of unexpected beauty began at Truk lagoon, also known as Chuuk lagoon, in Micronesia in the Second World War.

Chuuk lagoon is one of Micronesia's undersea phenomena. The giant lagoon is almost 40 miles in diameter and reaches depths of 300 feet. It has a beautiful undersea coral reef beneath the clear water, but it also is the final tomb for more than 100 ships, planes and submarines – the legacy of a Second World War battle between the Japanese Imperial Fleet and the American Air Force. American carrier attack planes attacked it on 17 February 1944 in an early morning raid called Operation Hailstone. The attack lasted for three days and resulted in the Americans sending 60 Japanese ships and 275 airplanes to the bottom of the lagoon. For over 60 years these wrecks have rested on the bottom virtually undisturbed, but creating the greatest underwater museum in the world.

The warm tropical water, prolific marine life and ocean currents have transformed the wrecks into beautiful coral gardens and artificial reefs that are home to hundreds of exotic marine animals and fish. Today, Chuuk lagoon is a favourite place for the world's sport divers, underwater photographers and marine scientists. It could be home to artists too interested in the transforming power of nature, and considering how to use this power in their art.

Artists have to at least understand the possibility of such transformations and to use them in their art. The transformation that takes place in a story would be quite different from the transformation of a war grave into a coral reef but it could be just as dramatic and just as beautiful. As writers we can transform the world in our work as much as nature does in the natural world. We might transform a setting in a story. We might transform characters. How many characters can you think of in stories that start out appearing to us in one light and end up through the progress of the story appearing in quite another. Can you think of someone beautiful who ends up ugly? Or someone, like Cinderella, who starts out ugly, or at least poor and at the mercy of her two ugly sisters, and ends up the beautiful princess who captures the heart of prince charming. Fairy tales have an understanding of the transforming nature of art at their heart. Think of the tale of Beauty and the Beast and how the beast starts out a monster and ends up a beauty. The transforming power of imagination is crucial to creative writing. In instances like these, seeing is a lot more than mere looking.

 ## Write

Study a familiar object. If you are in a café, it might be your cup of tea, or the salt cellar. Make notes about this object in the same way as you have just been doing. Then, using your notes, write a short paragraph as if you were describing it to an alien who only had the sense of sight. Do not use sound, smell and taste or texture unless you can describe those things visually. The alien can only see and you have to describe the object so they can understand what it is and what it does.

(750 words)

This might seem a silly idea but poet Craig Raine developed an entire poetic approach from something similar, starting with this collection *A Martian Sends a Postcard Home*. And at least one major novelist, Graham Greene, with *Our Man in Havana*, published in 1958, has made mileage out of something similar. It is claimed that certain aspects of the plot of this book, in particular the importance of rocket launchers, appears to predict the Cuban Missile Crisis of 1962. The novel is set in Cuba during the regime of Fulgencio Batista. Batista was later overthrown by Castro. James Wormold is a vacuum cleaner salesman. He meets Hawthorne, who offers him work with the British secret service. Wormold lives alone (his wife has left him for another man) with his teenage daughter, Milly. Wormold needs money to get his beautiful growing daughter all she wants, so he accepts the offer from Hawthorne. But he has no real information to send so he starts to pretend. He uses his imagination mixed with observation to claim that he has a network of agents. These are actually people that he knows only by sight. But he gets very enthusiastic in his reports by sending London a circuit diagram of a vacuum cleaner. He tells them that this is a sketch of a secret rocket launching-ramp. This proves to be a very lucrative line as he excites his spy masters back in London.

Wormold's descriptions of the world he both sees and imagines are so vivid that he seriously worries London about the communist threat and earns himself a tidy sum on the way. He creates the 'story' for his spy master bosses by an amalgamation of two forms of seeing; seeing with the eye and seeing with the imagination. He looks very closely at the world around him and draws imaginative suggestions about it. He looks closely at vacuum cleaners and does very accurate drawings of them, turning them in the eyes of London, into rocket launchers. What happens is the dream of all writers: his imagined world becomes real. His messages are intercepted and the enemy begins to act on them; even to the point of killing people and trying to poison Wormold himself. The plot gets complicated, as you would hope, but it ends well for the imaginative would-be spy; as you would again hope. He gets an OBE for all his fraudulent messages; and he also gets a new wife.

Seeing properly and certainly writing properly involves the imagination as well as observation. You might well classify the imagination as another form of sight. There is only so far that observation can take you. If writing was only observation then it would be something factual, and not dissimilar to a piece of technical writing. But creative writing is not technical writing. It is essentially different from it. It is when a writer supplements the careful observation they have made with imagined detail, with a leap into the imagination, that a piece of writing can come alive in the way that *Our Man in Havana* comes alive. Another film that comes alive in a similar way through imaginative use of storytelling within a story is *The Usual Suspects*.

Writing and memory

Another thing to consider with the sense of sight is the importance of memory. If observation is fundamental to writing what we see and if imagination can transform observation into a wonderful new creation then memory can also come into observations and work with the writing. Memory acts as a supplement and a motivator. It can bring forgotten details to an observed piece to fill it out and make it more.

When we live we store experiences. We store them naturally without any deliberate intention to do so. They just come along with us. As humans it is the way we are. We experience things, good and bad and we remember them; or at least we remember some things about them. The memories can be fragmentary or very particular; a smell, a sudden flash of touch or taste. We quite often forget most of the details about something but a significant part can stay with us; it can get under our skins so deeply that we can't shed it; and sometimes we don't want to shed it because it is important to us. At other times we would love to shed it because of the pain it brings to us – though writers would know that in those memories could be the potential to release some writing gold. Sometimes the memories we have become so important to us that they, in some ways, encapsulate and contain our lives. We do not want to shed them because that would be shedding our lives. These memories come into us as we write. They come unbidden and sometimes that can be a problem. Part of the problem with writing, with what we remember, can be of using it well, of controlling and organizing it so that it serves the writing we are producing. Another problem can be that of truth.

If we are using a memory in a piece of writing, the question nearly always comes up about how truthful we are to that memory. Do we have to put it down exactly as it happened or can we take from it some of its energy or its detail and use that in the service of creating a good piece of writing? People can be divided on this though for any real writer that is hard to imagine. The writing must always come first for a writer; writing the best possible writing. And if the best possible writing is to make use of a memory or part of a memory in order to add to the picture being painted, then that is what the writer must do. The memory must be made to fit the requirement. It is not a question of lying or of twisting the facts, but of using whatever is necessary to create the best possible work of art.

 ## Write

Find a building that you can observe comfortably. It might be an apartment block, a house or an office block. Study this building in the way that you have been observing other places and objects in these exercises. First of all note the details about the building: things like the material it is built of, its size and shape, what manner of building it is. When you have an accurate record of it, think of a similar building that you know quite well. Maybe it is a building you lived in, or someone close to you lived in or worked in.

Remember what this other building was like. Remember what it was like to come and go; to enter and leave the building. If you live there remember details of your existence and write them down. Remember some of the people in the building. Write all this down.

(750 words)

 ## Key idea

In creative writing, one is not trying to tell the same sort of truth as we might be in science or history. The truth of creative writing is a truth of being true to life. In order to be true to life it is essential to invent.

After you have done this writing you will have a piece that is a mix of the observed and the remembered. You will have started with observation, accurate, detailed observation and supplemented, adding to the writing with memories. With memories of a particular place different from the observed place. You will have material here to build up a convincing picture of a place, or office, acting in a story.

In this chapter we have been looking at the sense of sight and considering ways that we can use and develop sense of the visual in our writing. We can start with clear, simple and accurate observation of people and things in the world around us. If we only do this, however, our writing will be indistinguishable from technical writing. Creative writers, when looking at a building they are considering using as a setting in a story may, for a brief while, put on the spectacles of an architect but they must not leave them on. Creative writers must supplement observation with imagination. And must add to that picture, and will, inevitably, add to that picture with remembered detail drawn from their own wealth of experience of life.

Summary

In this chapter you have begun to explore the senses; considered the range of senses; explored in detail the sense of sight; learned to look as a writer and learned about the movement of a piece of writing through observation – memory – imagination. And you have seen that the best possible creative writing is a mix of the observed, the remembered and the imagined. In your reading, find and make note of writing that uses the senses. Pick up one of your favourite authors, read a passage and see how much use they make of theses and which sense predominates.

Next step

In the next chapter we will continue our work on the senses and learn to explore the senses of touch and sound. We will build up bigger passages of writing based on these senses.

7

The five senses (2)

In this chapter you will learn to explore the sense of touch; build up passages of writing based on touch; explore the sense of sound; and build up passages of writing based on sound.

The sense of touch

Snapshot

Fill in the missing gaps:

1   You have more _____ nerve endings than any other type of nerve endings?

2   The least sensitive part of your body is _____ .

3   The most sensitive areas of your body are _____ (list them).

4   Shivering is a way your body has of _____ .

5   There are about a hundred touch receptors in each of your _____ .

6   _____ use their skin to feel the body heat of other animals.

7   _____ use the sense of touch a good deal in their writing.

Answers:

1   You have more **pain** nerve endings than any other type of nerve endings.

2   The least sensitive part of your body is **the middle of your back**.

3   The most sensitive areas of your body are your **hands, lips, face, neck, tongue, fingertips and feet.**

4   Shivering is a way your body has of **trying to get warmer.**

5   There are about a hundred touch receptors in each of your **fingertips.**

6   **Rattlesnakes** use their skin to feel the body heat of other animals.

7   **Good writers** use the sense of touch a good deal in their writing.

OK, we made the last one up, but we believe that it is true and we are going to explore it.

Key idea

To tell the truth – learn to tell lies.

While our other senses (sight, hearing, smell, and taste) are located in specific parts of the body, our sense of touch is found all over us. That seems quite obvious when you think about it, but it is only when you think about it that you realize how amazing that is. It is true; we hear with our ears, smell is centred on the nose, sight in the eyes, taste on the taste buds, but we can *feel* with every part of our bodies. This is because your sense of touch originates in the bottom layer of your skin called the dermis. The dermis is filled with many tiny nerve endings which give you information about the things with which your body comes in contact. They do this by carrying the information to the spinal cord, which sends messages to the brain where the feeling is registered.

It is our nerve endings that tell us if something is either hot or cold or if something is hurting us. Our body apparently has twenty or so different types of nerve endings that all send messages to our brains, but the most common messages we get are to do with heat, cold, pain and pressure or touch. Some areas of the body, such as the tongue, are more sensitive than others because they have more nerve endings that are sensitive to pain, which is why when you bite your tongue it hurts as much as it does. However, the tongue is not as good at sensing hot or cold, which is why we can so easily burn our mouths when we are eating something hot. The other part of us that is very sensitive is our fingertips.

Snapshot

Write 20 words for touch. For example: stroke, rub, graze. Try to find words that are exact and precise for the sensation you want to write down.

You probably came up with a lot of these, but in case you did not here are some examples – graze, scrape, shave, brush, glance, kiss, pinch, flick, tickle, scratch, creep. Some of these are close to being onomatopoeic words. An onomatopoeic word is defined as a word which sounds like the thing it describes. In this case these words have an onomatopoeic quality. You can almost see and perhaps even hear the action in words like graze, or brush. Words like glance, perhaps because of the meaning it carries with it, suggest something striking another thing very briefly and moving on. Kiss suggests both the coming together, the touching, even the lingering sensation of touch but also seems to bring with it the sound of the touch. It is not the purpose of this discussion to focus on writing about sound; we will do that later, but it is interesting to note here the interrelation, the complexity of how our senses relate.

Key idea

Our senses combine to provide us with the essential information we need about the world we inhabit. This combining is a most useful and dynamic thing when it comes to writing creatively. It is a power that we can tap into because it informs our writing. It can give our writing potentially multiple meanings and multiple effects.

Write

Find a favoured object; something you can hold in your hand. Sit somewhere you like, where you are comfortable, and close your eyes. Spend a few moments feeling this object; explore its texture.

- What is its size and shape?
- Is it long, thin, big, round?
- Is it heavy or light?
- Press it against your skin. What does it feel like?
- Is it soft, hard, lumpy, smooth or spongy?

- What is its temperature?
- Is it cold, hot, warm?

Write down your thoughts and sensation about this object.

(200 words)

Edit

How have you managed with this familiar object? In what ways have you described it to yourself; familiarly? One of the problems about describing something we know quite well is that we might tend to see it and therefore to describe it familiar ways; i.e. the writing might perhaps not be fresh and new. Has this happened with you? Look the piece over and see if there is anything that is commonplace and hackneyed; anything that is rather obvious? If there is, see if you can find a new word or two instead, a new way of putting it. You might also try the exercise again.

Focus point

We often think when we have done a thing once we have done it. But actually we have only just begun to learn about it and it is a good thing to do many of the exercises more than once. We often have to fight against the idea of boredom; the idea that once we have done something we have done it. But, in fact, going again over something we have done once can help us understand a task or technique or bring us new insights into the particular technical aspect we are studying, or about the creative process itself.

Repeat the last exercise and try to feel more intently than you have done before. Watch your hands touch and explore the object; really feel your hands move over the surface of the object. While you are doing this think how fantastically dexterous and clever are our fingers. Think of how they are transmitting the information they are gathering through the flesh of your fingertips, down the nerve ends, up your arm, through your body into the receptors in your brain that are turning these sensations into data that you can record and reuse in order to create the experience for readers on a page.

While your hands are spotting and exploring any scars or dents or nooks and crannies in the object, enjoy the smoothness and the roughness; enjoy the angularity and the roundness; enjoy the dampness or the dryness. While you are holding this familiar object imagine it being manufactured. If it is a metallic object, think how it was milled and ground, or moulded. Where was this done? Think of the hands that brought it into being. Think of the life this object has had. Think of how the scars and cuts on its skin got there. Is it possible to bring the entire history of this object up before your mind's eye? If you were a psychometer, you would believe it was possible to do this, at least according to an article by Michael O'Hanlon in the

Journal of the Royal Anthropological Institute, vol. 5, 1999. O'Hanlon wrote about a nineteenth-century man in British New Guinea, Professor William Denton. At a time when photography was evolving fast, Denton got very interested and excited about the way photographic plates of the period retained an image. It seemed to him that objects might carry such a latent impression of their original surroundings in much the same way. He took this a step further hypothesising that by coming into contact with the object, through holding it, certain, sensitive individuals might have the ability to revisit these original surroundings. He called these sensitive individuals 'psychometers'.

It is not an uncommon belief that objects contain certain, perhaps, mystical properties. Hence people pay huge sums for articles that have belonged to famous people, such as items of clothing, jewellery or other valuable possessions. People can feel they are brought or kept near to people by having some article associated with that person in their presence. Lady Bess Raleigh carried the head of her executed husband around with her for the rest of her life as a rather macabre way of being near her dead husband. There is no doubt that we invest objects with properties that scientific examination may find hard to 'prove' are actually there. That does not mean that they are not there for us.

So that even though it is a mighty leap to believing an object to carry its whole history with it, for people who can loosen their minds that way it is not an unimaginable belief. One can imagine a very plausible and persuasive piece of fiction built around this notion, which might say a good deal about human relations or the human condition. But for science it would be an unproven assertion. O'Hanlon was not persuaded. He went on in his article to talk further about Denton and his view that people could be psychometers:

> *Happily, Denton's close family proved to be 'psychometers' and, variously clutching mastodon teeth and stone fragments, they made astral visits to the prehistoric world and ancient Egypt and Pompeii, dictating what they saw to Denton. One day in 1869, and long before he visited New Guinea in the flesh, Denton was favoured with a glimpse of the country through the agency of his psychometric son, Sherman. In the years that followed, Denton ranged even more broadly, reporting on 'Winter sports on Mars' and 'Modes of travel on Jupiter'. Then, in 1883, Denton complemented his earlier astral journey to New Guinea with a visit on the physical plane. There, he joined an expedition to the hinterland of the capital, Port Moresby, a journey on which he soon died.*

The ideal subject for a science fiction or fantasy novel, perhaps.

This idea of an object carrying its history with it, also brings into focus the idea of closeness, intimacy, the intimacy of the object and the intimacy of the touch. Touch almost by definition is an intimate sense. Smell is intimate in that you smell the smell, but the smell could be coming from a fair distance off. A sound that is heard could be distant or could be close. The same can be said of our sense of sight. We can see things close or far away. The sense of touch, however, is something that we need to do close up.

Rebecca McClanahan

'Touch, by definition, is an intimate sense. It requires a body's immediate presence.'

We cannot physically touch something if it is a long way distant from us. Perhaps, because of this sense of intimacy, a piece of writing about intimacy would seem to cry out for the use of the sense of touch. A story about a mother with a new-born baby would be brought to life by the use of sensory description about the closeness of the touching between them. Similarly, a love story or a sex scene in a story would be greatly enhanced by details of touch, about how things felt, the touch of skin, the touch of lips and of fingers.

Even when the piece of writing is not such an intimate one, the sense of how things feel is very important. A scorching hot day; sand sticking to your skin on the beach; the smooth or rough bark of a tree beneath your fingers or against your back; the solid heavy weight of a bag on your aching shoulder or a rucksack on your back; the softness of material such as velvet and silk. All these details, put in the right place in a piece of creative writing can help bring that writing to life.

Focus point

When you are observing you should note the different textures, feel the difference between stone and wood, metal and brick. They are all hard but they are hard in different ways just as other materials are soft in different ways. Examine different fabrics, the material of clothing, see which ones you prefer and which you can write about.

When you come to write and revise, remember what we said about the key tool of our trade, language. Try and get the right word for what you want to say. Often, that comes through trial and error. But as to the importance of it, we can underline it with lessons from other writers.

Robert Frost

'I never knew what was meant by choice of words. It was one word or none.'

Mark Twain

'Use the right word and not its second cousin.'

Somerset Maugham

'All the words I use in my stories can be found in the dictionary – it's just a matter of arranging them into the right sentences.'

For the next set of exercises you need a helpful partner, someone close to you or a friend who is willing to let you hold their hand.

Write

Take hold of your partner's hand. If you are by yourself, take hold of your own hand.

It sometimes helps if your partner shuts their eyes so that they are not staring at you. It stops both of you from laughing. Or you might shut your eyes as you hold the hand; get a sense of what it feels like.

- Is it soft and warm, dry and cold?
- Is it large or small?
- How strong does it feel?

Think about a memory that this evokes; maybe of holding your father's or mother's hand when you were a small child. Can you think yourself back to that time when you were walking down the road by their side? You might get a particular memory; you might just get a sensation or series of sensations of texture.

When you are ready, write down your thoughts; whatever has come.

(200 words)

Next time you shake hands with anyone, pay attention to what sort of handshake it is. Think about the feel of the hand: is it a strong hand, does it give a feeling of power or confidence? Is it weak and wispy, suggesting weakness, lack of commitment or lack of interest in you? What is the difference from one handshake to another? Why does one handshake make you feel one thing and another handshake lead you to feel quite another? Think about the ways personality comes through the handshake. You might also pay attention to the way that other communities greet each other; whether they use handshakes or some other form of greeting. Anthony Trollope in *Barchester Towers* gets a great effect from describing people as always to be seen walking away wiping their hands on their clothes after they have shaken hands with the Reverend Slope. He does not need to tell us how damp the man's handshake is.

Workshop: describing objects you can't see but only touch

For this exercise you need to have someone do some preparation for you. Your partner will need to select and put various random and different objects that you don't see, inside a bag or pillowcase. Ask your partner to make sure there are all sorts of different objects. Make sure they have different shapes and textures; some soft and squidgy, like children's toys, others spiky, others hard and wooden or metallic. Your partner might use a ball, a nail brush, or a stapler; they might fill a balloon with hair conditioner; if they do, remember to seal the end!

Another way of doing this is to blindfold yourself or close your eyes and ask someone to get an object that you have not seen and then to hand it to you. The issue is that you should not see what you are going to feel because knowing what it is affects the way you experience and describe it. So keep your eyes closed while you are handling the object. Either take the object in your hands or feel it in the bag. Handle it carefully and sensitively for as long as you need. Feel for bumps, flat bits, rounded bits, sharp edges; feel for where it is smooth and where it is rough. Though you are exploring the sense of touch here, you might want to shake it, and see if it makes a noise. You might want to smell it if you can; difficult if it is inside a pillowcase or bag, but you might be able to do it. Does it smell? What of? You might even taste it if it is edible, but you might first like to get advice from your partner on whether it is safe to do that or not. When you have finished, ask your partner to put the object back in the bag, or otherwise conceal it, then open your eyes and, still without knowing what the object actually was, write down the sensations you experienced. Think about:

- size
- weight
- shape
- texture
- does it make a noise?

Do not worry about what it is. Afterwards, you can check what it actually is but that is not the point of the exercise. If you guess what it is, try to put it out of your mind and describe what it feels like.

(200 words)

Do not worry about what it actually is. Once you have your writing you can check, but what it actually is is not the point of the exercise. Have you come up with any weird descriptions or ideas? In the end, it does not really matter what you came up with. What matters is the process of learning to think about the world in terms of touch and finding the right words to describe those sensations.

In the next exercise you will be asked to pick up the description you just made of the familiar object and this time describe it to another alien. This alien can only relate to our world through touch. Think of the ways you might describe this object to the alien but also try to carry with you the sense of being a psychometer; convey some of the history of the object to the alien as you describe it. Concentrate only on how it feels.

 Write

Imagine that you are a psychometer. Using your notes, write a few short paragraphs as if you were describing the object or objects you have been touching to an alien who only had the sense of touch. Do not use sound, smell and taste or visual appearance unless you can describe those things through the sense of touch. The alien can only *feel*, all the other senses are meaningless to it. It may have antennae that are its equivalent of eyes, but using only touch you have to describe the object so they can understand what it is, what it does and what its history is. Imagine you can feel that full history coming through. Let it come and remember, the alien has touch receptors over its entire body.

(200 words)

Focus point

Try writing without one of your senses. Restrict yourself. Through restriction sometimes comes great freedom.

Write: feeling good

Think of an activity you like doing, for example:

- swimming
- running
- having your hair washed and cut
- riding a horse/motorbike
- playing a sport you are good at
- eating a meal
- being stroked
- sunbathing.

While you are thinking of this activity concentrate on the sensual aspect, the feeling of it. If you can it is a very good idea to go and re-experience this activity. This is often very important. It is a form of research.

Make notes and write about this favoured activity.

(200 words)

Key idea

Writing often appears very different if someone is writing from or about something they have experienced, then if they are writing about something they are imagining. The trick is to get the imagined bits as good as the witnessed bits. While you are in the middle of an experience, think about how you would describe it, and then as soon as you can, write about it.

Workshop: feeling bad

Look at this table.

Adjective	Noun	Verb	Comparison

- Draw the table in your notebook.
- In the noun column make a list of six things you hate touching, for example, spiders, frogspawn, insects, or cat poo.
- Make a list of six verbs that capture something about these things you hate. If they move try to get something about the way they move, their energy; if they don't move of their own free will find a verb that captures something about the way they move if pushed or slid, etc.
- Next, find six good adjectives to go before the nouns.
- The last column is for you to come up with a comparison.

Here is an example.

Adjective	Noun	Verb	Comparison
matted	hair	grabs/grazes/creeps/ kisses/tickles/brushes	like a spider in the bath hole

Take one of the images from the ones you have created and build up a piece of prose around it. Use this one image as your starting point and then try to include two more of your images somewhere in the piece.

Keep *touch* as the theme of the piece.

(750 words)

 Key idea

Often in writing, stating something is not the most effective way of getting it across. Writing is not always a matter of stating things; it is instead often a matter of pointing to things and letting the imagination take over.

This is what Seamus Heaney does in one of his best-known poems, 'Death of a Naturalist'. The poem is so carefully constructed around the senses to be so rich in concrete detail that it builds up a physical picture that allows the imagination to take the leap from the physical and the experienced to the imagined. And, as with so many things, like ghosts, phobias and fears, the imagined horrors are much greater than the explicitly seen and stated horrors.

The shark in the film *Jaws* is much more dreadful to our imaginations when it is made up of sound, implied movement and music than when we see the rubberised mechanical shark towards the end of the film. We do not need to labour the point or make everything visible. We must allow our writing to open doors and vistas that allow the reader's imagination to work.

Key idea

Successful writing is often a matter of what we leave out as much as what we put in.

The sense of hearing

Snapshot

Did you know that your ears not only enable you to hear but they also have a second important function? What is that? It is not just to keep your hat or your glasses on. Think about it and write down what you think it is.

Your hearing helps you to keep your balance. That is why you can feel sea-sick or suffer from motion sickness, or feel giddy after a fairground ride has whirled you round and round. Your balance is upset. Our sense of hearing and the world of sound are very important to us. A lot of us probably know the feeling when we go up high, for example, to the top of a mountain or in an aeroplane, where the change in pressure causes our ears to pop. Some facts which could well prove useful in producing a piece creative writing are:

• Children have more sensitive ears than adults. They can recognize a wider variety of noises.

• Dolphins have the best sense of hearing among animals. They are able to hear 14 times better than humans.

• Animals hear more sounds than humans.

An earache is caused by too much fluid putting pressure on your eardrum. Earaches are often the result of an infection, allergies or a virus.

Some people, of course, cannot hear. Some are born with hearing problems; others develop problems as they get older. This might lead you to develop characters where hearing is a central trait and a very important issue for them. Novelists J.M. Coetzee and David Lodge have both published books dealing with central characters suffering from diminished hearing. If you are going to do this, you will have to do a lot of research about sound and about hearing; both the way we hear and the way we can fail to hear. This research is no different from the work of observation that we have stressed in the previous chapters. It is simply observation of another sort.

In this section we are going to explore the way we hear, the world of sound and the way we write using the sense of sound.

Snapshot

Just to loosen yourself up, write down 50 onomatopoeic words for sound (onomatopoeic words are words that sound like the sound they are describing) – for example, click, tap, bang, boing, ooze, slap, slurp, crack, bray, etc.

(*50 words*)

Snapshot

This next exercise is based on one in *Taking Reality by Surprise*, edited by Susan Sellers.

Choose three different word sounds from the lists you made in the previous exercise; sounds, not actual words. From the examples given above you might choose sounds like *ack*, *ooze* and *ay*. Now write 12 words for each sound. The sound can come anywhere in the word and you can have words of more than one syllable.

For example, for the sound *ack* – back, crack, accident, accuse, rack, flack, etc. For the sound *ooze* – booze, flues, floozie, choose, bruise, cruising, etc. And for the sound *ap* – slap, bap, rap, crap, trap, map, aperture, apply, etc.

Now take these 36 words and include them all in a piece based on a theme suggested by the words. Do not worry about the piece making sense. Try to concentrate on the rhythms and sounds of the words as they work together.

(*100 words*)

Read it over out loud. Listen to how the repetitive word sounds set up an insistent rhythm. Listen for any changes in rhythm when the different sounds come in.

Key idea

It is often hard to state clearly where a piece of writing either comes from or will take you. Go with it.

Here is an example based around the word sounds *eck*, as in 'deck' and 'wreck', the words sound *ake* as in 'cake' or 'flake', and the words sound *ess*, as in 'best' or 'rest'.

First of all, we made a list of words – for *ake* these were: make, break, take, taking, etc. And for *ess*: essential escape, press, mess, test, best. For *eck*, we came up with deck, fleck, excellent, wreck and others. Here is the way we got 36 of these word sounds into the piece:

'On Sundays after a break by the lake slake your thirst and make time for a meal. Pasta is best dressed with flakes of cheese and pesto. Bake your excellent hake dish in the oven, 20 minutes estimate, letting excess steam escape; press the rest of the pastry with a woodpecker's beak and bedeck with a heck of a lot of pecks of salt. Raking downwards is essential so as not to wreck or fleck the neck of the dish and make a mess. Wake the family; get rid of the pests, taking all day if you wish. Break the bread.'

The key is to allow the words to suggest what it is they want to suggest, and to go with that. There is a good deal of complex thinking to be done to try to accommodate the different words like this. It is unlikely that you will be able to make complete, coherent sentences from a piece developed in this way. Though, if you like that particular challenge, no one is going to stop you from trying. But there is an essential use of creativity and accident and letting things happen in a piece like this. It is allowing the journey to happen and encouraging you to go with it. Here is another example built around three different sounds. The sounds *it*, *oo* and *aze*; as in 'hit' or 'flit' or 'pretty', *oo* as in 'blue' or 'loose', and *aze* as in 'lazy' or 'stays'.

'A pretty loose goose sitting lost in a maze on a hazy day flew high into the bitumen sky cooling its wings in the blaze of the wind where it now sits in true glue coloured sun. Zit, fit, flit go the insects and flies. Moo go the cows in the ooze mud below where sheep graze in a hazy daze of craze grass avoiding the gambolling of the shepherd's collie bitch. Leaving trays of lemonade in the labourers' mitts the Farmer's wife pulls up her itchy stays, pitching herself forward to hit the cheeky git who pops his head out of the chimney flue grabs her tit and says "boo."'

Well, it is not possible to say where this nonsense piece came from nor does it matter. The important point is that it is here and can anything be made of it? Whatever nonsense you have produced look at it in that light. Maybe there is something in the piece, in some parts of it, maybe something is suggestive or has potential. Maybe it is just a line, a combination of words, an image that you might be able to use somewhere else. But what you should have seen and felt and heard in this piece in the repetition of sounds is the importance of sound in our work.

Snapshot

Choose seven of the words you listed and write a short piece using only those seven words. You may use repetition. Here is an example using the word sound *ake* as in 'take'. And the word sound *ess* as in 'essential'. Here is a piece built around rhythm and only using seven words:

Make make

take make make break

take best take taking

essential essential essential

make escape.

Your turn.

What effect does the restriction or constriction have in this piece? When you have limited resources like this and have to rely on very few words, the first thing you need to do is choose them carefully. Once chosen, then you have to use them in intelligent and inventive ways because you need to get the maximum out of them. This works as a poem or perhaps we could try it as a speech in a play.

Perhaps we have a character who is desperate to get out of a prison. It might be a literal or a metaphorical prison. Imagine this character talking to himself, trying to convince himself of escape.

> 'Make make take make make break take best take taking essential essential essential make escape.'

The broken nature of the dialogue, the repetition, the build-up to the word at the end, escape, adds power as does the build-up in the fragmented words. The fact that the sentences are not whole and the person is repeating himself adds to the desperation. And the point of the build-up comes where it should, at the end. What about a character in a play trying to persuade someone else to make a plan of escape?

> 'Make make take make make break take best take taking essential essential essential make escape.'

The only word not repeated in one form of another comes at the end of the speech. It is the point of his speech; it is what the speaker is driving at; the desperate need to *escape*.

Focus point

It is often possible through such restriction to say more than when we have the choice of less. An important lesson for all creative writers; not just for poets or playwrights. Limit your resources; test yourself and see what more you can create with less.

Listen!

Wherever you are reading this, whether at home, on a train, in an aeroplane, shut your eyes and listen – what do you hear?

Listen – really listen. There may well be an overwhelming sound; a hum, perhaps of an engine or a computer. Within that there will be intermittent sounds; the sound of wheels on tracks. Other sounds will come and go; the sound of a seagull, or the thud of footsteps upstairs. Write down all the sounds you hear.

If you can, visit a supermarket, a station, airport, or a fair: somewhere where there will be a variety of competing sounds at different pitches, levels and of varying duration. Really listen to all of the sounds. If you can't visit anywhere, remember a sound from back in time. Think of a circus, a fair, the office, the train and imagine the sounds made by a circus, a fair, the office, the train or at home in the kitchen. Take your time; listen carefully and make notes.

Write

Once you have listened and made some notes, write a piece to another alien; this time the alien can only hear. Describe to the alien the world you have heard solely through sound.

(750 words)

Edit

Check the piece you have just written over. What areas work? What areas work less well? Have you used description? Have you used dialogue? Is everything clear? Is everything contributing to the whole piece? Cut any parts that you find weaker, anything that is not taking the piece forward. You can reduce your 750 words to a much smaller passage just by trying to keep the strong writing and jettison the rest.

Summary

In this chapter you have explored the senses of touch and sound and built up passages of writing based on touch and on sound. Find some more examples of similar writing in your own reading; note how the writers use these senses and what effects they are able to create with them. Try writing some passages in that style yourself. Imitation is a good way to learn.

Next step

In the next chapter we will look at the remaining two senses of smell and taste and discover how crucial they can be to creative writing, and the peculiar challenges and rewards they can give to writers.

8

The missing senses

In this chapter you will explore the sense of smell; build up passages of writing based on smell; explore the sense of taste; and build up passages of writing based on taste.

The sense of smell

Jean Lenoir, wine expert

'In our education, the greatest importance is attached to hearing and sight, but the sense of smell is almost ignored.'

It *is* fair to say that, though we are taught to read and write and to listen, unless we work in such worlds as wine tasting, perfumery or cuisine, we are never taught to smell or taste. Where education has gone, writers have followed because the same might also be said of them; the sense of taste is so often missing from good writing. There is not a complete absence of writing using taste yet both of the senses are so often not there, but why are the sense of smell and taste so underused in our writing? Both senses are vital to us as humans and both senses can be the most evocative in writing.

Key idea

The link between smell, taste and memory is a vital one that many writers have explored. Yet these senses remain underused in writing; we tend to be dominated by the visual.

One of the most famous examples in writing is of Proust and the small cake, the madeleine, he tasted which took him right back to his childhood. Smells are particularly good for evoking memory and place. Write about the smell of fresh mown grass, or straw in a barn, a leather saddle or leather shoes in a shoe shop etc. and we are immediately taken there as readers.

You may well remember some examples from your reading. If you do, it is because these tend to stand out.

Rudyard Kipling, 'The Roman Centurion's Song'

'Will you e'er forget the scent of hawthorn in the sun, or bracken in the wet?'

Siegfried Sassoon, *Memoirs of a Fox Hunting Man*

'The odiferous twilight of the Horticultural Tent ... the crushed bracken that the horses were munching, and the pungent unmistakable odour of foxes.'

Sassoon's *Memoirs* are unusually rich with references to smell, such as the smell of strawberry jam being made, but this is not common in writing.

Rudyard Kipling

'The first condition of understanding a foreign country is to smell it.'

The smells they came up with were:

Argentina – steak

Brazil – a glass of Pina Colada

England – After Eight mints

Poland – vodka

France – Chanel No 5

Germany – freshly baked bread

The Netherlands – cheese

Iran – saffron

Italy – pizza

Japan – green tea

Mexico – ripe mangoes

Sweden – pine and flat-pack furniture

United States – Coca-Cola.

In the 2006 Football World Cup, the German town of Holzminden, which is a centre for the ingredients which are used in the cosmetic and food industries worldwide, wanted to represent every competing nation in some way. They did not choose something visual, like national flags, or something aural, like national anthems. Because of the importance of smell in the life of their city, they chose to try to capture the essential aroma of a country. They erected a series of 'smelling posts' which people could touch and which would give them the essential scent of that nation. What do you think they come up with?

Snapshot

What smell represents each nation in this selection of different nations? Write your thoughts of each country in your notebook. What is the smell of: Argentina, Brazil, England, France, Germany, Iran, Italy, Japan, Mexico, the Netherlands, Poland, Sweden, the United States?

The *Daily Telegraph* took exception to the smell of England being After Eight mints and suggested instead, 'the smell of warm beer, tea, newly mown cricket pitches and Marmite in the morning'.

UNDERSTANDING AND CLASSIFYING SMELLS

We are going to take as our guide a nineteenth-century book *The Art of Perfumery*, in which the Englishman George William Septimus Piesse classified smells according to his invention the 'Odophone'.

In *The Art of Perfumery*, published in 1857, George William Septimus Piesse classified scents by taking an approach similar to music. He put forward the idea that odours were like sounds and that a scale could be made from low to high; i.e. from the heaviest smell to the sharpest, lightest smell. In between the top and bottom he proposed an ascending scale. To classify this he used the idea of 'top notes', 'middle notes' and 'bass notes' and he called this an 'odophone'. Top notes he said are the scents we smell first. They evaporate quickly and are classified as fresh and light. Middle notes come a little after the top notes have evaporated. They are the core of the blend and give it its character. Middle notes are generally floral, herbal and spicy. The bass notes are thick, heavy and richer scents. They are usually woods, resins, and spices. These bass notes are warming. They emerge slowly but they tend to stay around longer. They give roundness to a good blend.

 ## Snapshot

Think of various fruits and flowers and write down what you think the top notes would be as if you were classifying them according to Piesse's Odophone – don't only write the names of the fruits and flowers but think of words to describe the sorts of scents they give off.

(50 words)

Then write the names of flowers, herbs and spices that form middle notes; also write words to describe these tangs.

(50 words)

Finally, write the names of woods, resins and spices that form bass notes,

and also write words to describe these smells.

(50 words)

You may have some others but examples of top notes in this system are: basil, bay laurel, bergamot, citronella, eucalyptus, grapefruit, lemon, lemongrass, lime, orange, peppermint, spearmint and tangerine.

Examples of middle notes are: black pepper, chamomile, cinnamon, dill, fennel, geranium, juniper, lavender, marjoram, nutmeg, parsley, rose, rosemary, Scotch pine, spruce, tea tree, thyme, tobacco and yarrow.

Examples of bass notes are – beeswax, benzoin, cedar wood, frankincense, ginger, jasmine, myrrh, sandalwood, patchouli and vanilla.

Key idea

Use smell and taste to evoke place or time.

Snapshot

Supermarkets have all their foods under one roof but the fridges and freezers tend to kill the smells; and also the proximity of things one to another muffles and blurs individual smells. It is better to go to separate shops and smell them as discrete smells. So for this exercise go to three different shops – for example:

- a perfume shop
- a delicatessen
- a hardware shop
- a flower shop
- a butcher's shop
- a fish shop
- a cheese shop
- a coffee shop
- a bread shop

– and smell the produce. Try to classify the smells according to Piesses's classification; find the top note, the middle note and the bass note. Make your notes. (You might want to explain to the shop owner what you are doing.)

The ideal in perfumery and in blending aromatherapy recipes is to make a blend harmonious and 'in tune' by using all three notes: top, middle and bass. Using the notes you have just made write a scene set in a shop between a customer and shopkeeper in which you 'blend' all three, i.e. the top, middle and bottom notes. Perhaps the customer wants a particular cheese, perhaps the customer is complaining about a particular smell. At some point in the scene use all three levels of scent.

(200 words)

Write

Write a piece in which someone comes into a room and smells something; or perhaps wakes up to discover a smell in a room. The smell is important to them. Maybe it is the smell of flowers or of someone's perfume. Maybe the perfume gives away that person's presence. Maybe it is something nice; maybe it is something repellent. It could signal excitement, danger, anxiety or perhaps distaste. Describe the smell striking them in three phases; first the top note, then the middle note, and finally the bass note. Use the discovery of the smell to provide the structure to the piece.

(750 words)

We are all the same in that we all experience the world through our five senses. But as in everything, everyone is also different and we are probably stronger in one or two senses than other people and weaker in others. Some people will have a great sense of smell, others fantastic hearing. Even within ourselves these senses are probably not all experienced equally as strongly. At different times in our lives one sense may dominate more than the others. When we get a cold or feel ill we often can't taste or smell things as usual. This is a loss and a deprivation. It is the same with writers. The senses do not all seem to get used equally. One or two dominate.

 ## Key idea

Find out which of the senses are strong and which are weaker for you. Practise the ones you are weakest at.

 ## Write

Write a piece in which someone loses their sense of smell; they had it, but now are no longer able to smell. It may be temporary or permanent but put them in a situation where the deprivation is important. Perhaps they are a chef or a perfume manufacturer.

(750 words)

THE VOCABULARY OF SMELL

The vocabulary of smell seems limited. Look over the pieces you have written in this chapter and write down all the words you have used for smell.

 ## Snapshot

Having done this we imagine you will find what a limited choice of words there are for taste and smell. What do you think this points to? Write down your thoughts. It seems to point to the fact that you can't write smells the same way as you can write sound or visual observation. It isn't just a matter of saying, as you can with sound, the murmur of cars, the drip of water, or the creak of the door. As we have said previously, those words *are* the sound. Something like wonderful smells, on the other hand, doesn't say anything, does it? What about the damp smell of the sodden sycamore leaves? How close does that get? How else would you say that? Think of how those wine buffs on telly try to get across the smell of a wine – the say: 'It's like Granny Smiths, gooseberries, or burnt tar. I'm getting caramel and toffee, I'm getting mothballs and stewed cabbage.'

What they do is pile up words in images and description. When Ernest Hemingway wanted to describe the smell of the Spanish Civil War in *For Whom the Bell Tolls*, he piled detail over detail, pages of slaughter and bloodshed and violence in order to get across the powerful smell of war. If you want to see this repetition process at work, this piling up of word on word, of image upon image, read Patrick Suskind's novel *Perfume*. It is set in eighteenth-century France, an age that stank to high heaven according to this novel. The novel opens with a long description of smell and continues in that vein for quite a few pages. The opening reeks with the smell of manure, urine, the mouldering wood and rat droppings; of boiled cabbage and mutton fat; of stale dust, of greasy sheets, and chamber-pots. But if you look at it you can see how the picture is built up: concrete detail piled on top of concrete detail. The strong verb to stink is also used over and over. Perhaps there really was, in this case, no good alternative but, even if there was, the repetition succeeds in driving the point home: that the vocabulary/language used for smell is limited. This perhaps also shows us that we need not always search for another word.

Just because we have used a word once in a particular passage does not mean we cannot use the same word again so soon. If it is the word you need, use it. In this case to stink is used again and again and again because this is the method the writer uses: of piling up the words to create the effect. If there is a limited vocabulary for writing smells, the way some writers like Suskind and Hemingway have found to write smells seems to be to pile up the concrete detail. Clear nouns and strong verbs. We come back to the lessons of the previous pages.

Vladimir Nabokov

'Nothing revives the past so completely as a smell that was once associated with it.'

Smell is part of every living thing. It is believed that the average human being can recognize up to 10,000 separate odours from the ones that surround us. Consider the odours that are being emitted by vegetation such as trees, flowers, grass and earth; from animals such as cats, dogs, horses, and cows; from the food we eat or grow; from all the urban city activity, the traffic and trains and planes, and from all the industry around us. Smells come from our bins and rubbish tips full of decay. We also get, of course, a host of smells from other humans. Sometimes they are in close proximity such as in crowded trains or bars; sometimes further off but they are always there. Yet when we want to describe these many, subtle and varied odours, we find our language crude and unsophisticated. We will say that something smells like a rose, or smells like sweat, or smells like ammonia. We will say it is pungent or it is acrid. In her very interesting book *A Natural History of the Senses*, Diane Ackerman says:

> *Our sense of smell can be extraordinarily precise, yet it's almost impossible to describe how something smells to someone who hasn't smelt it.*

She says further about our difficulty with finding the right words for smell, that

> *Smell is the mute sense, the one without words. Lacking a vocabulary, we are left tongue-tied, groping for words in a sea of inarticulate pleasure and exaltation.*

Exaltation and pleasure because smell can be something we enjoy and delight in. We may even enjoy the struggle for words to express what it is we smell.

Writers have found ways around this dilemma and we will look at some of them in a moment, but first it will be valuable to consider why we have this problem.

Our culture is so dominated by the visual, and likely to remain so with our dependence on screens for working, for information, for reading, for watching movies and for being entertained, that it has placed a high value on sight and seeing and taking things in through the eyes and a correspondingly low value on smells and the way we smell. We have many more words to describe the look of something than we do the smell or taste of something. Because we do not value smell and taste we have never developed a vocabulary for it. Elsewhere in her *A Natural History of the Senses*, poet Diane Ackerman notes that there are names for all the pastels in a particular colour – but none for the tones and tints of a particular smell.

The sense of taste

Let's sample some facts about taste:

- We have almost 10,000 taste buds inside our mouths; even on the roofs of our mouths.
- Insects have the most highly developed sense of taste. They have taste organs on their feet, antennae, and mouthparts.
- Fish can taste with their fins and tail as well as their mouth.
- In general, girls have more taste buds than boys.
- Taste is the weakest of the five senses.

Snapshot

How many words can you come up with for the taste of something? Take your notebook and write down as many as you can. Do not make it a mix of good and bad; pleasant and unpleasant. That is, do not list things you liked and things you did not like. Try to be more precise. Think of particular things that were salty and things that were sweet, things that were sour and things that were bitter. Do it now.

Did you find it easy or hard to come up with your words? What type of words have you thought of? Are there similarities between them or are they quite different from each other? There are different sorts of taste, from hot to cool, spicy to zesty; do your words reflect that?

Taste can be divided into four kinds of things. These are the four kinds of tastes that the thousands of taste buds we have on our tongues and the roof of our mouths can recognize. These are salty, sweet, sour and bitter. Ackerman tells us that:

> *At the tip of the tongue, we taste sweet things; bitter things at the back; sour things at the sides; and salty things spread over the surface, but mainly up front. The tongue is like a kingdom divided into principalities according to sensory talent. It would be as if all those who could see lived in the east, those who could hear lived in to the west, those who could taste lived to the south, and those who could touch lived to the north.*

Everyone tastes things differently and our tastes change as we get older. Babies have taste buds on their tongues and on the sides and roofs of their mouths. This is why they are sensitive to a whole range of different foods. As babies grow into children and then into adults the taste buds actually begin to disappear from the sides and roof of the mouth leaving taste buds mainly on the tongue. Adults' taste buds also get less sensitive. This means that adults can eat food they hated as a child or baby.

Write

Imagine you are a taste bud. Write from its point of view using some of the words you found above. Taste one thing you love and one thing you loathe.

Write the sensations.

(200 words)

Write a short scene in which an adult tries to get a baby to eat something that is 'good for it' and the baby will have none of it.

(200 words)

Write a short scene in which an adult tries to stop a baby eating something the baby loves that is 'bad for it' and the baby will have none of it.

(200 words)

Tasting things can be vital for our survival. We need to know if what we eat is going to agree with us or not; it may even poison us. Monarchs and dictators of the past have used food tasters as a means of ensuring that they did not eat anything likely to kill them. A food taster for a dictator is not work with a lot of job security. Instead of food-tasters, the rest of us have to make do with our own taste buds and it is good that we can tell bitter from sweet. It is great that we can tell a poison by its bitterness. The bitterness and sweetness of things is so important to us and Diane Ackerman makes the point that we use the language of taste in big and important ways to describe people and situations. We will describe people as 'sweet' or 'bitter'. Sometimes when things go wrong against our wishes it becomes a metaphor: a 'bitter pill to swallow'. A footballer might describe a goal as *sweet*; in fact, any number of sports people might well describe tries or shots as sweet.

If taste is so important to us, imagine what it would be like if your taste was severely reduced or you could not taste anything? Some kinds of medication can affect taste, as can smoking, or not getting enough of the right vitamins. An injury to the head or a brain tumour; exposure to chemicals or radiation can all cause people to suffer a loss or a diminution of the ability to taste. Our taste buds also diminish as we get older.

Write

Try to imagine what it would be like if you could not taste anything. Put yourself into, or imagine another character in, a situation where you have been affected by some kind of medication, an injury to the head or exposure to chemicals or radiation and suffered a loss or a diminution of the ability to taste. Write a short piece about what this is like.

(200 words)

LIKES AND DISLIKES

Write

Think back to food you ate as a child; something you loved and looked forward to. The smell and the taste of this food was what life was about. Maybe it was a fish and chips supper on a Friday night, or your mother baking bread on a Saturday morning: first the smell and then breaking into that crust before lashing butter on it and watching it melt. Maybe it was buttered crumpets by an open fire or a sizzling gas fire. Think yourself back into it. Make notes, and then write a brief piece knitting those notes together into a short prose piece or a poem.

(200 words)

Think back to food you ate as a child; something you loathed and dreaded. The smell and the taste of this food was the bane of your life. Maybe it was overcooked cabbage or sprouts. Perhaps it was celery. Maybe it was horrible school dinners. It would be something the taste of which you loathed, but remembering the smell, look and texture too will help you write it. Maybe it smelt foul, maybe it was tough and chewy in the mouth; maybe it was rubbery like sea food. Think yourself back into it. Make notes, and then write a brief piece knitting those notes together into a short prose piece or a poem in which you just try to get across what it was you really loathed.

(200 words)

SMELL, TASTE AND MEMORY

The link between smell, taste and memory has been famously explored by French novelist Marcel Proust. In *The Remembrance of Things Past*, Proust described what happened to him after eating a piece of madeleine, a short, plump little cake which he had soaked in lime flower tea.

Proust makes the point that it wasn't enough to see the madeleine. The simple sight of it had not brought back these memories. He had to taste and smell it to get back into those memories.

The combination of taste and smell is essential. A good deal of the flavour of food comes from its aroma; the smells go up our nostrils into cells in the nose and they also reach these cells through a passageway in the back of the mouth. As we have said, our taste buds actually give us only four distinct sensations: sweet, salty, sour, and bitter. Other flavours come from smell. This is why when the nose is blocked by a cold, most foods lose their taste and seem quite bland. It is why smell and taste can be treated together in a passage of creative writing. They belong together and they can also give strength to a piece of writing that employs them.

In a piece called 'Hunger was a good discipline' collected in a series of short pieces under the title *A Moveable Feast*, Ernest Hemingway writes about the ideas of hunger and importance to his creativity. He gets across the sense of hunger he felt when struggling to make a living as writer in Paris and how wonderful food and drink tasted to him when he was hungry. At the beginning of the piece he walks through Paris avoiding all the places where there would be food to see and to smell and which would get his taste buds going. He uses the method we have discussed in previous chapters; he evokes Paris by using its place names; the Luxembourg gardens, the place de l'Observatoire, the rue Ferou, place St-Sulpice and the rue de l'Odéon. As he walks past and along these streets he thinks about hunger in relation to art and in particular in the work of the painter Paul Cézanne. Hemingway is trying not to think about food yet it is on his mind continually. Finally, he gets to Sylvia Beach's bookshop, the famous Shakespeare and Company on the Seine, opposite the cathedral of Notre-Dame – the famous bookshop from which Sylvia Beach published James Joyce's *Ulysses* when no one else would touch it. And he gets from her a little money for a short story he has had published. With this money in his pocket he goes to his favourite brasserie, called Lipp's, and orders a big glass of beer and potato salad.

He describes drinking the cold beer, then grinding black pepper over the potatoes and moistening the bread in the olive oil. After the first drink he eats slowly enjoying the taste of Frankfurter and mustard and olive oil. As he nears the end of his meal he describes how he mops up all the oil and all of the sauce with bread and how he drinks the beer slowly and then orders another, watching it being drawn and then drinking half of it. He savours the entire meal.

Hemingway is famous for having a plain, strong style. It is not true that he never uses adjectives or adverbs, but it is true that he uses them sparingly and sensibly. In his description of the meal he makes great use of strong nouns and active verbs. Here is a list of the nouns; *distingué*, mug, potato salad, beer, *pommes à l'huile*, olive oil, black pepper, potatoes, a *cervelas*, sausage, frankfurter, and mustard sauce. The verbs used are drank, ground, moistened, ate, ordered, mopped and watched. He uses one or two adjectives, big glass, cold, wonderful, heavy, special and twice he uses the adverb slowly.

But really this description of eating and drinking is built around the names of things and the choice of active verbs. It is a piece of writing well worth looking at several times in order to see how a master writer can evoke sense of smell, taste, and hunger by precisely knowing and using the tools of his trade. It took a long time for Hemingway to learn his craft and to evolve his style, and there is no substitute for that apprenticeship. Technically, there is a lot to be learned from a piece like this. Get a copy of it and study it. Note how he gets down on the page what it is like to be hungry and to finally assuage that hunger. It is called 'Hunger was a good discipline' and is in a collection of essays entitled *A Moveable Feast*. When you have read it why not have another go at smell and see what you come up with?

Workshop: hunger

Imagine you are hungry. If you want to be a 'method writer', you might do this when you *are* hungry. Write a piece in which a character is as hungry as Hemingway was in *A Moveable Feast*. Construct the piece in three stages:

1 beforehand (the feelings of hunger)
2 the meal (feeding the hunger)
3 afterwards (the hunger fed).

Stage 1 – the character is unable to not think about food. They try to avoid seeing food and catching smells, but sights and food smells are everywhere and they are sorely tempted. Your character imagines what it is going to be like to taste the food. They picture it in their minds, running over it with their senses, even as they are trying not to think of it. (If it is easier for you to write about yourself doing this, then use yourself as the subject.)

(250 words)

Stage 2 – they finally get the food and drink. Include the anticipation, the excited, even desperate build-up. Then they eat and drink: they might savour every mouthful or they might wolf it down.

(250 words)

Stage 3 – they are satisfied and replete or they have made themselves sick. Show how the world seems different to them now.

(250 words)

Edit

When you have finished, read it over and revise where needed. Read the piece for nouns and verbs. Circle all adjectives and adverbs, then read the piece again and see how it works without them all. Look the piece over once more and see whether any of the adjectives and adverbs are required; if so put them back in.

The aim is not to get you to write like Hemingway, or like anyone else, but to help you to learn from writers who have developed and honed their craft.

Focus point

You can learn from other writers all of the time. Study of another writer will show you the careful way to select the words you use; to keep the action simple and find clear and direct words to convey that to the reader. You can do much worse than the clear and simple naming of things. Follow the principle of using concrete nouns and strong verbs that we discussed in the earlier chapters, spiced with the right adjective or adverb and you can write some strong and solid pieces of writing.

Key idea

We do not think all writers are good, but we can learn lessons from writers we like and from those we don't like.

Write

Prepare and cook a meal. Use a similar skeleton framework:

- Stage 1 – the build-up of buying the ingredients
- Stage 2 – preparing the meal
- Stage 3 – serving and eating it
- Stage 4 – afterwards.

Make notes while you are doing this, and then write your notes up into a piece of no more than 250 words.

Remember these principles:

- Call things by their names.
- Use strong verbs to describe actions.
- Spice with carefully chosen adjectives and adverbs.

(250 words)

Workshop: à la carte

Choose a starter, a main course and a dessert from the following menu:

Salads and Starters

Soup of the day - wholesome home-made vegetable soup and fresh crusty bread

Honey and mustard glazed chicken salad - succulent strips of chicken marinated in honey and wholegrain mustard on a bed of fresh mixed-leaf salad, sprinkled with pine nuts

Greek salad (v) - cubes of feta cheese with marinated olives on a bed of fresh mixed-leaf salad and drizzled with Mediterranean olive oil

Main meals

Roasted vegetable enchilada (v) - wrapped tortilla filled with a medley of roasted vegetables, tomato and herbs, topped with melted cheese. Served with chips and salad

Homemade lasagne - fresh minced beef ragù with layered pasta sheets and a cheesy béchamel sauce. Served with chips and salad

Home-made roasted vegetable lasagne (v) - roasted vegetables with layered pasta sheets and a cheesy béchamel sauce. Awash with chips and salad

Stilton and black pepper steak - gorgeous prime rump steak with stilton, black pepper and cream sauce, with chips and salad

Fish and chips - Crispy, golden battered cod fillet with chips and salad

Desserts

Toffee pudding - hot sponge smothered in sweet, sticky toffee sauce

Chocolate sponge pudding - hot chocolate sponge drowning in a rich chocolate sauce

Cassis royale - soft vanilla ice cream pampered in a blackcurrant sorbet

*Parfait caramel*ice cream centre with a caramel volcano exploding chocolate

---

First make notes on the taste, smell, texture, sound and appearance of the food. (There is a sound to food – particularly when being eaten.)

Once you have written your notes, write a scene in which these elements are important. It might be a scene at home, a special anniversary or a Valentine dinner, a hopeful seduction scene or a scene where someone is going to be promoted or fired. Start off with two characters, build a disagreement between them and then bring in a third

The films *Chocolat* and *Babette's Feast* are both centred on food and are both based on books. *Babette's Feast* is an award-winning 1987 Danish movie written and directed by Gabriel Axel based on a story by Karen Blixen, who also wrote the story on which *Out of Africa* was based. *Chocolat* is based on the novel *Chocolat* by Joanne Harris. In it, a young mother opens La Chocolaterie Maya, a small *chocolaterie* in a fictional French village, and with her chocolate quickly turns the lives of the villagers upside down. Food is central to both stories, informing the plots and the themes.

Food and crime are central to an English television series broadcast by BBC TV between 1994 and 1997 called *Pie in the Sky*. In this series, a policeman, Detective Inspector Henry Crabbe, longed to leave the force and dedicate his life to his major passion – food. Many of the stories are centred on the frustrations of cooking a perfect dish, while having to do his day job and detect crimes. He is desperate to leave the force but he is such a good detective that his superior officer relies on him and will not let him go.

In *Pie in the Sky* you get important things that we shall look at more closely in the following chapters. In Henry Crabbe we have a character with a passion, and a character with a problem. His passion brings him into conflict. These, as we shall see, are essential ingredients in creating characters and in developing stories. But more of that later.

In summary here: you can use food in so many ways in writing. It can be a way of characterizing someone if they have a passion for food, or perhaps a fear or loathing for certain foods. Food can be the central issue around which an entire plot or story could be constructed. A story set in a time of famine would have the potential for great scenes and story lines. Admittedly, food has been used quite a lot in writing. The key to your using it would be, as with so many of these ideas we discuss, to find a way to do it differently.

Focus point

The senses do not all seem to get used equally. One or two dominate. Do not write solely visual writing: remember the other senses, too. Let readers hear, feel, taste and smell.

Summary

In this chapter you have explored the senses of taste and smell, built up passages of writing based on taste and smell, and used the senses of smell and taste together. If you recall any writing you have read that uses taste and smell strongly, find it, reread it and mark what made it stay in your mind. Can you learn from it and can you create similar effects in your writing?

Next step

In the next chapter we will build on all this work on the senses and look at how we create scenes replete with vivid sense detail, the sort of detail that bring scenes alive for the reader, making all the senses work together, and combining them in pieces of writing.

9

Making the senses work together

Separating our senses in the way we have done is not actually the way our senses work in life. It has helped us to understand and practise them but, in fact, all our senses work together in order to give us the whole picture of the world we enjoy. When we are born we are such a bundle of sensations that we probably smell, taste and feel more strongly than we see. Though, as adults, we may be consciously aware of only one or two of our senses at any one time when we experience something, we do, in fact, see, hear, touch and smell at the same time. But now that we have put each separate sense under the spotlight and tried to tease out what is unique and also difficult about each one, we must develop writing that uses all the senses together. Not only is this more accurate to the way we as human beings live in the world, it is also the way that we make passages of writing 'leap off the page' to employ that commonly used phrase.

Childhood memories

 Focus point

We are highly attuned to the senses when we are young. It often seems, looking back, that we apprehend the world in a more animal-like way; touching, sniffing and tasting our way around. Our childhoods are particularly rich in memories of smell. Smell will also take us instantly back into a remembered place. Remember the Proust example from the previous chapter.

 Write

Shut your eyes; think back to your childhood. Can you remember the house of a friend or a relative that had a different smell from your house? Choose a place that you had a strong reaction to – either of like or dislike. Let your mind wander over it; let the place come to you. Think of touching something there, tasting and seeing and hearing something, as well as smelling.

When you are ready, write down as much as you can remember of the different smells, for example, food, perfume, clothes, tobacco, people, pets, etc. But pay particular attention to all the concrete detail, all the 'things'. List all the smells and textures and tastes and record anything else that comes to mind. Look your notes over and, using them, write a page recreating this place. Do not worry about creating character or telling a story, let this emerge through the things and place you describe. Concentrate on using smell but get something in from all the other senses too

(250 words)

Workshop: a happy place

Think yourself back into a place you loved as a child. You were happy there. Maybe it was a room, a place by the sea, in a car, your grandparents' sitting room, a sofa, a cupboard or a loft. Perhaps it was outside: a tree house in the garden, hay barn or garden shed; a place on the river bank where you fished; or a sports field where you played sports. Take a moment to sift a few places and settle on the one strongest in your memory. When you have decided on the place, make notes.

- What did it smell like?
- Describe the smell of the place. Did it smell musty, dry, of coal fire or wood smoke, compost, mothballs, polish, perfume, paraffin?

(250 words)

- Is there any taste associated with this place?
- Did you go there to eat secretly?
- Did you take food with you, perhaps chocolate or picnic fare?
- Did you find food there, wild strawberries, peas growing in a field?
- Did you go scrumping apples or pears?

(200 words)

- What was the texture like?
- What does it feel like against your skin?
- Is it rough, smooth, soft, warm, dry, moist, damp?

(250 words)

- What sound do you hear?
- Is it an animal or animals?
- Is it human?
- Is it a voice, a trumpet, traffic, a boat on the river, or the wind? Try to capture the quality of this sound.
- Is it sharp and quick?
- Is it thin and reedy?
- Is it thick and bass-like?

(250 words)

- Finally, write anything visually striking.
- What did the place look like?
- Was it unusual or particularly beautiful?
- Is that why you went there?
- Was it sunlit?
- Were there interesting shadows?
- What was it like in the rain?

(250 words)

Look over what you have done and, using this as source material, write a longer piece in which you convey to a reader how you feel about this place. Do not say things like, 'I felt happy/unhappy/sad/euphoric there.' Try to convey the sense of happiness, joy or exuberance that you felt there through the choice of words and the way you use them. Remember the work we have done on using concrete nouns and verbs and think about the nature and power of the language you are using. Develop this writing into a piece on the place.

(750 words)

Here is a piece based on memory:

Mum took me into the school gate, then into an office where she started whispering to a woman in a window, asking if it was all right to leave me here because, she whispered, she had to catch the bus and take the eldest one to her school. Giving a look down her beak at me the whispery woman said it was all right and she'd look after me. But she didn't. When Mum had dashed off she just left me standing by myself in the corridor. She didn't even tell me where the toilet was. And I didn't know.

For hours the world clattered and echoed past. Children and teachers looked down at me as they went by. But I didn't cry. I wanted to. I knew something wasn't right; my eyes were darting about the place. Where was Baby Jesus? Where was the Virgin Mary? In Southend we had had Jesus and Mary with her blue mantle and her radiant smile of perfect innocence. Where was she now? And where were the nuns to nod at me with faces white as plates? I'd not seen one nun go past and the walls were totally bare. Something was wrong. The whole smell of the place was wrong.

It was like being in someone else's house except it was the smell of green walls, floor polish and varnish, warm, stale milk and coke from the heating pipes, all mixed with the smell of books preaching duty, denial, and of things being forbidden. It was the smell of Methodism. What had Mum brought me to? Why had she abandoned me here in this place?

Here we have something through which we can underline an important lesson we met very early on in this course. What is the author writing about?

He is writing about his early experience of different religions. How do you write about an abstract notions such as religion without it sounding empty, or without writing a religious tract? Read the passage over again and see what the author has done.

The author gives content to the abstract by using language which is concrete. He says the whole smell of the place was wrong and suggests religion has a smell. It seems fine as a statement until we ask what does that actually smell like? Saying that something smells wrong is saying nothing; it is empty. What the author needs to do is give the concept a content and a context and that is exactly what he goes on to do. He fills it in for us so that we can sense it, experience it, visualize it as he does. He fills it in by making it concrete and, by making it concrete, he makes it appeal to our senses.

It was like being in someone else's house except it was the smell of green walls, floor polish and varnish, warm, stale milk and coke from the heating pipes, all mixed with the smell of books preaching duty, denial, and of things being forbidden. It was the smell of Methodism.

When he writes the 'it was like being in someone else's house' we all know how wrong that smells. This whole passage is akin to the writing we have seen in the novel *Perfume* by Patrick Susskind, as well as the writing by Ernest Hemingway that we have looked at. The passage uses detail in order to get across the sense of place exactly as those other examples did. But we have included it here because it uses the senses in a combined way to create a sense of time and place.

Key idea

A writer alert to the power of language, to nouns and verbs and to the power of writing from the senses can bring time and place to life for the reader.

Write

Think of a subject you can write about. For the purposes of the exercise this ought to be an animate thing like a person or an animal, and not an inanimate object. Write five sentences that convey the essence of this subject to someone else without saying explicitly what you are writing about. Do not say what it is; suggest that through what it looks like, feels like, sounds like, smells like and tastes like. Write it in the form of a puzzle, or a riddle that someone else has to guess. Each one of the five sentences should be about one of the senses. When you have done it, show it to someone and see if they can guess what you are writing about. It is not a contest; you are not trying to beat this person so don't make it the sort of puzzle that nobody can get. Give clues, but overall the aim is to try to convey the essence of this thing without explicitly stating what it is.

Edit

Show your riddle to someone and see if they can see what you are writing about. Listen carefully to what they say. If they make any helpful comments to you, say they are confused by one part or another, or got lost, revise.

Using the senses in a scene

Look at the piece of writing that follows and, as you do, write down at least one thing used in the example for each of the senses.

At each of the suspect's denials Detective Chief Inspector Ross's nose twitched as if he'd caught the whiff of something nasty. He leaned forward, drumming his hands on the table. He rapped out three questions, wanting to hammer them into the man's skull. At each denial the suspect blinked to shield his eyes from the naked light. Seeing this, Ross moved so that the light shone straight into the suspect's face and asked him again. Still the man held out. DS Julie Holmes' chair creaked forward. Ross let her have a go. As Holmes probed the man's story, Ross's tongue dug into the cave-like cavity in his back teeth. Each time he worked a bit of the stuck beef burger loose, he coated his tongue with the grease and undercooked onions that seemed to taint everything that came out of the kitchen. It wasn't just the lies coming out of the man's mouth that made him want to go outside and spit but he had to stay; he had no choice. Then, suddenly, the man made a slip. DS Holmes' excited voice made a noise like a mouse in high heels on a parquet floor.

Ross practically threw himself over the desk and both officers went in for the kill. Why, when, how, what, where? They hammered at him and got what they wanted. When it was over and he had signed his confession, the man even held his hand out. Holmes' mouth tightened and turned sour-looking but for some reason Ross stretched his hand out. The hand he took gave him a shock. He had expected something stronger but this hand was soft and warm and unexpectedly dainty as a choir boy's. Ross looked down at it, pink and small and manicured and warm and lying gently in his. He let it fall. The man had strangled eight victims. What was the hand of a strangler supposed to feel like?

This scene gets all the senses in. As well as using all the senses, it moves the story on. There is character and action and we are in a different place in the narrative at the end of the piece than we are at the beginning, but the main focus has been on getting at least something in for each sense. What did you write down?

Write

You are going to write a similar scene.

- Decide where the scene is going to take place; inside or outside; time of day, time of year, etc.
- Then think of four things for each of the senses that would be present in the scene and that you could use.
- Write them down. What four things would you use for sight, sound, touch, taste and smell?
- Now write a scene using all five of the senses and using as many of the above as you can. Have something move on in the scene, i.e. something is different at the end of the scene from what it was at the beginning.

(750 words)

We can use the senses in prose passages to describe:

the **weather** – cold, sunny, hot, dry, wet?

the **characters** – cold, sunny, hot, dry, wet?

Sounds can be used to delineate places and set up stories – these sounds will be different depending on where the story takes place:

• inside or outside?

• in a big space or a confined space?

• distant traffic noises?

• garden machinery, aeroplanes, voices, crowds at a football match or in a pub?

Smells can come from people, animals, food, vegetation, the sea, the rain. (Don't forget the sound of the sea or of rain.)

Taste is closely allied to smell: the taste of food, of people (perhaps if you are writing an erotic piece).

Touch will be good for things like:

- texture
- feel of heat or cold on skin
- effects of heat and cold
- touch of fabric
- leather from shoes
- the touch of a metallic seat on bare skin
- the touch of a hand on an arm
- the touch of wind on a face
- the touch of a gun barrel against skin

Sight will be used throughout as it is the most commonly used of our senses to show the appearance of:

- people, places and things
- shadows, light, colour, shape.

Any such details can make a scene concrete and bring it to life. Try to use them.

Workshop: set the scene

Cover this page where marked below. The exercise requires you to uncover the following instructions one by one.

- Begin with the sentence 'I was walking along the road when I saw…' Write in a few words what you saw – for example, 'a dog chasing a cat up a tree.' Then read the next instruction.
- You hear something. Write what you hear – for example, 'He barked.'

By now you will have a piece which starts something like:

'I was walking along the road when I saw a dog chasing a cat up a tree. He barked.' Continue – read the next instruction and carry on. Follow the instructions through to the end. Try not to see what is coming and write according to each new instruction.

- You touch something.
- You smell something.
- You taste something.
- You touch something.
- You fail to hear something.
- You fail to see something.
- You fail to smell something.
- You fail to touch something.

- You fail to taste something.
- You see something.
- You hear something.
- You touch something.
- You smell something.
- You touch something.
- You see something.

(750 words)

Edit

When you have got to the end, go over it and see whether you can revise it. Change anything weak if you can think of something better. Add some pace or atmosphere by choosing words to convey the place or atmosphere you want. See whether you can come up with a more polished 750-word piece. Even if you find you are completely happy with your first attempt, you are fooling yourself. It is essential to do the revision.

Oscar Wilde

'I was working on the proof of one of my poems all the morning, and took out a comma. In the afternoon I put it back again.'

The following was done precisely following the instructions in the workshop exercise above, then worked over a little bit to add continuity, tension and atmosphere:

I was walking along the road when I saw the dog. He barked. I knew I should not show fear and I tried to push past him. His smell hit me. It was so strong I could almost taste it running down the back of my nose into my throat. I recoiled and fell back against the wall and didn't hear him growl. Nor did I see him bare his teeth. I was desperate to get away from the smell of him but he smelt my fear and came at me. I ran but he was too quick. I tried to fend him off, but I got only air. Fear filled my mouth as I turned and saw him on me, growling and snarling, the huge white teeth in his open mouth. A pain like a piece of broken glass going through me seized my leg as his teeth sank in. The stench of his breath and his oily fur was overpowering. I grabbed at the gate beside me and tried to crawl through the gap. I could see a light on and I started to scream ...

Try to write with all of the senses. It can capture the full experience of life in your writing and make your writing truly alive.

Synaesthesia

One other interesting thing about our senses is that for some people they are transferable. Things these people normally see or hear can be felt and heard, too. There is a name for this: synaesthesia.

Synaesthesia Research website – http://www.syn.sussex.ac.uk/

'Synaesthesia is a joining together of sensations that are normally experienced separately. Some synaesthetes experience colours when they hear or read words, whilst others may experience tastes, smells, shapes or touches in almost any combination.'

Musicians can describe notes as having colour. In writing we carry a sense of transference too. Voices are sometimes described as deep brown or dark and velvety, or smooth as silk. How can a voice have colour or have texture like silk? Our language stretches to allow this to work for us. Language used for a visual purpose can communicate how something feels. This, as we have seen, is how images work. Language pointing in one direction and giving light in another. We know the silky dark brown voice is not a colour, material or a texture yet we both feel and see the smoothness of silk and we get the colour in an understanding of the voice. This is part of the amazing power and flexibility of language.

Write

Try to think of something that can be described in this transferable way. Then:

- Describe someone's touch as a smell.
- Describe a visual picture as a colour.
- Describe a sound as a colour or a smell.
- Describe the touch of something visually.
- Describe a taste in terms of touch.

(200 words)

Summary

In this chapter you have explored the senses of smell and taste, seen how the senses are used to create and bring writing to life, looked at ways of accessing and using a range of sense material, built up written passages full of sense detail and life by using all of the senses. Try writing your own passages using all the senses in the same way. Keep practising it. This is how to make your writing come alive.

In the next chapter we will build all this foundation work that we have done with language, with images and with sense-based detail in these earlier chapters by going on to explore a key concept in creative writing, that of showing and telling, though as we prefer it, showing, telling and ignoring.

10

Showing, telling and ignoring

In this chapter you will be introduced to the concept of 'show and tell' and write several pieces using this key idea in creative writing. We will develop this concept and add to it the idea of 'ignoring'. We will discuss what should be shown in writing, what a writer should tell, and what a writer should leave out, that is 'ignore'. And we will also look at how the balance between these three concepts can be crucial for creative writing.

Show and tell

What would you prefer, someone who tells you they love you or someone who gives you diamonds? These days probably the latter! It is the same with writing. Readers don't want writers to tell them about fabulous cities or amazing diamonds or to promise them a fortune. In the words of Cuba Gooding Junior's character, Rod Tidwell, in the film *Jerry Maguire*, they want you to 'show me the money'. They want to see and touch and bite the diamonds; that way they know they are real. In this chapter we are going to show you the money.

To begin with we will look at the distinction between show and tell.

Key idea

The distinction between 'show' and 'tell' is one of the most important, useful and sometimes puzzling concepts in creative writing.

Some people grasp the distinction immediately, others find the idea confusing. But it need not be puzzling. In fact, you have already been doing showing and telling in the previous chapter. We thought it a good idea to get you writing this way without being told that you were using a particular concept. Being told that you are doing something particular can make you so conscious of it that it can sometimes stand in the way of doing. You begin to think about it. What we are going to go on to do in this chapter is now make the concept explicit and clear so that you know what you are doing when you are using it; and so that you know when to use it and when not to use it.

Children do 'show and tell' in school, where a pupil brings in something, like their pet tortoise, shows it to the class and then tells them about it. That is not the show and tell we are talking about. What we mean by show and tell in the creative writing field can be seen as the difference between giving information and firing the imagination; the difference between telling readers about the diamonds and letting them see the diamonds for themselves.

Most times when you see this subject written about in books on creative writing the title is not 'show and tell' but 'show *don't* tell'. The implication being that: to tell is bad, to show is divine. But there is another important element to show and tell which is often overlooked.

Orson Scott Card

'You've no doubt heard of the slogan "Show, don't tell." Under certain circumstances, that advice is good; under others, it's exactly wrong. Storytellers constantly have to choose between showing, telling and ignoring.'

You cannot show everything. Nor can you tell everything. Some things, many things, you have to leave out.

Key idea

In your writing you need to show some things and you need to tell some things and you need to IGNORE many other things.

You actually need to *tell* the vast majority of your story; you need to show (dramatize) a good deal of material, and you also need to leave out lots of other details that are irrelevant: events, characters, settings, scenes, inconsequential dialogue that will clutter and hold up the story. So, a better slogan than 'show and tell' is 'show, tell and ignore'. For example – if you have a character in a story who is journeying from the UK to the United States, you need to make some decision about how you will present this. If the journey is not important, just the fact that she has travelled, then you can just tell us that:

> *She left London and landed in New York, x hours later.*

Or, with a smidge more detail:

> *Mary left Heathrow and landed at Newark six hours later. The cab took her straight to her meeting on the Upper East Side.*

This is swift. You have got your character from one side of the Atlantic to another in a matter of seconds. No queuing up for security checks or baggage. All ignored.

But if the journey is going to be important to the story, either because she meets someone, or something happens at security or on the plane, then you may need to take the reader through it. You may need to make more of it to make sure the incident stays with us. This is where showing comes in.

Snapshot

To warm up …

- Write 50 words about isolation without saying the word.
- Now write 50 words about hunger without saying the word.
- Write 50 words about boredom without saying the word.
- Write 50 words about football without saying the word.

(200 words)

Workshop: openings

Read the openings to these novels. You will be asked to answer some questions about them after you've read them.

'No one who had ever seen Catherine Moorland in her infancy would have supposed her born to be a heroine.'

This is the opening sentence of Jane Austen's *Northanger Abbey*, it dates from 1818. Read it again. Now read the next extract.

'The title of this work has not been chosen without the grave and solid deliberation which matters of importance demand from the prudent.'

This is the opening to Sir Walter Scott's *Waverley*, from 1829. Read it again. Now read the next extract.

'In the latter day of July in the year 185–, a most important question was for ten days hardly asked in the cathedral city of Barchester, and answered every hour in various ways – Who was to be the new Bishop?'

The opening to Anthony Trollope's 1857 novel tells us that we are in Barchester, the setting for *Barchester Towers*.

'All happy families resemble one another, each unhappy family is unhappy in its own way.'

Extract four is from Tolstoy, the opening to *Anna Karenina* which dates from 1877.

'Under certain circumstances there are few hours in life more agreeable than the hour dedicated to the ceremony known as afternoon tea.'

This final extract comes from Henry James's 1881 novel, *The Portrait of a Lady*.

What do these extracts have in common? In your notebook, write down four different things the extracts share.

Now read the following openings to novels. Again, it will be a good thing for you to read them twice. You will be asked to answer some questions about them once you've read them.

'"Morning Jeeves," I said.

"Good morning, sir," said Jeeves.

He put the good old cup of tea softly on the table by my bed and I took a refreshing sip. Just right as usual. Not too hot, not too sweet, not too weak, not too strong, not too much milk, and not a drop spilled in the saucer. A most amazing cove, Jeeves.'

The excerpt comes from 'Jeeves Exerts the Old Cerebellum', in *The Inimitable Jeeves*, published in 1924 by, of course, P.G. Wodehouse.

'To the red country to part of the grey country of Oklahoma the last rains came gently, and they did not cut the scarred earth.'

This is John Steinbeck's opening sentence to *The Grapes of Wrath* from 1939.

'The boys, as they talked to the girls from Marcia Blaine School, stood on the far side of their bicycles holding the handle bars, which established a protective fence of bicycle between the sexes, and the impression that at any moment the boys were likely to be away.'

This is Muriel Spark's opening to *The Prime of Miss Jean Brodie* from 1961.

> 'I would like to write down what happened in my grandmother's house the summer I was eight or nine, but I am not sure it really did happen. I need to bear witness to an uncertain event. I feel it roaring inside me – this thing that may not have taken place.'

This is from the beginning of Anne Enright's novel *The Gathering*. It is the latest extract of them all, published in 2008.

What things do these extracts have in common? Before reading on, in your notebook write down four different things the extracts share.

Did you spot that the first five extracts are all openings to nineteenth-century novels and that the next set of openings date from the twentieth century, with the exception of the last which is from the twenty-first century? Can you write down in what ways the nineteenth-century extracts differ from the later extracts? Below are some suggested answers, but please write your own before you look at them.

Here are some answers you might have given in relation to the first set of extracts:

- They are all opening sentences.
- They are all extracts from classic authors.
- They are all from the nineteenth century.
- They are well polished; a couple of them are almost epigrams.
- They establish the tone of the story at once.
- The author's tone of voice is very important. (You can already hear the irony in both Jane Austen and Anthony Trollope's opening lines.)
- In each of these extracts we know we are in the hands of a master storyteller with a story to tell.
- There is a vision and a sweep that is broad.
- The writer is the controlling voice, controlling the narrative and sweeping across characters, story and setting in a confident, godlike way.
- None of the extracts contains any dialogue.
- We are not plunged into the action.
- They are all examples of telling.

You may well have thought of other things but the point we seek to make here is that fundamentally all these openings are narrative, they are telling. No one said narrative writing was boring. In good narrative, the voice is strong and distinct. The choice of words can be dramatic, or they can suggest or intimate a dramatic situation to follow and in all these examples we are in the hands of excellent, skilled narrators who are *telling* us things.

Now here are some possible answers to the second set of extracts:

- They are all opening sentences.

- They are all extracts from classic authors (with the exception of the last one who may become classic – who knows?).

- They are all from the twentieth century (with the exception of the last one).

- They all start in the middle of the action – something is going on and they start with scenes that take us straight into the action. We are plunged straight into what the characters are doing and saying.

- Each of these extracts starts in particular places at particular times with particular people, for example, Edinburgh or Oklahoma.

- Several of them use dialogue – the first two extracts introduce us to characters immediately and through dialogue.

- There is a lack of certainty or confidence in the voice – and about what actually has happened – explicitly stated in the last example.

- They are all quite different from the nineteenth-century extracts.

- We are introduced to characters and not the mediating voice of the all-seeing narrator.

- They are all examples of *showing*.

- Some of them are in the third person; others are in the first person. If you are unsure what third or first person means, do not worry about this; we will cover that aspect later.

There are many ways we could approach these differences but we shall concentrate on unpicking those elements that relate to showing and telling.

In the Jane Austen extract we know we are going to be presented with an ironic story about Catherine Moorland. We learn that immediately from the writer's tone, but there is no action going on as the story opens. There is no scene that we immediately enter and share with the characters. We do not *meet* Catherine. The same can be said of the examples by Walter Scott, Tolstoy and Henry James. You could argue that the Trollope example opens up on the goings-on in Barchester, but we are still not presented with a scene; we are not actually plunged into any action.

The more recent examples all introduce us to characters, or people in particular places at particular times. The example from the *Grapes of Wrath* is description but in an immediate scene because we see the rains come; we are there when they come. The example from *The Prime of Miss Jean Brodie* is also description but again in an immediate scene; we are with these boys and girls in this place at a particular time.

A couple of the examples are written in the first person, taking us directly inside one character's heads. This is something not done at all in the 19th century examples given. This is because those authors are telling the story; the authors and not the characters are in control. The stories are in the control of the characters in the twentieth and twenty-first centuries and in so many ways the narrators are less certain about their own stories.

Why this difference between works from the two centuries? Why has novel writing changed so much? Think about this question and write down your thoughts about this change in your notebook.

There are probably many reasons but the American publisher and writer Sol Stein, in his book *Solutions for Writers*, makes a good case for the twentieth-century development of film having considerably influenced writing and reading. Because of film and television, Stein says, the way we read and write has become more dominated by the visual and more and more dramatic. Stein's argument is that readers are so used to *seeing* stories that writers have had to write stories they can see while they are reading. Stein says:

> *'If you examine twentieth-century fiction, you'll find a dramatic increase in immediate scenes and a corresponding decrease in narrative summary.'*

Focus point

Don't spoil your chances of ever getting published. Learn how to tell, show and ignore.

Showing through images

> *Claire looked up at the other children in the playground. Three of the older ones loomed over her. They had no faces. Their backs against the sun, they had only big heads and shoulders with huge humps on them. They were monsters; ugly, deformed, hungry monsters.*

Snapshot

You can see how this extract uses images to make a visual picture, but what is the scene trying to show? If you could write this in a simple sentence that tells what it shows, what it would be? Don't read the suggestions below but get your notebook and write your answer down. There may be more than one sentence.

Here are some suggested answers:

- It was Claire's first day at school.
- Claire was being bullied at school.
- Claire was small for her age.

The fact that there are several sentences implied is not a bad thing; it brings out something vital about showing. There is often a sense of decision making about scenes. As a reader you are shown a character doing something in a certain way and are invited to make up your mind about what they are doing. This means that as a reader you are active. You look to the context and you use what clues you have about a character to decide what is going on. Because you are not told everything but are encouraged to make up your mind about things, there is the potential for a real dynamic in the writing and for a dynamic relationship between writer and reader. Readers like to have their minds engaged and that dynamic relationship is what writers should aim for. In this example the simple sentence about Claire has been transformed into an image. But there is even more to showing than this. An essential element to showing is action.

Showing through action

In plays, people reveal themselves by what they do and say. Actors look for this when rehearsing their parts. They also look for what other people do to and say about their character and what their character does to and says about other people. All of this can be revealing of character and help the actor form a true view of that character. We will consider dialogue in a moment, but first we are going to focus on action.

 Key idea

Common advice given in playwriting is that, when a character first appears on stage, you should have them do something typical or say something typical. This helps fix them in the audience's mind. This advice is also good for story writers. When a character first appears in a story, have them doing something typical.

 Snapshot

Write three brief, different descriptions of the same person coming through a door into a room in three different ways. Find things for them to do that show how they feel. For example:

1 John was nervous about meeting Sue's parents. (How does he show this nervousness?)
2 John was ecstatic about meeting Sue's parents. (show)
3 John was depressed about meeting Sue's parents. (show)

 Focus point

Get your characters to do things; put them in action and they will reveal themselves to the reader.

Snapshots

Write a scene in which two people are walking. They can walk fast or slow, up and down corridors, steps or escalators, in and out of lifts – perhaps one on the up escalator and one on the down escalator, or in a train corridor or in a plane, with one trying to find something out from the other which the other one is trying to conceal. Don't think about character or story too much: just write.

Write a piece in which two people are in the middle of a row or disagreement, or a search for something. This involves the two people switching things on and off, like light switches, televisions, or opening and closing doors, cupboards, drawers. This should result in a very active piece of writing. Don't think about character or story too much: just write.

Write about someone in a situation of danger, for example, someone has fallen on a railway line or is about to fall off a wall or out of a window, or a car crash with the driver trapped and petrol spreading everywhere. It need not be physical danger – someone could be in danger of making a wrong decision in a relationship, or perhaps adopting a mistaken cause. Two people arrive and have to try to rescue them. Will they or won't they succeed?

Showing through action and description

Workshop: another world

Read the following extract:

'Once off the M3 you felt as though you entered another world; the world of a washing powder commercial or an advert for lawn mowers. In every identical square of front garden identical men went up and down lawns with identical mowers. All the houses were identical. They all had Georgian bay windows, car ports, carriage lamps and front lawns with garden gnomes in them. These identical houses were on identical streets with names such as Saracens Way, Temple Close, Corinthian Drive, Zeus Walk, and Roman Road. Driving there was like being caught in one of Dante's circles of hell without an *A to Z*. Cars had been known to wander in off the main road and never be seen again for a hundred years.'

Either rewrite or continue this piece of 'telling' with 'showing'. Remember also to ignore – leave out whatever you don't need. Invent characters who live there or who get lost while driving there, or elaborate the setting in any way you wish: add description, action and dialogue as required.

(750 words)

Key idea

Don't just describe your character – describe them in action.

Showing through action and dialogue

You may already have discovered in your work on the exercises you have done that, as well as action, dialogue can add a key element in showing and telling. So let us add some dialogue.

Look at this sentence: 'Dick was always nervous around Annie.' This is a general statement that tells us about Dick and his way of behaving around Annie. If we are writing a story do we need to ask ourselves whether we show, tell or ignore it? If we decide it is important to our story and that we want to the reader to get a sense of how Dick behaves around Annie rather than simply be told about it like this, possibly among a lot of other information in the middle of which it might get lost, then we need to make more of it. If it is really important to character and to situation, perhaps to the plot of the piece, then we need to dramatize it; we need to make it into a scene. We do not want to leave it as a general statement but we want to turn it into a particular scene in which we see Dick behaving nervously. How do we do that?

Let's ask some questions.

• Who are Dick and Annie and why is he nervous around her?

• Is his nervousness going to manifest itself differently if he loathes her rather than loves her?

Let's go for the obvious and say he is nervous around her because he is attracted to her; maybe he wants to ask her out but he is afraid to because she is brighter than him. She always has her head stuck in a book and he does his reading from TV. Having decided this, how do we play our scene out?

• Where do we set it?

• Where are they and what place does it happen in?

• What is going on?

• What is going on when we join it?

What has happened to them before the scene you are going to write? (It is essential to ask this, because though it will not explicitly appear it will have a bearing on the scene as it plays out.)

 ## Write

Find yourself answers to these questions: make notes. Come up with a situation, and think of some way of showing his nervousness and her attitude to it. Perhaps she secretly adores it; who knows? Decide. Then, when you are ready, without looking at the example below, write a passage which *shows* 'Dick was always nervous around Annie.'

(*750 words*)

Here an example response to the above exercise:

> *'Anyone sitting here?' Dick asked with a grin, bouncing back on his heels so that he looked like his socks were on springs.*
>
> *Annie's eyes went to the empty seat beside her and then back to her book.*
>
> *Dick took it as a good sign. She hadn't actually said 'Drop dead' or told him to clear off.*
>
> *'I suppose they can't be, unless they're invisible, eh?' He laughed the laugh his last girlfriend had told him made him sound like a castrated hyena and bent forward on his springs to look under the bench before bouncing upright again.*
>
> *Annie sighed. Dick eased himself down on the cold metal bench beside her, perching on the very edge of the front rim like a man about to be fired from a cannon.*

As well as the dialogue we have used images and body language to try to convey his state of mind; and hers. The simple act of her eyes going to the empty bench beside her and then returning to her book without looking at him and without saying a word says quite a lot about her character; but it leaves it up to the reader to decide what that is. We have made the point before but will make it again; showing is suggestive. It allows the reader to use their imaginations to interpret the scene as you present it. That is why the reader enjoys it; they are asked to actively participate in the engagement of reading, to use their imaginations.

Nowhere in this example is the word 'nervous' used, but the idea is to get Dick's nervousness across in an implicit way. Whether it does or not, you can decide.

Edit

How did your piece work? Is there anywhere that you can work it over a little to make it work better? Read it again, and if there is do so. If you did not use dialogue then get your characters to speak to each other; listen to what they say.

Snapshot

Here are two sentences that tell:

'Simon had an inferiority complex.'
'Gavin did well with girls.'

Let us see what we can do by combining these pieces of narrative. Without looking at the example below, put these two characters in a scene letting what they do and what they say convey this information to the reader. Do it in 200 words.

Example:

> *'I can't tonight,' said Simon, covering himself with his towel.*
>
> *'You've got to. You said you would. Stacey'll be there,' said Gavin towelling himself vigorously in front of the mirror.*
>
> *Simon ducked away from the sight of his white skin, hairless chest and bony ribs against Gavin's already hirsute body. How come Gavin was so hairy and had such muscles considering he was the same age?*
>
> *'You fancy her, don't you?" said Gavin. 'You can't let me down. You've got to be there, and then I can have her mate, for sure.'*
>
> *Simon looked down on the locker room floor and sponged water off his bald legs.*

This is a scene built around action, dialogue and description. How did your version compare?

Read the following extract of a dramatic scene built on dialogue, action and description:

> *'You will be back early tonight?' said Mark.*
>
> *Mary stabbed buttons on the TV remote.*
>
> *'Only we're going around to Ben and Penny's later.'*
>
> *The screen burst into life. The Jewellery Channel; the same one she'd been watching until the early hours. Mark winced at the volume.*
>
> *'They invited us last week; remember?'*
>
> *A cuticle and a fingernail of gigantic proportions bearing a sapphire ring filled the screen, glowing under the spotlights like a fluorescent maggot that had just got engaged.*
>
> *'What time?' He moved in front of the screen.*
>
> *Mary peered around his legs.*
>
> *'I need to let them know.'*
>
> *Mary reached for the mobile and her credit card.*

 Snapshot

What is the narrative here? What sentences do these passages show?

Cover what is below and write your thoughts down in your notebook – there may be more than one suggestion:

Our suggestions for this exercise are:

- Mary was obsessed with TV shopping.
- There was something missing from Mary's life.
- Mary was a spendaholic.
- Divorce was in the offing.

148

Did you come up with anything else; perhaps a sentence or two seeing the piece from Mark's point of view? In reality, it does not matter what you wrote. The main point is for you to see how dialogue and action combine to animate a scene, create characters and develop a situation so that it is active, engaging and moves a piece along.

Key idea

In your writing you must be able to move fluently and easily from telling to showing and from showing to telling. You need to be able to do both; and you need to know when to do both; and when to ignore.

Summary

In this chapter you have explored the concept of show and tell (and ignore), written pieces using this key idea in creative writing, practised identifying telling and showing, practised writing a piece of telling as showing, and practised writing a piece of showing as telling. To develop this still further, practise it for yourself and, once again, read your favourite authors to see if and how they use the concept. Write out favourite passages in your notebook and read them over several times until you fully understand how they are using narrative and how they are dramatizing scenes and why they have chosen to do it.

Next step

In the next chapter you will further use show and tell to explore the technique of description, describe places, and describe people through places.

11

Description

In this chapter we will look at description and take the understanding of creative writing a stage further. Building on the previous chapters, we will look at how integrating the concept of 'show, tell and ignore' with the use of sense-based material can lead you to create descriptions of people and places that are resonant, alive and engaging for the reader.

What is description / what isn't it?

Consider these questions in relation to a piece of creative writing (e.g. fiction, play script or poem):

- What is description? What do you understand by the term description?
- Think about this and write your definition down in your notebook.
- What is description *not*? Sometimes we can be clearer what we mean by a term by saying what it is not.
- Think about this and write down your ideas of what description is not.
- What is good description?
- What is bad description?

The *Concise Oxford Dictionary* defines 'description' as:

> a) the act or an instance of describing; the process of being described. Or
> b) Spoken or written representation of a person object or event.

As ever with dictionaries, one definition points us to another and the verb 'to describe' is defined as to

> state the characteristics, appearance, etc., of, in spoken or written form.

It is not clear how much this helps us, so it may be that a writer can come up with a definition more useful for other writers. In her helpful book *Word Painting: A Guide to Writing More Descriptively*, Rebecca McClanahan writes,

> Description is an attempt to present as directly as possible the qualities of a person, place, object or event.

If description is an attempt to present as directly as possible the qualities of a person, place, object or event, what exactly do we mean by 'the qualities of a person, place or object'? What qualities do persons, places and objects possess? Think about it and write down in your notebook two or three qualities for persons, places and objects.

Let us see how Shakespeare shows us the qualities of people, objects and events in a famous speech from Act 2 scene ii of Shakespeare's *Anthony and Cleopatra* where Enobarbus describes Cleopatra.

> DOMITIUS ENOBARBUS
> The barge she sat in, like a burnish'd throne,
> Burn'd on the water: the poop was beaten gold;
> Purple the sails, and so perfumed that
> The winds were love-sick with them; the oars were silver,
> Which to the tune of flutes kept stroke, and made
> The water which they beat to follow faster,
> As amorous of their strokes. For her own person,

> *It beggar'd all description: she did lie*
> *In her pavilion – cloth-of-gold of tissue –*
> *O'er-picturing that Venus where we see*
> *The fancy outwork nature: on each side her*
> *Stood pretty dimpled boys, like smiling Cupids,*
> *With divers-colour'd fans, whose wind did seem*
> *To glow the delicate cheeks which they did cool,*
> *And what they undid did.*
> *Her gentlewomen, like the Nereides,*
> *So many mermaids, tended her i' the eyes,*
> *And made their bends adornings: at the helm*
> *A seeming mermaid steers: the silken tackle*
> *Swell with the touches of those flower-soft hands,*
> *That yarely frame the office. From the barge*
> *A strange invisible perfume hits the sense*
> *Of the adjacent wharfs. The city cast*
> *Her people out upon her; and Antony,*
> *Enthroned i' the market-place, did sit alone,*
> *Whistling to the air; which, but for vacancy,*
> *Had gone to gaze on Cleopatra too,*
> *And made a gap in nature.*

So much is conveyed here though Enobarbus' words. Shakespeare shows us a good deal about the qualities possessed by Cleopatra but this is not all he does. As with other concepts we have looked at in this book, description can only be separated out from the other elements of writing and studied in a theoretical way. In any piece of writing, description is combined with and works with all the other elements. It can have a number of jobs. It can, for instance, form part of exposition and narration. Exposition is the giving of back story; narration is the onward movement of the story. Both of these elements can be conveyed to the writer through and with a large amount of description. Description might also give information and it might also drive the plot along. While it is doing all or any of these jobs it can be giving us the qualities of people, objects and things. It would be wrong therefore to imagine that description is something that is added later; something the writer puts on top to decorate the writing and make a show of it.

Key idea

Description is fundamental; not something you can choose to leave out. It is part of the writing. It is often, as in the example from Shakespeare, at the heart of a poem or a piece of prose.

To return to the example, Enobarbus' purpose in describing the scene is not only so that we will see how majestic and beautiful Cleopatra is, but so that she will impress. He intends that the audience in the play, the Romans, as well as we, the audience in the theatre, will get an impressive sense of the Queen of Egypt's majesty, wealth and power. The description here furthers our knowledge of Cleopatra but also of the forward movement of the narrative and the politics of the play. So how does Shakespeare do it?

 ## Snapshot

This writing from Shakespeare springs to life because of the use of detail, and also because of the imagery, which is sense based. Read the speech again and as you do, write down any images you can hear that are based on any of the five senses. Do that now before you read on.

Can you see how this entire picture is built up on concrete, sense-based images? The images are predominately visual, as would be expected, the burnished gold, the silver oars, which scream wealth and opulence. But note too, the use of images of smell as well as sound and touch. 'A strange invisible perfume hits the sense.' Cleopatra is strange and mysterious and she is best suggested by a strange, invisible perfume. You might argue that all perfume is invisible, but her mystery is being added to here. This strangeness of smell even seems to taste at the back of the throat. The very sails of her barge were 'so perfumed that the winds were love-sick with them.' Cleopatra is a live, sensible, hot-blooded creation. She is a creature of smell and touch as well as having amazing visual appeal.

Study the imagery as marked up in the following passage and compare it with the notes you made:

> 'The barge she sat in, like a burnish'd throne, [SIGHT]
> Burn'd on the water: the poop was beaten gold; [SIGHT]
> Purple the sails, [SIGHT] and so perfumed that
> The winds were love-sick with them; [SMELL]
> the oars were silver, [SIGHT]
> Which to the tune of flutes [SOUND] kept stroke, and made
> The water which they beat to follow faster, [SOUND]
> As amorous of their strokes. For her own person,
> It beggar'd all description: [SIGHT] she did lie
> In her pavilion – cloth-of-gold of tissue – [SIGHT]
> ... on each side her
> Stood pretty dimpled boys, like smiling Cupids,
> With divers-colour'd fans, [SIGHT] whose wind did seem
> To glow the delicate cheeks which they did cool, [TOUCH]
> ... at the helm,

A seeming mermaid steers: [TOUCH] the silken tackle
Swell with the touches of those flower-soft hands, [TOUCH]
That yarely frame the office. From the barge
A strange invisible perfume hits the sense [SMELL]
Of the adjacent wharfs. The city cast
Her people out upon her; [SIGHT] and Antony,
Enthroned i' the market-place, did sit alone, [SIGHT]
Whistling to the air; [SOUND] which, but for vacancy,
Had gone to gaze on Cleopatra too,
And made a gap in nature.' [SOUND]

Snapshot

What technique that we have studied in the book does this description fully exemplify?
Read it over; think about what we have studied and write your answer in your notebook.

Have you spotted that this description connects with the concept of show and tell that
we studied in the previous chapter? Enobarbus does not just *tell* us about Cleopatra
here, he *shows* us Cleopatra. He presents a dramatic scene the better to make her come
to life before our eyes.

And how does Shakespeare the writer dramatize his subject, Cleopatra? By employing
the techniques we have discussed throughout this book: he uses concrete images, good
detail and sense-based description. Read the speech again. Look at the sense-based
imagery that pervades this speech. Look at the way he dramatizes, makes a scene of
what he wants us to know.

Write

Describe someone as striking as Cleopatra. They could be amazingly beautiful or stunningly ugly,
if you wish, but whatever you choose, make them impressive. Perhaps it is someone you know;
perhaps it is a model, film or pop star whose image you have seen in papers and magazines.
Start with key words that sum them up; for example, tall, thin and birdlike, granite head, etc.
Just put down single words or phrases, then add to the description what will help you – what
you know about the person, what they do, what they'd like to do, what they say. When you have
made the notes, imagine the person doing something characteristic. Give them something to
do, put them in a scene. Dramatize. Employ the same techniques as Shakespeare. Do not just
describe flatly but dramatize the person. Put them in a scene in which they are doing something
or in which something is happening to them or around them. Make use of all five of the senses.
Write as much as you like to start with, then edit it back to 200 words.

Describing people and places

John Braine, *Writing a Novel*

'People are places and places are people.'

Note how in the Shakespeare example we have looked at, he unites person and place. The person of Cleopatra is inseparable from her surroundings; the barge with all its riches is a part of her. It helps create the vision of her before our eyes as much as anything said about her. In fact, very little is said directly about her. He does not tell us how tall she is, what colour her eyes or hair were. In fact, Enobarbus says he cannot describe her. Her description, he says 'beggar'd all description'. He could not find the words to describe her. All he could do is describe the world around her and how 'she did lie in her pavilion – cloth-of-gold of tissue' surrounded by cupids and handmaidens. He tells us too how all the city came out to watch her. It is like the red carpet at Hollywood Oscars' night, the people all agape.

John Braine, *Writing a Novel*

'Whenever you write about places, you also write about people. It isn't always that you mention the people when you write about the place. Sometimes it's necessary, sometimes it isn't. On the whole the best way is to concentrate on making the reader see the place.'

Braine says that the most revealing place about the character is the home. He is right that if you could enter people's houses just when you are in search of a character you could find a lot about them from the things that they have around them as well as from the very house they choose to live in. Ask yourself – what sort of house do they live in? How full of books is it? Is it dominated by a large television? Is there a television at all? Do they have a child's paddling pool in the garden, or large swimming pool and tennis courts? Do they cook; are there house plants? A whole host of observations would spring to mind and some of these would reveal a lot about a person who lives there. In his book, Braine quotes an example from *The Acceptance World* by Anthony Powell. It is a fairly long description of the interior of the Ufford, the favourite hotel of his uncle, Giles. The description of the halls and reception rooms; of having tea in the lounge with its permanently closed doors; of the wallpaper with its intricate floral design; the chintz-covered sofa and armchairs; the gilt mirrors and a single picture, 'an engraving placed over the fireplace, Landseer's *Bolton Abbey in the olden time'*. This is a picture rich with concrete detail; it is from this detail that we are able to form a picture of the man who spends his time there but we have not a shred of description of the man himself. His environment, his world, carefully brought out for us on the page is what creates the man. Take a look at it: *The Acceptance World* by Anthony Powell.

Write

Think of someone you know well. Then think of a room that you associate with them. It could be a kitchen; it could be a bedroom, a study, or workroom. It might be a garden shed. Describe this place in such a way that you tell us about the person who inhabits it. Do not introduce the person. Describe the place with the person absent but make them present through your description of their favoured place.

(750 words)

Key idea

If you want to describe a person for a reader, don't describe them, describe the place they inhabit.

Non-fiction is about the giving of information and of imparting facts. In textbooks, handbooks, academic work, articles and travel books we tell people about things. A guidebook about Venice might try to capture some of the atmosphere along the way; the best guidebooks probably do.

Write

Find a travel book; perhaps of a place you know well or have visited. In this book find a factual description of a town or part of a city that you can use as the basis for a scene in a story. Dramatize it by writing a scene for one or more characters. Do not worry much about the characters.

Concentrate on trying to breathe life into the place as a setting. The aim is to transform the factual description by using the techniques of concrete detail, and by employing all the five senses. In terms of narrative you might imagine someone arriving at this place at the start of a story in which some adventure is going to happen. The place is going to be significant; make it significant in the writing.

(200 words)

Write

Remember an incident you have experienced and that left its mark on you. It might be a disagreement at work or with a fellow driver. Write it up in a narrative way. Tell what happened. Where it happened, who was there, what was done, and what was said. Use reported speech – that is, *tell* us what people said; do not actually have the characters speaking.

(200 words)

Edit

Take this last piece and rewrite it as a dramatized piece, an immediate scene. Write it as if it is happening now, in front of your eyes and make it filmable. Don't just concentrate on the visual details and how the place looked. Try to capture the sound of the world you are writing about, the feel, smell and taste. Include action, sensory details and dialogue, i.e. have the characters speaking to each other in dialogue exchanges.

(750 words)

Write

Take two of the locations in the following list and describe, in short paragraphs yet in some detail, two or three places, real or imaginary that spring to your mind.

- a place of great mystery
- a place of horror
- a place of secrecy
- a place of quiet and harmony
- a place of imprisonment
- a place of great magic and unknown power

- a place of happiness and celebration
- a place of great loneliness
- a place of great destruction
- a place of decay and desolation

(200 words)

Combining showing and telling

Read the following:

> *We'd known Granny Rose for years but we didn't feel like we really knew her until that first time when we saw her in the shed at the bottom of the garden, leather jacket complete with skull and cross bones on her back, spanner in hand, surrounded by all those cannibalized motorbike parts, heavy metal music thumping from the radio nailed to the wall.*

This piece combines telling us the writer had 'known Granny Rose for years' with showing us the detail about character – the leather jacket complete with skull and crossbones on her back, spanner, cannibalized motorbike parts, and heavy metal music thumping from the radio nailed to the wall.

Combining showing and telling in this way can be most effective in pieces.

Write

Write a piece like the example above in which you tell us something about a character in the first sentence or two, and then go on to show this in the rest of the piece. Keep it short. The example above is well under 100 words. You can have 200 words, maximum.

Edit

Read the piece below. Underline what is showing and ring what is telling:

'She was exhilarated. The whole thing was exhilarating. The sun was shining and she felt so free, riding so high. The horse seemed to know exactly what was required of her and Madge had only to give a little encouragement here and there; a squeeze of the legs, a feel of the rein, never the whip, for her to turn to face the next fence, approach it smoothly and sail over it with the lightest of leaps and a feather-like landing on the other side.

'The multi-coloured spectators seemed to be miles beneath her as she swept over the water jump and after the last fence she left the ring to cheers and a lot of applause. She saw her sister, Molly, making her way through the throng, shaking her fist triumphantly in the air. Gasping for breath but exhilarated Madge got down from the horse and fell straight into the arms of her sister who congratulated her on the ride and seemed so pleased that she had done so well.

'The sisters hugged and screeched for sheer joy. It was good, Madge felt, to share this moment with her dearest sister and her oldest friend. Molly had always been there whenever Madge had needed someone to share her success and failures with. Madge hadn't felt so excited since her first year at school when she had got into the show jumping team and today she had felt convinced that she would make a mess of it after the dressage. She explained to Molly how seriously she had doubted herself. Molly told Madge that she knew Madge had doubted herself and that she hoped now that this would prove she could compete. She told Madge that she was a more than a competent rider. Now she ought to believe she could do anything if she set her mind to it. Madge was so pleased when her name was announced over the loudspeaker and she went up to the rostrum, to collect her winner's rosette; something she would treasure for the rest of her life.'

What do you think of this piece? Can you think of three things you like about it and three things you don't like about it? Read it again and write your thoughts down in your notebook.

There are several things that we are told that Madge said to Molly, or Molly said to Madge. Reporting on a conversation like this is called 'reported dialogue'. We will look at dialogue in more detail later, but for this exercise rewrite this piece using show, tell and ignore. Try to put some of the reported speech into direct speech; i.e. create a scene in which Molly and Madge actually speak to each other. Remember the senses, remember concrete detail.

Now that you have practised these techniques in depth, it must be said that a combination of showing, telling and ignoring is an ideal to be aimed at. But it is important to redress the balance in favour of narrative here and remind you not to underestimate telling. A writer like Anthony Trollope creates scenes but he also has all the nineteenth-century control of narrative. In Chapter 4 of *Barchester Towers* he tells us that 'Of the Rev. Mr Slope's parentage I am not able to say much. I have heard it asserted that he is lineally descended from the eminent physician who assisted at the birth of Mr T. Shandy, and that in early years he added an "e" to his name for the sake of euphony, as other great men have done before him.'

This is wonderfully amusing character presentation. The tone of voice carrying such irony is entertainment itself. We learn so much more about the man once we know that he changed his name to Slope from Slop 'for the sake of euphony'. It is marvellous writing and it is pure telling.

There is so much to admire in it, but the point to be made in the context of our subject is that we could turn this into scene, and if we were turning it into a script for film or television we would have to dramatize it; we would show it. But in terms of writing the novel would we want to show here? Probably if this was written today it would be shown, but in showing we would lose the wonderful narrative writing. This reminds us that telling is good. We must not show everything.

 Key idea

Telling is good. Do not try to show everything. Show, tell and *ignore*.

Revision

What **telling** is good for:

- taking less time than showing
- filling in detail quickly
- giving background information about a character or situation
- moving through time – you can cross time and place in an instant
- linking scenes that show.

What **showing** is good for:

- revealing characters and the interplay between characters
- creating empathy, which allows the reader to get inside a character and see the world with their eyes

- allowing the reader to be active
- allowing the reader to use their imagination to see characters, scenes, places
- revealing information through showing can be dramatic.

What **ignoring** is good for:

- everything that has no place in your story
- unimportant details
- digressions
- rambling descriptions
- boring, inconsequential dialogue.

Elements that help to show:

- Action
- Dialogue
- Making an image
- Concrete details
- Sensory detail.

Showing …

- happens now, before our eyes, in real time
- is filmable
- is presented in a scene – which usually has a specific purpose in a story – to introduce a character or a piece of plot. It usually has a beginning,
- middle and end and it moves the story forward.

Note the dictum 'Resist the urge to explain', or 'RUE', as Renni Browne and Dave King have it in their book *Self-editing for Fiction Writers*.

Here is an example in a piece of reminiscence done for a writing class. A writer remembered his sister playing with dolls as a child. He wrote a delightful scene where he and his sister operated on one of them. The writer fashioned some good, believable dialogue and created an effective scene, which included this:

> *'We're going to do a heart transplant.'*
> *The world's first heart transplant was in the news that year.*

He was criticized for having his authorial voice popping up in the middle of a strongly established scene to explain the background to the dialogue. This was felt to be lazy and amateurish, and the writer was advised to find ways of getting the information across better.

Key idea

Writing should stand alone without such authorial comments to shore it up.

Focus point

Writing is a balance of showing, telling and ignoring. Don't forget the ignoring. Do not put everything in. There are lots of unimportant details you can leave out. You might put everything in when you are writing a first draft; perhaps you should because you do not really know what is going to be important or not. But as you revise you need to cut and trim and focus on what you really need to make any particular scene, character or dialogue work.

Why do beginning writers want to tell not show?

Beginning writers want to tell not show because it is more natural and seems easier. At the beginning we do all seem drawn to narrative summary because in some ways it is a natural way to tell stories and it looks easier. Constructing fully rendered dramatic scenes has to be learned and it is not easy. In fact, writing fully dramatized scenes is quite a challenge. For instance, it is much easier to write 'Simon and Claire loved their house' than to write a scene or scenes which show their love for their house and allow the reader to share and experience their love for their house from the inside as Simon and Claire do. For that you need to handle more technical elements. You need to be able to create atmosphere and a sense of character and place. You need the ability to write from the senses and, more than probably, handle dialogue, as well as the ability to dramatize. Showing therefore has a lot more elements to it.

But showing everything can be just as bad for your story. If no one cares whether Simon and Claire love or hate their house why spend time on it? If Simon and Claire are not important to the story why spend time on them? This is why the three elements of this chapter, show, tell and ignore are so important.

Edit: a checklist for showing and telling

When you have written a piece, look it over and ask the following questions:

- Is there too much description? Can you cut it back?
- Is there too much narrative summary? Can you turn it into dramatic scenes?
- Where you have told, can you use action?
- Can you use dialogue?
- Have you used dialogue in which characters say things they would not say just to give information to the reader? Avoid this.
- Do you describe your characters' feelings?
- Have you told us that they are angry or sad; depressed or exhilarated?
- Could you find a way to show it?
- Do you mention feelings outside of dialogue? If you do you might be telling. Check.

What to ignore:

- the bits that come between scenes and passages
- the bits where characters go shopping, or eat, or sleep, or travel somewhere (unless they are absolutely germane to the plot or to revealing something indispensable about character – for example, they go shopping because they are a kleptomaniac, or they eat, or don't eat, because they have an eating disorder).

In films, people only have to say a line like 'See you in Cairo' and we can cut to Cairo and we're there. Fiction can do that too, so use the jump cut technique.

Summary

In this chapter you have explored the use of description, using the concept of 'show and tell' to describe a character, see what telling is good for, see what showing is good for and see what things you can leave out (ignore). Practise doing this for yourself in your own notebooks and find examples in your reading that you like and from which you can learn. Study these examples, make notes with a view to helping yourself to learn. That is to say, write down what will be helpful for you; you are the only one who will see them.

Next step

The next step will be to look more closely at ways of conjuring up the key creation at the heart of your story – the characters.

12

Character from outside in

In this chapter you will analyse and create characters. We will develop characters from outside in, show you how to develop characters using yourself and develop characters using props.

Remarks made by Marks and Gran at a master class on comedy writing for TAPS at the Riverside studios, September 2000

'We want to know the people. The people are who we like. We need their truth, need them to be believable. Ninety per cent of what's wrong with stories for new writers is that they don't know their characters. Plot is only what your character will do in a situation.'

What is a character?

Character is the lifeblood of any piece of creative writing. But, first of all, we need to ask: what is character? Consider the following questions in relation to a piece of creative writing (fiction, play script or poem):

- What is a character? What do you understand by the term 'character'? Think about this and write your definition down in your notebook.

- What is a character not? Sometimes we can be clearer what we mean by a term by saying what it is not. Think about this and write down your ideas of what a character is not.

- What is characterization? Writers and critics talk about characterization. What do you think they mean by it? What is your understanding of that word?

Writers and critics also talk about good characterization and poor characterization:

- What is good characterization?
- What is bad characterization?
- Where do characters come from?

Only after you have answered these questions should you continue reading below.

The *Concise Oxford Dictionary* defines 'character' as:

> *1. the collective qualities or characteristics, especially mental and moral, that distinguish a person or thing.*
>
> *2. a person in a novel, play, etc.*
>
> *3. a part played by an actor, a role.*

'Characterization' it defines as being 'to impart character'.

Let us stick with 'the collective qualities or characteristics, especially mental and moral, that distinguish a person or thing'.

How do we know our characters? We need to know their collective qualities and characteristics. What kinds of qualities and characteristics can a character have?

A character can be kind, good, patient, impatient, irritable, morose, intelligent and much more. A person's characteristics will be what makes them stand out from other people. It can be a combination of physical and verbal mannerisms. It might be the way they walk or talk. So good characterization will be writing that does this well; bad will be writing that does not do it well.

The second definition says a character is a person in a novel, play, etc. or a part played by an actor, a role. Characters are the people in a story but they are *not* people. We must not make that confusion. They are not real people because they are created by the creative mind of the writer and shaped by the editing mind of that same writer and interpreted by the reader and/or viewer. One mistake that people can make in writing classes is to discuss characters as if they were real people; as if they do what real people would do or say.

Focus point

The idea of a character having verisimilitude is important but it is also important to keep clear that characters are not real people; the two are very different. Characters can often be more interesting than real people.

Walt Disney

'Love your characters. I love Mickey Mouse more than any woman I have known.'

Some people say that characters are the single most important element in a script or story. That probably depends on the type or genre of story being considered. It is arguable that the characters in a genre book such as a fast-paced thriller or a chill-a-minute vampire story are as important as they might be in, say, a character based work of literary fiction. Obviously every aspect of a script or story is important but the claims of characters are fundamentally important. They often give the life blood to a story.

As we have already said in this book when you read a story you should read as a writer would. That is to say look at how the story is made; try to find a way into how you might have come up with such a story. You should always read so that you can get things for your own writing. In terms of character, read for character. When we are writing ourselves we may start off with an initial idea but how do we know about our characters? Where do characters come from? How do we find them? We can't go and buy them in a shop. Are there any tricks and devices that can help you learn?

Key idea

Characters can be the single most important element in a script or story.

Creating characters

How do we create characters? You can create characters in many ways, but here you are going to consider two ways: creating characters from outside in and from inside out. In this chapter we will look at the first option – outside in – and we are going to do this in three ways:

- using you yourself
- props
- other people.

We will look at the second option – inside out – in the next chapter.

USING YOU YOURSELF

 ## Snapshot

Look at your hand. Study it carefully; look at the lines and pores, the nails. Are there any scars, any hairs, any tan? Are there any rings? Can you remember the finest achievements or biggest failures of this hand? Did it once take or drop the winning catch at a cricket match? Did it once shake the hand of someone famous or important? Write any of this down and make notes about your hand.

Put your hand on a page in your notebook or a piece of paper and draw round it. Write your name on the page below the hand you have drawn.

Fill in the finger and thumb spaces with a list of things you do. In the palm space write a physical description of the hand. Fill in the palm space with details of what the hand looks like and what makes it individual; rings, watches, scars or mannerisms.

 ## Write

Again, put your hand on the page and draw round it. This time think of someone you know well, a friend or a relative, and put their name on the page below the hand you have drawn. Fill in the finger and thumb spaces as you did last time but this time with a list of things *they* do, such as in the example. When you have done that, using these notes, write a 200-word description of this person: include what they look like, say, do, want, etc.

(200 words)

 ## Anton Chekhov

'When men ask me how I know so much about men, they get a simple answer: everything I know about men, I learned from me.'

Key idea

You are the single most useful resource you have as a writer.

Yes, we are the single most useful recourse we have as writers. Most of what we need is in ourselves: from experience and knowledge of life, to the magical faculty of the imagination. We draw on what we know and what we have learned to write and using ourselves for the creation of character is something we do pretty naturally too. We don't always use our own physicality to create character but we are probably always using some of our own psychological, emotional and intellectual knowledge as well as elements from our past. We probably do this without being conscious of it. It is natural to draw on what we know and what we are and to use small parts of ourselves to create larger, rounded, full-bodied characters. We can start with a memory or an experience and give that memory or experience to a character. We can then add other memories and experiences, not our own, but from other people we do know, or from things we have read or seen so that the character moves on very rapidly to become something other than us, something very much its own self. We can do this with our own bodies. Starting with our own hands and feet and faces can give us this same small core of information, detail and inspiration to begin the creation of a full rounded character.

Feet first

Starting with something such as our hands or feet, as we will go on to do next, is an amusing but useful way into character. Here we have started with a drawing of our hand and used that as a blueprint on which to stamp the character of someone else whom we know well. Starting with what you know is always good advice; here you have started with the person you know best in the world, in theory, and have used that as a base on which to build the character of someone you know well. Neither portrait will be really you or really them: they will be an approximation; a characterization of them. We have not gone far with this yet but however lively and interesting you make them will depend on your skill as a writer. Your skill as a writer is often dependent on your skill as an observer. Having done hands, let us see we what can do with feet.

First of all, feet are odd things. Those disabled or unable to walk probably view feet differently but most people use them all the time to move, whether to walk or run; they are also crucial to our sense of balance. We share feet with animals, and they use them for the same purposes as us: for locomotion and balance; to move towards something and to move away. But we use them also to kick balls in sport. We use them to dance; they are obviously basic to the art of the ballet dancer and the contemporary dancer. For the rest of us they are useful for holding doors open and for driving cars.

Feet are both robust and delicate. They can suffer from a variety of conditions such as arthritis, athlete's foot, bunions, ingrown toenails, corns, warts and stress fractures; all of which tend to have their comic and serious side. Feet are full of delicate bones that get bruised and broken. When soccer player, David Beckham, broke his foot before a

World Cup campaign, the newspapers, through diagrams and illustrations, introduced the world to the wonders of metatarsal bones. These are the bones in the middle of the foot. His foot became vitally important to the nation as did speculation about the nature of the latest slipper-like football boot and whether this had contributed to the injury. But most of the time our feet in our culture are not front page news. In other cultures it is different. Other cultures have treated feet with great importance.

In certain cultures it is customary to take your shoes off at the door and enter a building barefoot. In Japan and Korea it is such a prevalent custom that the interiors of buildings are built of material that would not survive being walked on in shoes and boots. Between the tenth and twentieth centuries in China young women's feet were bound to produce a foot that was thought to be aesthetically pleasing. In the Middle East the female foot is thought to be a beautiful thing and given special care. Within Christianity foot washing is given great prominence, a custom developed from Jesus' washing of his disciples' feet at the last supper. And there is foot fetishism which is an erotic obsession with feet.

Feet, then, are important to us in so many ways in our lives; yet how much attention do *we* normally give them? Unless you are a sports person or a dancer you probably look at your feet very little, generally look after them badly and take them for granted. They can be very odd and ugly things too. The feet of a gymnast, of any sports person, dancer or ice skater can be very bruised, battered and misshapen from the constant beating they take.

As for writers, they have not used feet too much. There are books on the Chinese custom of foot binding and English author, P.G. Wodehouse, wrote an amusing story called 'The Man with Two Left Feet' in a story collection with that name, about a man who wanted to learn to dance to please his new bride – with subsequent Wodehousian comic results. But there is still a market for the great foot novel to be written. You could write a story in which a character suffers from a condition such as athlete's foot, bunions, ingrown toenails, corns or warts. It could not only be a part of his character but germane to the plot. Imagine a story in which a character practised reflexology; an alternative therapy which relies on stimulating the feet to produce well-being. Such a character could come into contact with a variety of characters – all through the feet. But let us see what mileage we can get from writing about feet with an exercise.

Workshop: feet first

Take your shoes and socks off and draw around your foot in the same way you did with your hand. Then think of someone you know well, a friend or a relative, and put their name on the page below the foot you have drawn.

Ask questions and note down the answers:
- What do they use their feet for?
- Are they a dancer, or sports person?
- What do their feet look like bare?
- Do they look after their feet – what sort of condition are they in?
- What size shoe do they take?

- What style of shoe?
- Do they look after their shoes? How – polish, dubbin?
- Are their shoes scuffed or in good condition?
- Do they have their shoes mended or just wear them out and throw them away?
- What do their shoes look like empty?
- Do their shoes smell? Of what – boot polish, feet, dubbin?
- Describe the person's walk. Are they light or heavy on their feet?
- What foot-related habits do they have (kicking walls, impatient tapping)?

Write a piece built around your notes that is centred around feet.

(200 words)

Self-portrait

Using ourselves in the style of a portrait is something that has a long tradition in art. Painters have seen themselves as a legitimate and interesting subject for a long time. Rembrandt used himself as a regular model for his own self-portraits over a long period of time and these portraits are some of the most moving and interesting paintings you can ever see. Seeing his translation from confident, optimistic young man with the world at his feet, to the older, battered, sadder man in the later portraits is a wonderfully moving and stirring experience. What happens with portraits is that you will possibly start with the outer appearance, the face, age, colouring, etc. and gradually move inside. This is what we get from the Rembrandt portraits. He is painting the outer man but through the outer man rendered in pigment the soul, sprit and mind of the inner man comes. Using yourself as a model for a portrait can be a good ways of practising. Once you get over the initial hurdle of looking at yourself, which can be as big a barrier as hearing yourself, then you have a readily available model for you to study. Make use of it.

Write

Position yourself comfortably in front of a full-length mirror or something that will show your face; study your face, its shape, colouring, etc. Make notes about everything you see: colour of hair, eyes, etc., and then write a self-portrait of yourself. Either be honest or describe yourself to someone who hasn't ever seen you and who you want to impress.

(750 words)

USING PROPS

As well as their physicality, people can also be characterized by things they carry or wear, by the world around them. The contents of a handbag or wallet are very revealing of character. If you were able to go through three or four different handbags in order to think about the sort of people who owned the handbags you would be able to construct a variety of interesting characters. These characters might not actually be one hundred per cent the people who own the bags; but your imagination would have quickened and stirred, and that is the point.

 ## Key idea

Creative writing's relationship with truth, or what actually is, is at best tenuous.

Handling objects that people own is very evocative and can inspire interesting and successful character studies. It is why people treasure letters and objects that famous people have touched; why rooms that people have occupied are hallowed, as if something of them has been transmitted into the place. From things like tickets for a plane, a train or a cinema; from receipts and shopping lists, you can conjure up very believable pictures of someone's age, background, hair colour, and where they've been.

Handbags

Workshop: the contents of a handbag

Take a look at this + list of the contents of a handbag; torch, travel tickets, matchbox, cigarette lighter, lipstick, house keys, glasses, a pen, a kitchen knife, sweets, hair brush, necklace of plastic pearls, pack of tissues, bottle opener and corkscrew, brochure for a holiday cruise, mobile phone, address in Cheltenham scribbled on a piece of paper.

Imagine that it belongs to a woman who has gone missing. Take some time to assess the contents; make sure you consider everything, make notes and then start to put down your ideas about the character and identity of the bag's owner. What sort of character do these items suggest to you? Think about it and make notes. Build up a picture of the woman in as much detail as you can. Consider questions such as:

- How old is she?
- What is her name?
- What background does she have?
- Does she work?
- What is her job?
- What address has she written down?
- What is she doing with a brochure about yachts?
- Why is she carrying a kitchen knife?

Is there anything else that occurs to you?

What do you make of the items in the handbag? The first thing to ask is, is there anything that stands out from the ordinary? Everything is quite as expected, apart from the kitchen knife. Most women could be expected to have lipstick, a hair brush, tickets for bus and train, a pen, and sweets but the item that stands out from this collection is the kitchen knife. What do you make of it? Why would she be carrying a knife around? This is a dangerous weapon. Is she in danger? Does she need it for protection? Is it perhaps not her knife but something she confiscated from someone: from her son perhaps? Perhaps she is a teacher and she confiscated it from someone at school. It is always a good idea to ask as many questions and to let as many ideas as you can go through your head before you settle on one.

Edit

The handbag exercise is a good thing to do when revising a piece of writing. It may be that you feel something is not quite working with a character; perhaps they haven't quite gelled and remain out of focus. In which case you could make a list of things they carry in their handbag, pocket or other bags. You may in all likelihood not use any of these things in your piece but the very act of thinking about them can often help you get a new insight into the character and result in you writing them better. Any extra insights you gain can only enrich an already complex character and a make a dull character more interesting.

Focus point

The first thing to ask of a character; is there anything that stands out from the ordinary? If there isn't, then find something that does.

Edit

Look over the piece you wrote earlier in the chapter based on the hands and feet of a friend or relative. Imagine either their wallet or their handbag. Think of the appropriate style to suit them, then list the contents of either wallet or handbag. When you have completed a comprehensive list of the contents of the wallet or handbag, go back to your original piece and see if your perception of the character has changed. Can you write some more about them using the insights gained from their wallet or handbag?

Hats

Look at this list of headgear:

- astrakhan
- babushka
- biretta
- chef's hat
- cricket cap
- crown

- deer stalker
- derby
- fedora
- fez
- flat cap
- folded newspaper

- forage cap
- homburg
- leghorn
- panama
- pillbox
- pilot's helmet

- policeman's helmet
- pork pie
- rain hat
- riding helmet
- sombrero

- sou'wester hat
- Stetson
- stove pipe
- straw boater
- tam

- ten-gallon hat
- topee
- trilby
- turban

 Write

Choose a couple of hats and write a short piece about the wearer(s). This could be a dialogue or a short piece in a situation or a place. Choose a title such as 'The Journey', 'The Angry Customer', 'The Underground'. Write what you like but the hats must be central to the piece.

(200 words)

Clothes

Look at this list of clothes:

- boiler suit
- dungarees
- trilby
- bra and pants
- rugby shirt

- Doc Martins
- pink tutu and top hat
- trainers
- shorts
- gym slip

- floral skirt
- little black dress
- corduroy trousers

 Write

Choose a couple of items which don't normally go together and write a short piece about the wearer(s). This could be a dialogue or a short piece in a situation or a place. Choose a title such as 'The Lost Ticket', 'The Missed Bus', 'The Doctor's Waiting Room' – write what you like but the clothes must be central to the piece.

(200 words)

Hats and clothes are interesting props for developing character. Some actors like to explore the physical sense of a character because that helps them get the character. Some like to get the walk; if they know how someone walks they can get a sense of the person they are. Others like to don a costume and use that as a way of getting to the character. There are a lot of similarities between actors and writers and writers too can approach character creation in similar ways.

Clothes have been used by writers in stories. In the film *My Cousin Vinny*, the judge takes exception to the leather jacket that Vinny, the inexperienced lawyer wears to his court room. He orders him to turn up next day in a suit that is made out of 'some kind of cloth'. When Vinny turns up in the same leather jacket the judge jails him for contempt of court. Vinny only then begins to appreciate how serious the judge is about procedure. He buys a suit but at the climax of the film, on the day that his court room skills are to be tested to their limit his suit ends up covered in mud and he has to go to a local second-hand store and buy the only suit they have.

Key idea

Clothes can make the man and the woman. The writer of *My Cousin Vinny* makes a lot out of the idea that 'clothes maketh the man'.

Casting against type

Think of someone wearing a form of dress that belies the reality of their appearance, for example a woman wearing a man's shirt and waistcoat and man's baggy cords. This might tell us something – but what? When we know her husband died two weeks earlier and they are his clothes, we may have the basis for a story, and this could be written up by getting the person involved in some action. Other variations could be a vet who hates animals and is wearing a woman's dress – why? A doctor, who is a hypochondriac, wearing a policeman's helmet.

Uniforms

Uniforms of all sorts have been used in films and stories to give viewers and readers a sense of the characters in the story. Thinking of a character wearing a uniform can begin to give you a way into a character or story. Imagine that you have someone in one state of mind donning a uniform and changing his state of mind as he puts it on, so that he or she is in a different frame at the end than the one in which they started. Perhaps you might think of a policeman or woman on his or her first day, or an experienced policeman becoming chief constable; maybe a nurse on her first day or on moving up to Matron. They might start anxious and lacking in confidence, maybe feeling they don't deserve to wear the uniform but the very putting on of the costume gives them the confidence they need so that they stand there at the end resplendent and full of confidence. Or you could write this in reverse, of course. Perhaps the putting on of the uniform brings about doubts. It could be turned again so that the change occurs in the taking off of a uniform. The character starts in one frame of mind and through removing the uniform ends up in another. If you want to build a story around something like this remember that uniforms are not just something for the armed forces, police or nurses. Sportsmen and women wear a uniform of sorts. When we join clubs we often have to put on a uniform that signal that we belong. Think of the clothing everyone wears to the gym. Think of the uniform that lawyers and judges have, or priests and nuns. Uniforms mark out a territory. They are a sign of belonging or of not belonging. Characters in your stories can either want to wear the uniform badly or want not to wear it badly. Whichever approach you take can yield the beginnings of a story for you.

What if someone falls for someone in a uniform, *because* of the uniform? What happens when they take the uniform off or if they want to take the uniform off? What if the attraction goes with the uniform? There is story potential in this idea. Imagine a scene in which a policeman, doctor, nurse comes home. Do they shed their persona with their uniform? Are they able to shed it? You could ask a story question here and possibly develop a story out of it.

In the film *Scent of a Woman*, the character played by Al Pacino, a blinded officer, dons his uniform for one last visit to the city where he intends to have one last great night on the town and then shoot himself. He needs to be in uniform to die. His donning of his uniform changes his persona.

Write

Imagine someone in one state of mind donning a uniform and changing their state of mind as they put it on, so that they are in a different frame at the end from the one in which they started, e.g. they started out hopeful, excited or solemn and end up disappointed, depressed or unhappy.

(750 words)

USING OTHER PEOPLE

We are taught by our mothers not to stare at people. For a writer this is bad advice. For a writer, staring at people is good. We can learn a lot from observing people closely. Putting those bits of observed details together to make a person can be great fun, too.

You are by now very familiar with both the process and importance of observation to the writer. In the earlier exercises you practised looking at stationary and moving objects; at buildings and at animals. People are animals too and are fascinating sources of study for the writer interested in creating characters. Keep in mind the lessons learned about observation and note-taking as you do the next exercises. There is no difference here; if there is, the only a real difference is that you will be studying people with a view to developing them as the characters in your work. The first exercise will be to study people from real life, or you could study people from photographs. These are not different activities, but they can result in different outcomes. Sometimes things done from life have more juice in them, more energy than things done from a still photograph. Artists that work from photographs often create very different work from artists that work from life. But that is not always the case.

Focus point

If you want to be a writer, be rude. Stare at people. Write down what they say. Look, listen, write and learn.

Key idea

Good writing is a marriage of what is researched and what is imagined but don't let anyone see the join.

A character's inner life

Up until now with character we have focused quite exclusively on external considerations such as hats, coats and uniforms. Working from the outside in, by using externally observed things like the clothes they wear, their mannerisms of speech, their physical attributes, is an excellent way of creating characters. All characters by doing and appearing also suggest an inner state. If we see a character in a top hat, striped tights and a pink tutu doing something like digging a garden or getting on a bus, we can infer something from their behaviour and appearance. So that external appearance and characteristics do suggest inner states, but, at some point, you need to get inside the character. You need to get to the real inner workings of the character. This is what the real work of the writer is about. No amount of external detail will energize the character enough for it to leap off the page.

CHARACTER STUDIES

Whenever you are beginning a piece, it is a good idea, say in about 500 words, to do a character sketch for each character. In this, you should go into their background, considering such things as family, school, work etc. Ask about the character's past – schools, home life, relationships, work. Consider their social network – who their friends or colleagues are. A young mother at home spends time with different people to someone at work.

This will give you a pretty comprehensive view of them and their external background. One idea, once you have really got to know the character's setting and world is to take them out of their setting and plunge them into another one. Good stories can come from this. It is something that Alfred Hitchcock knew well and did in many of his best films such as *North by Northwest*, *The 39 Steps* and even *Strangers on a Train* where the innocent tennis pro meets the evil Bruno in a train carriage.

Write

Take one of the characters you have written about in this chapter and build a character sketch. Ask what the person's habits are, good as well as bad. Think about their attitudes to things. This is a good way to reveal the way a character's mind works. Ask questions of them such as

- Do they ever apologize if they've done something wrong?
- Do they ever do anything wrong?
- What are their needs?
- What do they really want above everything else?
- What do they want with regard to others in your story?
- What else do they want?
- What is their point of view?

(750 words)

When you have done that, you can ask why what they want clashes with what others want. And at some point they must clash because from clash comes story.

Summary

In this chapter you have found out what a character is, analysed and created characters, developed characters from outside in, developed characters using yourself, developed characters using props, developed characters using hats and clothes and looked at characters from within. As you read, note how other writers create character and bring them to life. What tools do they use? You should have enough by now to be able to identify one or two.

Next step

The next stage is to develop characters further. In the next chapter you will develop characters from inside out, using other people, and you will help a character to find their voice by writing monologues for them.

13

Inside-out characters

In this chapter we will develop characters from inside. You will develop characters from:

- a questionnaire
- monologues
- interior monologues
- inside to outside.

A character is not only what he or she does, but also what he or she wants or means to do (and, incidentally, what he or she is prevented from doing). You need to get to know what they desire, want, need and how they will behave in situations because that way you will be getting to know your characters from inside as well as outside.

Internal affairs

When you are trying to think up characters for piece, it can be a good idea to divide what you consider into *internal* and *external* components. An external component can be something like someone's job or career – are they a policeman or woman, teacher, doctor, carpenter, etc.? Or their speech – do they have little catch phrases, dialect, foreign language, a stutter? Do they have mannerisms like giving a little cough at crucial moments. Ways of walking, dancing or playing sports? Ways of doing things with their hands? These are the sorts of attributes we looked at in the previous chapter. These physical characteristics are very important, but there are other very important ways of characterizing people too.

Internal considerations can be a character's dominant attitude and the dominant impression they give – and these two things can be different. Someone's dominant attitude might be bullish but their dominant impression might be that of a wimp. They may think they are a great football player, they may genuinely believe they have the talent, but the rest of the world can see something different. Casting a character with this sort of inner tension or ambiguity can bring a good deal to a story.

DOMINANT ATTITUDE

Each of us will have a dominant attitude. It is the way we look at the world. Do we look at it romantically? Do we look at it scientifically or technologically, thinking of it as something for our use? Do we look at it hoping to make money out of it? Whatever our dominant attitude, this too affect story and plot as well as having an effect on the interplay with other characters.

DOMINANT IMPRESSION

Someone's dominant impression can also be very useful to decide because it can give you predictable responses for your character in a story. How do they come over? Do they come over as timid, angry, crude, sexy, etc.? If a man is a wimp, he'll behave wimpishly; a woman who is consistently a bore will behave boringly etc. That gives you predictable ways for characters to behave in scenes, which helps you write scenes for them, but also gives you ways to surprise.

Once you have established the type you can turn this around; have the bore suddenly become very interesting; have the wimp suddenly become macho. The coward might become a hero; the timid woman sexy; the liar be forced to tell the truth etc. How a character appears outside can differ very much from the way they are inside. This difference also gives the character a potential journey. We will come on to this later when we consider characters in relation to stories, but every character needs a journey. They need to start somewhere and go somewhere. They need to finish at a point in the story that is different from the point on which they started. Characters need to travel. Starting with a wimp who becomes a hero is a good journey. Your character will need a dynamic; they will need movement. A change in their inner being is fundamental to this.

POINT OF VIEW

Another internal consideration is point of view. A character's point of view is very important. It relates character to story. When building a character you must ask what does your character want from the story? Deciding that can not only help you form your character but will help you form your story line, or plot. A point of view will link with desire and intention and give a character ways of behaving in a situation. These, in turn, will provide ways of turning the story in one or another direction. Because a character is pursuing their intentions, what they want, they can both react to the plot and turn and drive it in certain directions.

GOVERNING EMOTIONS

Another important way to characterize is to look at dominant types, and dominant elements in the character. Characters can have a governing emotion like anger or sadness or bitterness. All these emotions seem to be in the central character that John Wayne plays in the classic Western *The Searchers*. This can relate deeply to the theme of a story too.

A CHARACTER'S INTERESTS

Interests are another thing important for characterization. A person's interest can tell us a lot. What are each character's interests? Are they a collector of stamps or cars or memorabilia of any sort? Do they go to football matches? Are they a keen amateur astronomer? Knowing *each* character's interests is vital for the creation of lively and alive, full-blooded characters that will inhabit your stories with warmth and vigour and stay in the reader's memories long after they have put down your elegant, carefully written prose.

Focus point

Readers will not remember the twists and turns of your carefully wrought plot or story. But they will remember your characters, if they are good enough. The characters will be like real people. And we remember real people who have had a big effect on us all, or played a significant role at some point in our lives.

Write

Choose one of the characters you have created while doing the exercises in this book or elsewhere. Choose one that appeals strongly to you, that, for whatever reason, you have a strong reaction to. Write what you think of the person. Write about how the character makes you feel. Write what you felt first. Did your initial feeling change? Write about that change. What did the character make you think of? Write down anything else that seems important to you.

After making your notes, write a short piece in which you convey a sense of this person to someone else. To give the writing urgency, write from the point of view that it is important you tell the other person about the person. It could almost be life or death. Maybe you are telling the police about a suspect or an incident you have seen. Whatever 'story angle' you take on it, make it important and get across your feelings about the person. You should also try to make *us* care about this person and empathize with them.

(200 words)

Key idea

Care about your characters; cherish them, love them. Then your readers can.

EMPATHY

As we have said, to write about any character convincingly and with energy you need to know them and what sort of person they are. It is important that you feel strongly about them. If you feel strongly about them then you will write strongly for them and a reader is much more likely to care for them or hate them. You want your reader to feel something; the worst thing in the world is if they feel indifference. If readers don't like a character, that is a strong reaction. Hopefully, they will like someone else in the story and identify with them. How are they going to if you don't? If you don't feel anything, then you are going to be on a loser right from the start. Readers want to like and care for somebody. They *want* to empathize. It is your job as a writer to create that empathy with your characters. It is also much easier and more interesting to write about a character if you care about them. The more you like and are interested in a character, the more you care, the more the reader will care.

Workshop: developing a character from a questionnaire

Using one of the characters you have been writing about so far, copy down and fill in the character questionnaire (opposite) in your notebooks.

If you look at the questionnaire, you will see that the chart has three main areas. We start with the physical, move on to the psychological; the inner life and finally the social. Laos Egri has something similar in his book *The Art of Dramatic Writing*. He calls it the 'Bone Structure' of a character. His subject is theatre and he believes it is essential for a playwright to develop this or something like it when working on a play. But it is not just playwrights who need to develop this sort of picture of their characters. Short story writers and novelists should do the same. If you look at the categories of the CV you will see that there is interconnectedness here between the external and the internal. This detailed questionnaire aims to provide information for both and to connect them.

 Key idea

It is not too strong to say that this sort of approach should underpin all the work you do on character. You will need to look closely at all the external, observable stimuli that you can. But you will also need to explore, expand and develop the character's inner life; their attitude to themselves, to other people and to life. You can get all the external, observable things right but if there is no inner life you will have no character.

A lot of stories are quite simply how this or that person responds to this or that stimulus or situation. You need to know your character's attitudes and motives so they may act and respond.

But in talking about this we have begun to touch on another measure of interconnectedness; the interconnectedness of character and story. Character has all sorts of ramifications for story. Your characters relate deeply and fundamentally to all areas and levels of your story.

Character questionnaire	
Name	
Physical details	
Sex	
Age	
Height	
Weight	
Hair	
Scars	
Defects	
Illnesses	
Dress/style	
Background	
Place of birth	
Marital status	
Residence	
Occupation	
Education	
Family	
Parents	
Children	
Siblings	
Friends	
Pets (and pets' names)	

Inner life
Strengths
Weaknesses
Obsessions
Ambitions
Religion
Positive traits
Negative traits ('foibles')
Desires
Fears
Most traumatic event
Most wonderful experience
Major struggle (when, past, present)
Other
Good/bad habits
Hobbies and interests
Politics
Drugs
Favourite beverage(s) (brands?)
Smoker (brand? matches or lighter?)
Drinker (favourite tipple?)
Erotic history
Favourite reading (books, magazines, papers ...)
Favourite movies
Favourite music
Work habits
Favourite food/colour/car

Creating character biographies

There are books full of biographies that are very useful to the writer – from *Who's Who* with crisp entries like:

> '*He once killed fifty salmon in fifty hours of fishing. His writing on fishing revolutionized the sport.*'

> '*A man of great wit and charm, he appears to have been an alcoholic.*'

And there are more intentionally colourful books such as *Rogues, Villains and Eccentrics: The Honourable English Gentleman in Literature and Life*.

Or you might look in an obituary collection like the *Daily Telegraph Book of Obituaries*. In the collection subtitled *A Celebration of Eccentric Lives*, you will find a whole series of entertaining obituaries about highly individual characters.

From the obituary of Viscount Barrington

'Patrick was so steeped in poetry that it became part of his daily life. His method of timing a boiled egg, for instance, was to recite a fixed number of the quatrains of Omar Khayyam.'

These collections reward those who have lived colourful lives with colourful accounts of their lives and they are both interesting to read for their own sake, and potentially full of things that a writer might be able to use in character creation. Even the driest facts can be useful in this quest. A combination of dry facts put unexpectedly together can make quite a lively and unexpected character.

Workshop: create a character biography

Look again at the raw material you wrote from the handbag contents in the previous chapter. Build up a character study of the person you created there. If you have not already done so, give them a name; use the questionnaire to go into their background – family, school, work etc. Ask about their past, schools, home life and relationships. Consider their social network and who their friends or work colleagues are. For example, a young mother at home spends her time with different people from someone out at work all day. Ask what their habits are – good as well as bad – and most importantly their attitudes.

Ask questions like this of them:

- Do they ever apologize if they've done something wrong? (Or even if they haven't.)
- Do they ever do anything wrong?
- Did they feel loved by their parents?
- Was their childhood happy?
- How do they cope in a crisis?
- Which do they put first: money, power, family, love, ambition, health, or something else?
- What are their virtues and vices?
- What are their motives in life?
- What big unfulfilled need do they have?
- What is their idea of perfect happiness?
- Which historical figure do they most identify with?
- Which trait do they most deplore in others (and themselves)?

- What do they most dislike about their appearance?
- What is their favourite smell?
- What is their greatest regret? (Do they regret anything?)
- Which talent would they most like to have?

Using this material and material generated by the handbag, write a biographical entry of for this person in a book of biographical entries, such as *Rogues, Villains and Eccentrics: The Honourable English Gentleman in Literature and Life*, or an obituary in the style of the *Daily Telegraph Book of Obituaries*.

Key idea

A combination of dry facts put unexpectedly together can make quite a lively and unexpected character. But do not necessarily stick with the facts regardless.

Mark Twain

'Get your facts first, then you can distort them as you please.'

Creating characters through monologues

In this section we will look at combining finding out facts about a person and creating an inner life.

Snapshot

What do you understand by the term 'monologue'? Think about this and write your definition down into your notebook.

Sometimes we can be clearer what we mean by a term by saying what it is *not*. Think about this and write down your ideas about what a monologue is not.

A monologue is a long speech spoken by someone in a play. It's a speech delivered to the audience or to another character or even to an object. Shirley Valentine, in the play of that name, spoke to her kitchen wall. A monologue is different from a soliloquy which is a speech not explicitly delivered to the audience or to another character but the words spoken by an actor that reveal the inner workings of his mind. A soliloquy has to be spoken out loud otherwise we would not hear it but we accept the device that the actor is only speaking the words in order to allow us access to his inner thoughts. Other people in a play could hear a monologue but not a soliloquy. Monologues can also appear in books where we can get a character's thoughts in a direct speech or his inner thoughts in an interior monologue. This, in one way, is more like a soliloquy because no other character in the story or novel is privy to these inner workings in the same way that we the reader are. Virginia Woolf and James Joyce used monologues to try to get across the stream of consciousness of a character's mind. They recorded the thoughts, observations, memories, feelings and to convey the sense of the busy mind often removed all punctuation. Yet we don't feel confused or lost. It is both easy to understand and follow.

Alan Bennett's well-known series of monologues called *Talking Heads* is well worth looking at to see both how you can create stories out of monologues but also very importantly how you can create characters through monologue. Monologues depend on things which are crucial to stories. They depend a good deal on shape and structure; they need to be going somewhere, to have a point to them, just as the story around them does. The voice speaking the monologue has to be well formed and distinctive. The voice needs particular speech patterns and phrasing to make it believable. It needs to be speaking in a particular place. If they are speaking their monologue to an audience, who are they speaking to? Again, this can lead you into other characters. What is the main thing your character is saying in the monologue? Does he or she bang on about anything particular? Are they obsessed with anything? Are there any recurring themes? If you were to write monologues for the characters you are interested in developing you would find that you had to confront many of these issues and therefore writing monologues for your characters can be a very fruitful way of getting to know them and of tackling other areas of your story.

The comedy writing team of Marks and Gran often do this for characters in their sitcoms. Their suggestion is to write a monologue for each of your characters as if they were at the doctors telling them of their symptoms. It is also advice given by James N. Frey in his book *How to Write a Damn Good Novel*. He gives examples there of successful character creation that began with character details which were developed into a monologue. In many ways your character only fully begins to come alive from the lifeless matter of facts and biographical detail laid down on the page. The act of speech is almost like the breath of life flowing through them. As they speak they get up off the page and address you and the reader. It is this coming alive of the character you are aiming for. Writing a monologue is a very good way of exciting that process into action.

In mechanical terms, writing monologues for our characters gets them speaking. It develops their speech patterns and their ideas; it allows them to tell you what it is they want to say. In doing this it allows you to learn about them. They say things that might surprise you; things about their background, upbringing, parents, early life; love life, etc.

Focus point

Nothing that comes up in the monologue may actually appear in the finished work, but the very process of doing it can release information about the character's desires or ambitions and this can fuel your character development.

On the other hand, the monologue you create may appear in your finished piece. The Alan Bennett work we have referred to is a series of monologues building up into a whole. The Irish playwright Brian Friel built his 1979 play *Faith Healer* entirely from three monologues. Seeing the play is a bit like listening to witnesses at an accident; everyone sees the same events differently. The fact that the monologues don't physically overlap and interact seems in one way wasteful from a theatrical point of view when resources are sparse and ought to be maximised, but hearing them all separately makes the play very interesting.

 ## Key idea

Let your characters speak; they will tell you things about themselves.

WRITING MONOLOGUES

Writing a monologue for a finished piece as opposed to writing a monologue for yourself in order to try to develop character, is no different from writing anything else as a finished piece. You should start with a hook, something that will grab the audience or reader. You could start in mid-sentence puzzling the reader and encouraging them to read on. You could start at the end of the story and then loop back to the beginning hoping to keep the reader interested in finding out how the journey took place. However you start, you should take hold of the reader's attention with something strong and clear and simple. As you move into the monologue have a clear goal in mind. Have a point. Do not just have a character talk for the sake of talking. Give them a reason. Make sure the piece is going somewhere. It must tell a story so construct it with a beginning, middle and end. While they are talking, through what they are saying, your character must reveal themselves. They do not have to *tell* the reader or listener or speak explicitly about themselves; in fact, it is better that they do not. Some of the most moving and amusing moments in Alan Bennett's *Talking Heads* and Brian Friel's *Faith Healer*, come from the dramatic irony of the characters not being fully aware of the implications of what they are saying. The audience is able to draw conclusions about situations and characters in ways of which the characters are ignorant. Characters must not know too much about themselves; this is one sure way for them to be dead characters on the page. But as they talk in the monologue they should reveal things about their background, about their attitudes and about their desires and disappointments. They should begin to shape themselves as characters for you on the page and for the reader. Once we know about their hopes and dreams and disappointments, once they start talking about them, they will begin to live. And if your characters live, your story will live.

 ## Key idea

Your characters must not know too much about themselves. Keep them ignorant of important facts about themselves.

Write

Write an interior monologue of someone engaged in a tense activity – for example:

- a policeman on stake-out
- a doctor about to operate or operating
- a traffic warden about to swoop
- a shoplifter about to steal something
- a store detective about to pounce.

Go through the stages of

- anticipation
- event
- outcome (success or failure).

(*750 words*)

A character can be created through the viewpoint of another character; the way one person observes and makes judgements about a second person can enable a double characterization to take place. The sort of things they pick out and the way they express them tells you quite a lot about the person observed and the one observing, about the viewer and the viewed.

Character in crisis

A character's personality also comes through in how they handle people or situations – particularly difficult or fraught situations or people. Character is revealed when it is stretched by a crisis.

One of the greatest crises in drama occurs for Jocasta and Oedipus in *Oedipus Rex* by Sophocles when they both discover the old prophecy that Oedipus would kill his father and marry his mother has come true. That she, Jocasta, is Oedipus's wife and mother. What do they do? Jocasta finds out shortly before Oedipus. She begs him not to continue with his quest for the truth, rushes off stage and hangs herself. Oedipus, when he finds out the truth, stabs his own eyes out so that he will not look on the world in which he has sinned. This is exactly in character for the man who has driven the play along; a man who will not compromise, and who seeks the truth regardless of the consequences. It is entirely fitting and natural, though tragic, for him to act this way. It would be out of character for him to deny it or to grovel and run away and try to escape the consequences of his actions like many other men might have done.

As with crisis, someone in the grip of an addiction gives more scope for writing about than someone who is not beset by such compulsions. We are told in society that addictions are bad and unhealthy – perhaps they are, but they are important for writers. An addictive character is a character with a purpose, at least in one narrow sphere, and as such provides good material – Molière builds a lot of his plays around characters with narrow, addictive purposes, for example *The Miser* and *The Hypochondriac*.

Key idea

A character in crisis is a character with a story to tell.

 Write

Write about someone in the grip of an addiction – love, sex, money, food, books, shopping. Try to structure it in some way by having them, for example, in a situation where they have to hide their addiction from another person. This could link with the following exercise. Write a scene in which the character deals with the crisis of the addiction becoming known.

(200 words)

 Focus point

Put the cast of your story under pressure; make them react. This will reveal their character.

Workshop: a character acrostic

Look back at the work we did on acrostics in Chapter 2. We are now going to develop the acrostic exercise further by developing a character from a name. It is an interesting way to consider different types of characters and the roles they might play in stories. Our aim here is to help you to

- think about character in a different way
- think about the ways that characters play different roles in stories
- show that characters need to change in stories, and give practice in writing a piece in which a character does change.

Write a list of ten ordinary names, the most ordinary possible:

- How do we develop this ordinary name into a character?
- Given that finding the name for someone is one of the most vital things in creating characters, what if you did an acrostic of a name to see if you can develop it?

Choose one of your names and write an acrostic for it.

We are going to start with the name Jean. For our acrostic, we have decided:

Jean is …

Just

Earnest

All right

Nice.

Just considering the name to start with, we cannot do anything about it in this case because it is a given, but names are very important for characters. You might ask does the name have to fit? Eventually, yes; a character needs an appropriate name. But as a writer you can work with a working name for quite a long time before you hit on the right one. Eventually the right name could well suggest itself for your piece. Don't hold things up just because you don't feel you have the right name, just write with the one you've got. It often turns out that the character tells you, the writer, the right name.

In this case, we have the name Jean. Jean is described as just and earnest which seem to be good qualities, but she is also all right and nice. What role could a character that is 'nice' and 'all right' play in a story? Some will feel that this Jean sounds like a victim in a crime story; ideal for being bumped off, or the sort of wife who would get left. But:

1 Would she be the lead character in a story?

2 Would she be a minor character?

3 Why?

4 What characteristics does a character need to drive a story?

5 What characteristics might be changed to make her more dynamic?

Answer the above questions in your notebook.

Edit

Go back to the name you have written and now change two of the characteristics. We will make Jean awkward instead of all right and naive instead of nice. She is now:

Just

Earnest

Awkward

Naïve.

- Is she still a character to whom things happen, rather than one who can make things happen?
- How would we turn nice Jean into someone dynamic who is capable of driving a story?

Well, what if she was, as a student wrote in one class:

Jealous

Eavesdropping

Ambitious

Narcissistic?

What do you think this time?

You might think this Jean sounds a mess (great!); you should think she is dynamic. She is jealous and ambitious and she eavesdrops. This Jean could be a victim OR a mover and shaker. This Jean wants things. She eavesdrops on people and she finds things out which drive her crazy with jealousy; her ambition makes her act on them but her narcissism brings her unstuck. This Jean *could* energize and *drive* a story.

So:

• What it would be if these two Jeans were the same person?
• What if the nice Jean was how she appeared on the surface or how she was at the start of a story, and the other Jean what she was really like or how she ended up?

This Jean might start as the minor character you don't notice but through the story *because something happens to her* she develops into something much bigger and more dynamic. When we ask ourselves what this something might be and how we would get her to make this journey, we are touching on the relationship between story and plot, which we will come on to later in this book.

Key idea

Do not have perfect characters; give your characters flaws.

Write

Look at the ordinary name you wrote, or choose a new one from your list of ten names. List some ordinary, humdrum characteristics in an acrostic form. List a second set of very different, more dynamic characteristics. Think of an event that might connect these two and lead to change. Write a short piece in which the character makes the change from the one at the start to the other one.

(200 words)

As a follow-up to this exercise, when you have time, you could:

• develop the beginning into a longer story
• connect it with a plot and start thinking about how to plan this as a story
• take the character further and develop some background.

Workshop: the 'Furniture Game'

We met this game in the chapter on metaphors. It is an ideal way of working on metaphors and similes without knowing it. It can also give us a way of looking at character which can be fun. It is a highly valuable and valid exercise because the qualities suggested this way can help you, as an author, learn a lot more about the character for yourself.

Think of someone you know. It could be someone famous, a celebrity, or a friend or someone in your family. As you have done so often, you are going to ask questions about this person. You cannot ask questions like: is this person a man or a woman? Do you work in politics? Are you alive or dead? These are questions that are trying to elicit facts. We do not want facts – we want character. A list of facts is not a character.

For the Furniture Game the sorts of questions you ask are *what if* questions, questions that try to elicit qualities. For instance you ask this sort of question: if this person was a car, what car would they be? NOTE, *not* what car would they *drive* or *own*, but what car would they *be*. A person might drive a mini but really *be* a Ferrari. And vice versa. What you want to know is what car would represent their personality.

Keep in mind the person you are thinking of and ask questions like the following. Note your answers.

- If this person was a piece of furniture, what would they be? (This question gives the name to the game.) For example, we might say a throne because we are thinking of the Queen of England.
- If this person was a time of day, what would they be? For example, we might say 3.00 p.m. because this is the traditional time for the Queen's Christmas Speech.

Think of the Queen of England and fill in the rest of these questions, Write down what the Queen would be if she was…

a piece of furniture	a time of day	a fruit
an animal	food	a place
a type of movie	a car	an item of clothing
a drink	a colour	a flower.

This list is not exhaustive. Add any category you can think of. The real requirement when you do it for yourself, is for you to think of some other thing by which to describe the person *you* have in mind.

Now repeat the exercise, not with the Queen of England, but with a person of your own choice. Make it a real person. When you have answered all the questions, using these answers, write a short piece, 6–8 lines, about this person. This can be either a poem or piece of prose.

For example:

- This person is a blancmange.
- They are scones and jam at tea-time.
- They are a Disney cartoon.

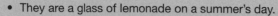

- They are a glass of lemonade on a summer's day.
- They are striped pyjamas and a bobble hat.
- They are a broken ski.

(Is this a 'nice' 'fun' person or a 'baddie'?)

(200 words)

Edit

Read your picture over and see how accurate it is. Have you conveyed the character and attitudes of the person you had in mind? If not, where can you change it to improve it?

This exercise makes very clear the point that has been central to this chapter: that characters in stories are made known to us as readers through our experience of them; i.e. through what the characters say, do and get involved in, more than through a list of things about their physical appearance, clothes they wear or the initials they have after their name. When they show qualities of mind and a degree of emotion it allows us to share their travails; hence we get to know them better and care about or fear and dislike them more. Either way we read with more involvement and depth.

Things to keep in mind when you are creating characters are:

- Do not have perfect characters, unless you deliberately want to test them.
- Do have characters with flaws.
- Do have characters that change over the course of a story.
- Do have characters who make choices (good and bad choices).
- Do have characters who can drive a plot or story.
- Do have characters doing things.
- Do have characters with an inner life.

The life of the character is vital. If you can capture the life, then you've got a character that moves and who will be able to move your story. Actors try to find the life in a part they play; the writer must put that life in.

If an actor acts the verb of a part, the writer must write the verb.

Key idea

Characters make a story; and often the bad characters are what we remember. They have more about them.

Plot ramifications and complications are difficult to remember over time, and fundamentally not very interesting. It is characters who stay with us. If, as writers, you can capture the life in your character, you will create someone people will remember. Characters want and need things. They are people who yearn, want and do. Their doing makes the story, your writing, happen.

Key idea

It is important also to realize that not all the characters in any piece are going to be heroes or heroines. You are going to need minor characters and walk-on parts and they are just as necessary and valuable.

The novelist E.M. Forster hit on the idea of describing characters as 'flat' and 'round.' The flat characters were types that a reader could recognize immediately. The round characters were fully rounded individuals, not types and not people that readers would recognize immediately. They were more complex and developed. It is a handy way of grouping characters. It can help in your understanding of a piece of writing; it can help in your own writing. You might take some of the same routes to character that we have described here, but how far you develop them might depend on how important they are to the plot. You will need less detail to delineate a minor character and you might not need an inner life at all. Obviously the richer you make all your characters, the potentially richer your story will be, but at the same time you would not want to allow your minor characters to take over and swamp the story to the detriment of the hero. This is the sort of scene stealing that you see in some films, where one actor in a minor role will totally take over and dominate the film, dwarfing the major star in the process. Flat (minor) characters have their roles as do the heroes and heroines.

Summary

In this chapter you have developed characters using monologues, interior monologues and an inside to outside approach for character. Find some monologues for yourself and read some; see how they work. How characters are created by what characters say and don't say in monologues. Read some of Alan Bennett's monologues; look at some play scripts by Brian Friel.

Next step

In the next chapter we will consider the intricate, interesting, and vitally important notion of viewpoint; of who tells your story.

14

Character and viewpoint

Although the adverts in the press saying 'Why not be a writer?' suggest writing is easy, it is not. No writing is easy. Writing a novel is certainly not easy. Nor does anyone really know how to do it.

In this chapter we will look at who tells the story; the viewpoint character; finding the right voice, and the unreliable narrator.

Danielle Steel

'Anyone who tells you how to write bestsellers is a sham and a liar. I can tell you how I write books. I write them with fear, excitement, discipline, and a lot of hard work.'

Orson Scott Card, *Characters and Viewpoint*

'Who is telling your story? You are, of course. You choose what story to tell, which incidents matter, which scenes to show, which events to tell about. It is out of your mind that all the invention comes, all the characters, all the background details, all the ideas.

'But when it comes to speak the words of the story, whose voice will the reader hear?'

The choice of viewpoint character is one of the most important decisions you will take as a writer. Viewpoint character means the character whose head you will get inside as the writer and therefore through whose eyes your readers and viewers will experience the story. Whatever you decide will have a huge influence on your character and how the story is expressed and experienced.

Viewpoint

There are several modes you can take to tell a prose story but the most frequently used and therefore the most relevant to look at are first person and third person.

FIRST PERSON

This story is told by a narrator who is also a character in the story. This form is easily identified because the author writes using 'I'. 'I did this. I did that. I wanted this. I wanted that.' Many acclaimed novels have been written from this viewpoint: *Catcher in the Rye* by J.D. Salinger, Mark Twain's *Adventures of Huckleberry Finn* and *The Sun Also Rises* by Ernest Hemmingway are three very well-known first-person stories. Alice Sebold's 2002 novel, *The Lovely Bones,* had a lot of success in many ways because of the choice of narrator made by the author. The narrator was a teenage girl who had been raped, murdered and dismembered, narrating her story from heaven. A murdered narrator had famously been used before, of course, that of the dead body floating in the pool in Billy Wilder's much lauded movie *Sunset Boulevard.*

The first-person narrator may not always be liked or laudable but their 'voices,' the sound their words make, the resonance they strike in the readers, is a crucial part of the story fabric. We get to know the character well and are drawn into the story and its world through the voice of the first-person viewpoint character. The narrator may be intelligent or dim, rich or poor, articulate or inarticulate, victim or aggressor, alive or dead but what they have to say and the way they tell it are a very important part of the involvement, enjoyment and meaning of a first-person story. It is as if a real person was speaking directly to us and telling us their tale.

THIRD PERSON

This story is told by the author using 'he', 'she', 'it' or 'they', and never by using 'I' or 'we'. For example:

> *He went down the road and bought a newspaper from the sweet shop. The woman behind the counter spoke to him. As he left he spoke to her dog which was tied up outside the shop. It was wet and unhappy and it was very hungry.*

The voice telling the story is not a character in the story but an observer. This does not mean any necessary loss of immediacy or that we are not drawn into the story. On the contrary, third-person narratives can be both immediate and involving. The majority of novels published are written in third person, not first person.

But third person is not so clear cut as first person. There are two forms of third-person viewpoint that you need to know and master: third-person limited and third-person omniscient or omnipotent.

Third-person omniscient or omnipotent viewpoint

This was the most commonly used form of narration up to and well through the nineteenth century. Classic novelists such as Jane Austen, Charles Dickens, George Eliot, Henry James, Leo Tolstoy and Anthony Trollope all wrote their novels in the voice of the third-person omniscient narrator. This mode is, of course, written in the third person, that is using 'he'. 'she', 'it' or 'they', but the clue to this voice is in the description 'omniscient' or 'omnipotent'. The voice in this form is an all-knowing, all-powerful, 'godlike' voice that sees into all the characters heads, into all the places in the story and moves effortlessly from character to character and from place to place.

Style and, again, 'voice' is a crucial element of writing in this form. The classic writers using this form all developed distinctive 'voices'. The tone of a Jane Austen novel is very much an essential part of the story she tells, equally so for Wodehouse, Trollope and Dickens. A large part of the enjoyment of their stories is enjoyment of their voices; of the way they use language to present worlds that are rich and full of characters and situations. This story telling voice is characterized by both closeness and distance. Both Austen and Trollope can present characters to us in a way that, with deft touches of insight or irony, at the same time undercuts them. A character like Mr Collins in *Pride and Prejudice* might see himself in one light, while other characters in the story see him quite differently but it is the all-knowing voice of the author, through the way she both presents and comments on him ironically that we are able to see him in this other, amusing light. The same is true with the character of the Reverend Slope in *Barchester Towers*. When Trollope tells us that Slope had at some point in his life added an 'e' to his name 'for the sake of euphony' we are able to laugh with the author at the former Reverend Slop. We learn a good deal about these characters while also enjoying the authors' wicked humour at their expense.

Characteristic of the omniscient viewpoint is that the author has both closeness to the characters (they tell us what they are thinking and feeling) and distance from them (they comment on them) Characters in this sort of story are held at a distance by the author because it is the author and their strong voice that we are listening to. We do not get inside the character's heads and hearts, except by invitation and direction of the author. The author conducts the story and directs our responses, both emotional and intellectual. With the great authors, a large part of the enjoyment of the tales they tell is the way they tell them, how they guide us.

But as confidence in authority in all its forms waned, and as movies and television developed and affected the way audiences experienced narrative, the third-person omniscient narrator became much less used in the twentieth century and remains less favoured in the twenty-first century. It is still possible to write novels in this mode but the most used form today is third-person limited.

Third-person limited

This, as a phrase, explains itself. Writing in this form is again written in the third person, that is using 'he', 'she', 'it' or 'they' but it is 'limited' not 'omniscient'. It is 'limited' in that it is not all-seeing, it is not godlike. It is human and it takes a limited perspective on characters and events. Instead of the wide overarching view encompassing as many characters as it wishes of the omniscient viewpoint, the limited viewpoint is closer to first person in that the author confines himself to one head, one brain and one pair of eyes, at least *at a time*.

To see the difference between the two third-person viewpoints, let's look at some examples:

Let's start with the third-person omniscient or omnipotent viewpoint:

> *He went down the same road where 2,000 years earlier a Roman legion had marched over the bones of his Celtic ancestors and bought a newspaper from a shop on which a Roman villa had once stood. The woman who spoke to him took his money, deeply hating him all the while. Out of sight behind the dirty window she cursed him as he bent and consoled her hungry, wet and unhappy dog that lay looking up hopefully into the only pair of human eyes that had ever been kind to it.*

This narrator knows everything; about the road's Roman past, the woman's present hatred of the man and the unhappy state of the dog. We are not solely confined to the thoughts and perceptions of the woman, the man, or the dog. We are in the hands of a narrator who does not feel solely confined to one character or to one time frame either. This narrator is capable of telling us about the characters and the situations in which they find themselves, both in history and at the same time in the here and now.

The difference between omniscient and limited viewpoint can be shown if we rewrite the same scene in third-person limited. Unlike the omniscient, we *will* be limited to the man, the woman *or* the dog:

> *He went down the same road where 2,000 years earlier a Roman legion had marched over the bones of his Celtic ancestors and bought a newspaper from a shop on which a Roman villa had once stood. The woman who spoke to him*

took his money while giving him a funny look. He thought he glimpsed her trying to stay out of sight behind her dirty window as he bent and consoled her hungry, wet and unhappy dog.

Our viewpoint here is the man. We are with him as we experience the scene. He knows about the Roman past and the villa and his Celtic ancestors, so maybe he is an archaeologist. But he does not know about the woman's hatred for him, though he senses something 'funny' in the look she gives him. If we wanted to give a different picture we could write 'angry look' or 'irritated look' or something else. But whatever we chose to write, it would be *his* perception of it and not necessarily what *she* was feeling. He also does not see inside the dog's head. He is limited to what he sees or senses and what he makes of it. He definitely thinks he sees her trying to stay out of sight while he pats her unhappy dog. And he judges that the dog is hungry and unhappy, that is an assessment that he makes from its body language, and possibly a judgement that is critical of the woman too. But all of his perceptions are limited. They have boundaries and the limits are what he can see, hear, touch, taste and smell; what he can apprehend or otherwise reason out.

Let's look at the same scene limited to the woman's point of view:

She watched him come down the same road where 2,000 years earlier a Roman legion had marched over the bones of his Celtic ancestors and come into her shop on which a Roman villa had once stood. She took his money, deeply hating him all the while. Keeping out of sight behind the dirty window she cursed him as he bent and said something to her dog.

In this version we are very strongly inside her head and her hatred comes over powerfully. *She* sees him coming down the road. *She* knows about the Roman past this time, so in this version *she* has the archaeological knowledge. But here you somehow get a sense of her taking pleasure in thinking that the legions had marched over the bones of his ancestors. She also takes his money while deeply hating him all the while. We can feel that hatred as she takes the money, possibly with a smile; after all, money is money. Of *his* feelings or reaction we know nothing, because she does not know or try and guess them. Maybe her own feelings are so strong that she does not care what he is feeling. When he goes outside she watches him pet her dog; not her 'hungry, wet and unhappy dog' because she does not see the dog that way. To see it that way would be making a judgement on herself. The 'hungry, wet and unhappy dog' is the judgement of someone else's eyes. To her the dog is just her dog. It is her possession. Somehow you can feel her rage burning through the glass that he dares to pet *her* dog.

Interestingly, if she did judge herself from *outside*, that would be a viewpoint slip, an inconsistency in viewpoint. We will look at this issue in a moment but from this brief exercise you can see how subtle, complex and interesting viewpoint is.

The viewpoint character in your story is the one through whose eyes the reader will experience what happens. In the third-person limited viewpoint the limited viewpoint character is human not godlike, there are limits to what they can therefore see and hear; they do not hear everything. The limited narrator may partially know themselves and have some knowledge of some people, but they not know everything about all people at all times. They can only tell us about what they see or know or believe or have found out. They cannot, for instance, tell us what another character is thinking, as can the omniscient author.

The limited viewpoint character can guess at what another character is thinking, or surmise it from their behaviour but they are limited to the evidence they can come up with, and the thoughts and perceptions of their own heads and are not privy to the private cogitations of others.

You can also see how the narrative can alter or be altered by changing your viewpoint character. The same scene can appear different depending on through whose eyes it is seen. Our example shows clearly the differences in third-person limited and third-person omniscient.

Focus point

In the limited version we are either in the man's head or we are in the woman's head. We are not in both, as we are in the omniscient method.

Changing viewpoint and viewpoint slips

If you are to make the characters and the narrative convincing in a third-person limited viewpoint piece you must not slip in viewpoint. You must not move from one head to another without signalling it clearly to the reader, but slips can occur in other ways, for example as we just mentioned allowing the woman to judge herself from outside herself, with the eyes of another. You could also slip by having a character tell us something they could not possibly have seen or witnessed or known about.

Sol Stein, *Solutions for Writers*

'If all but one of the instruments on a surgeon's tray had been sterilised, that exception would be a danger to the patient. It can be said that one slip of point of view by a writer can hurt a story badly, and several slips can be fatal.'

Key idea

Slipping in viewpoint can seriously affect the credibility of your story, so you must be consistent. But slipping in viewpoint and changing viewpoint are not the same thing.

It is not the case that you can and must only have one viewpoint character throughout a whole story, though there are often very good reasons for doing just that, and certainly when you are starting out that is not a bad decision to take to limit the number of viewpoint characters. Where omniscient authors move freely between the thoughts of one character and another and do this in the middle of scenes, and in the middle of sentences, writers using the limited mode need to signal a change of viewpoint character carefully, ideally changing from one character to another at the start of different chapters, or different scenes, never in the middle of scenes and never in the middle of a sentence. To do that is most confusing for the reader.

Key idea

If you are in one head, stay there. When you vacate that head, to go to another, help the reader by making it clear when you leave and where you go.

Let's look at the same scene we have already looked at and try to see what happens if we slip between the woman and the man's point of view while writing in third-person limited viewpoint.

She watched him come down the same road where 2,000 years earlier a Roman legion had marched over the bones of his Celtic ancestors and enter her shop on which a Roman villa had once stood. She took his money, deeply hating him all the while. He thought she gave him a funny look and also thought he glimpsed her trying to stay out of sight behind her dirty window as he bent and consoled her hungry, wet and unhappy dog that she left all day tied up outside and who now lay looking into the only human eyes who were ever kind to it.

We start with her watching him come down the road and we end up in the dog's head! The viewpoint is set up clearly at the start; we are with *her*, so where does this switch take place? Read it over to be sure. Yes, there are two.

The first one comes after the word 'while'. 'He thought she gave him a funny look' is *his* thought about their meeting. Maybe you think this viewpoint switch works. It does change in a clear place; one moment we are with the woman, the next we are with the man but there is a second switch, a switch from inside the man to inside the dog. What do you think of this viewpoint switch? Read the last sentence again to make sure you understand where the switch takes place and then decide what you think of it.

The problem here is that the piece begins in third-person limited and third-person limited is not third-person omniscient.

Focus point

In third-person limited the writer agrees a contract with the reader to tell a story, or at least a part of it, from a particular point of view. It is a contract entered into by both parties. The contract states that the writer will construct the narrative from a particular point of view and will not deviate from that. If he wants to change he will make the change clear and firm. Both parties know the contract and generally abide by it. If the contract is broken, then consequences ensue.

Rather than break the contract by slipping from one head into another, from man to dog like this, it is much more helpful to the reader if you change viewpoint character at the end of a scene or at least a paragraph and not mid-scene or mid-paragraph or mid sentence.

Let's try it again:

> *He went down the same road where 2,000 years earlier a Roman legion had marched over the bones of his Celtic ancestors and bought a newspaper from a shop on which a Roman villa had once stood. The woman who spoke to him took his money while deeply hating him all the while. Out of sight behind the dirty window she cursed him as he bent and said something to her dog.*

We appear to be in the man's head at the start but through this paragraph we go from his head to hers and we do it mid-sentence. We are with him up until the word 'money'. He does not think the thought that follows, 'while deeply hating him all the while.' She does; that is where the transfer takes place. She has become our viewpoint character. But do we stay with her? Where are we as she watches him with her dog 'out of sight' outside the shop? Are we with her viewpoint or back with his? She cannot be out of sight to herself, so is it his? But then how can he know she is there if she is out of sight? Does it mean she is out of *his* sight behind the window? Maybe it is just carelessly written but you can see how dangerously slippery viewpoint can become if it is not handled precisely.

Again, you might want to argue that writing it like this is all right; we worked it out. But can you imagine how potentially wearing and confusing this would be in a long piece if the writing continually slid from one character to another and you had to check back to see which character you were with?

 Key idea

Writing in third-person limited viewpoint your choice of viewpoint character is an important decision to take, at any point in the story it is an absolute position to take up and one you must be consistent with *until you change it.* And if you are to change it must be deliberate and clear. You must not slide in and out of viewpoint characters carelessly. To do so runs the risk of destabilizing your writing and your reader who will not know where you are or they are.

In summary, you can bring a lot of interest to a story through changing viewpoints from one character to another, but you must not make it confusing for the reader to follow. In third-person limited, if you do change from one character to another in your story you need to signal the change clearly so that the reader knows through whose eyes they are now witnessing the events because each time they change the new character is also limited to what they observe, know, believe or surmise. But changing viewpoint can add new dimensions to a piece of writing. If handled interestingly and well viewpoint can bring out a range of different features of a character and of a story.

To demonstrate this, let's look at the following excerpt:

He walked up the steps cutting the steep lawns, past signs to the library and the Schoenberg music block till he found the spot, the walkway between the library and another building. The walkway was lined with cypress trees and cast iron street lamps with glass bulbs on top to illuminate the path at night. They were unlit now except by the quiet glow which came from the daylight resting in them. He wondered what light they gave at night particularly how dark and safe this walkway was. He walked up and down the walkway twice, looking very carefully from side to side and behind each bench and cypress tree then stopped and sat on a flat stone bench next to some scattered peanut shells. They lay broken open by something human or something rodent like, a squirrel or a rat.

What narrative mode is this written in?

You should be able to tell that this is written in third-person limited viewpoint. We are limited to the thoughts and perceptions of the central character and this stays consistently so throughout the piece. But in order to further examine viewpoint and to see what effects it can have, let's try rewriting this in the first-person mode –

Here is a possible answer:

> *I walked up the steps cutting the steep lawns, past signs to the library and the Schoenberg music block till I found the spot, the walkway between the library and another building. The walkway was lined with cypress trees and those cast iron street lamps with glass bulbs on top to illuminate the path at night. They were unlit now except by the quiet glow which came from the daylight resting in them. What light did they give at night? How dark and safe was this walkway? I walked up and down the walkway twice, looking very carefully from side to side and behind each bench and cypress tree then stopped and sat on a flat stone bench next to some scattered peanut shells. They lay broken open by something human or something rodent like, a squirrel or a rat.*

How did your version compare?

This is the same piece with one or two changes but is there any difference, apart from the fact that it is written with 'I' instead of 'he'? The changes now make this an eyewitness account, something that happened to the person telling the story, which they witnessed and experienced personally and *want to tell us about.* Perhaps this seems to make the character's movements up the steps faster and the way he assesses the place seem more urgent and over all the whole piece appears quicker. This is something the narrator wants to tell us. It is important to tell us. This urgency draws us in. Compare the two versions and see whether you agree.

The first person, eyewitness nature of this version illustrates both the strength and the weakness of first-person writing. One of the strengths is the immediacy, the desire, the urge to communicate something. There is a story to tell and this person wants it to be heard. If they grab our attention, we will listen. One potential problem in all first-person writing is that if you choose this mode to tell this story then the 'I' character has to witness and experience everything in it. They cannot tell us about anything they do not know about, so that means they have to be present in every scene. That can be difficult both to manage in terms of the writing and the plotting and so hard to sustain in a convincing way. How does your character learn about events or conversations that they have not witnessed or been part of? A second difficulty with first-person viewpoint can be that the reader wants to ask why they are being told this information at this time and why? As the first-person narrator obviously knows the end, why don't they just 'cut to the chase' and tell us the ending? Why keep us waiting? If we get tired of the storyteller's voice we might easily skip to the end. That is true of all writing but it is particularly so with first person. If you write in the first person you have to make the narrators interesting, involving and arresting.

 ## Snapshot

Now you try rewriting the same piece again, this time in third-person omniscient viewpoint. Do it now before you look at the example below.

(400 words maximum)

He walked up the steps cutting the steep lawns, past signs to the library where inside all its reading rooms the rows of bowed heads were already busy and the Schoenberg music block, where the second nervous student that morning was presenting his composition to the fearsome professor, and where two young female students were huddled in the rest room together, crying in advance of the treatment they would receive from the cruel maestro. He found the spot, the walkway between the library and another building. The walkway was lined with cypress trees that had once been specially imported from Greece and cast iron street lamps with Murano glass bulbs on top that the Dean, three deans ago, had raved about on his Grand Tour. They were unlit now except by the expensive glow which came from the daylight resting in them. He wondered what light they gave at night particularly how dark and safe this walkway was, without knowing that in these more stringent times the institution's management had slashed the budget for lighting right across campus and that there had been a semester long campaign from the women's section of the students union to get better lighting installed on this very spot because of a spate of attacks on females students. He walked up and down the walkway twice, looking very carefully from side to side and behind each bench and cypress tree then stopped and sat on a flat stone bench next to some scattered peanut shells that lay broken open by the squirrels that feasted there each evening on the bits of scattered food that always fell beneath the benches.

How did yours compare?

This is recognizably the same piece but with several noticeable differences. It does not matter whether it is better or worse in this form, but is it different? If you are unsure how it is different, read it again.

One difference is that it is quite a bit longer. That is because we are told a lot more. We are told about the background to the purchase of the lamps and the Student Union's concern about attacks on female students. We are also told about what is going on in the library and the music room. But let's look at it in terms of viewpoint. There are questions we can ask: if this was written in third-person limited, then we would ask how the character knows what is going on in the library as he passes. He might be able to see some of the bowed heads in the library windows as he goes by but is he capable of seeing inside *all* its reading rooms? And as for the Schoenberg music block where it is the 'second nervous student that morning' who is 'presenting his composition to the fearsome professor':

- How does he know it is the second student?
- How does he know exactly what the student is doing?
- How does he know that the professor is fearsome?

The scene continues 'and where two young female students were huddled in the rest room together, crying in advance of the treatment they would receive from the cruel maestro'. We might wonder:

- How does he know there are two young females in the rest room? Has he been in there?
- How does he know they are huddled together crying?

- How does he know they are crying about the treatment they might get at the hands of the cruel maestro?
- Whose perception of the maestro is that he is cruel?

It would be possible to write this in limited viewpoint so that the character did know or could have observed it all but you would not write it in the way it is written above. The way the piece has been rewritten has to be omniscient narration.

Can you see and understand the difference? If not, then look again at all three viewpoint versions. If you do understand the difference, then you can ask the next question; does the piece of writing work better in third-person limited, third-person omniscient or first person? Different people will answer differently. It does not matter here, but whether a piece of writing works better in one mode or another is the sort of question you will find very helpful to apply to your own writing.

Key idea

When you are trying to find the right 'voice' for a piece of writing try writing it in one voice then another to see what difference it makes both to the character and the narrative.

Write

Take from your writing, or write new, a brief scene in which a single character is performing an action and thinking. Do it in three different ways:
- first person
- third-person omniscient
- third-person limited.

250 words are enough for each, though you might find the lengths vary according to the mode you use. Do it now.

(750 words)

What did you learn?
- Did changing the viewpoint change the nature of the piece at all? How?
- Did it change the nature of the character and/or the story? How?
- Did it make you write different actions, and/or different thoughts in a particular mode?
- Did you prefer one version to another?

If one version was longer than another, why was that and what can you learn from it?

Key idea

Viewpoint is a very subtle tool capable of adding a different dimension to character and to plot.

The unreliable narrator

Does your narrator always tell the truth?

It is very important to note that narrators whether first or third person can be reliable or unreliable; they can be telling us the truth or they can be spinning us a yarn. Which side of this coin you decide they are on can add interest to their character. Liars can be very engaging.

Dr James Sheppard, the narrator of Agatha Christie's first detective novel, *The Murder of Roger Ackroyd*, assists Poirot, a job done in later stories by Captain Hastings, not least because Sheppard turns out to be a very unreliable assistant and narrator indeed. He narrates this story for us and mainly through omitting to tell us the precise meaning of certain events and timings, or directing our attention away from important facts, a sort of literary sleight of hand, hides from us until the end of the story that he is, in fact, the murderer. Miss Christie saw well the use to which she could put the viewpoint technique. Wilkie Collins in *The Moonstone* used a 'multi-narration' method with several voices telling us the story. This is rather like having witnesses at an accident making their statements. They all see the events differently, so that we experience the story told from various viewpoints that contradict each other; and the truth lies somewhere in between, for the detective to uncover.

The fact that certain characters only have certain limited views of events, limited by their knowledge, their ability to witness them or by their desires or prejudices can work in a very helpful way in all stories, particularly when it comes to plotting, and especially with the dissemination and withholding of information. Much of the power of sensation novels and contemporary thrillers comes from fragmenting the narrative and doling the story out piece by piece to the readers through the fierce activity of some committed hero or heroine. Murder-mystery writers by having one limited-viewpoint character, the detective, attempting to piece together a narrative through the method of interviewing and interpreting the answers and evasions of another set of limited viewpoint characters, build their stories around the opportunities presented by viewpoint. It is probably no accident that the whole murder-mystery genre grew from a time when belief in the omniscient viewpoint was collapsing. Murder-mystery writers are basically handling the vagaries and shifting subtleties of a third-person limited world. They are turning a technical exercise into engaging, enthralling writing. Each of the characters in a murder mystery has seen only part of the story at any one time and the detective tries to piece together a whole narrative from their fragmentary perceptions (or lies). A large amount of the very character and meaning of a murder mystery is built around an exploration of limited viewpoints and this is not confined to that genre. A good deal of contemporary writing explores the piecemeal nature of limited viewpoint. Somewhere in the writer's head or notebook there may have been a complete narrative but each of the characters in the story only has a part of it and the story progresses by the bringing together of those limited perceptions until the narrative is understood whole.

Focus point

In a murder mystery a slip in viewpoint can be used deliberately to show someone is lying or to muddy the narrative.

In the Sherlock Holmes stories, Doctor Watson is the viewpoint character. He writes down his and Sherlock Holmes' escapades. Giving Watson the pen was another masterly decision taken by Conan Doyle, both in characterisation and in viewpoint. Watson is the filter and lens through which we view, witness and see in action the amazing character of Sherlock Holmes. He has the narrative voice. This is hugely important for the characters of both men. If Holmes had written about his own successes at solving crimes, if he had proclaimed his own genius he would have been even more insufferable than he sometimes is. That Doctor Watson, the brave, honest, hero worshipping, faithful Doctor Watson narrates by far the huge majority of the stories, allows him to sing Holmes' praises in a way that makes Holmes more admirable not less.

And Watson is very much the reliable narrator. He is good old English stock, born when gentlemen were gentlemen and the unreliable narrator was not the leading man in fiction. What Watson tells us we can believe and what he tells us about Holmes allows us to witness a genius at work.

Write

Choose one character to write about another character. Don't tell us about the narrator. Concentrate on the narrator's view of the subject and let their own character come through what they see and say about the other character. It could be husband on wife or vice versa, boss/employee, or whatever you like. The feeling for the other character might be love, admiration or loathing. Let the attitude come through the writing. 750 words

The secondary character

The secondary viewpoint character is also us, we the reader. This character can stand in for us at important moments in the narrative, asking the questions we would like to ask while also moving the narrative forward and so have an important relationship to the plot. Choosing a secondary character as the narrator of your story can be very important for the way the story is told and experienced.

Summary

Read some of your favourite books with a view to understanding how they use viewpoint. See which character the author chooses to tell the story and whether it works or not. Are they consistent with viewpoint; do they stay with one character or do they switch? If they switch, how do they do it?

Next step

Now that we have created characters and considered viewpoint we need to turn our attention to the matter of structure. Structure is vital in all creative writing whether it be a poem story film script or a novel. In the next chapter you will study the difference between story and plot, examine causality in plotting, look at using fairy stories to tell stories, and find an original structure for a short story.

15

Story and plot

In this chapter you will study the difference between story and plot; examine causality in plotting; look at using fairy stories; and find structure for a short story.

Definitions

Snapshot

We often use the words 'story' and 'plot' interchangeably, but if we say that plot and story are not the same thing what do we mean? Why are they different?

What is a story? Get your notebook and write down your answer.

What is a plot? Write down your answer to this question before you read more of this chapter.

Ansen Dibell, *Plot*

'The common definition of plot is that it is whatever happens in a story. That's useful when talking about completed stories, but when we are considering stories being written, it's about as useful as saying that a birthday cake is a large baked confection with frosting and candles. It doesn't tell you how to make one.'

One answer could be that the story is the whole thing – all the elements of character, mood, atmosphere, and setting; while plot is what happens, the events in a particular order. But this is not as focused a definition as we can get. If we return to E.M. Forster, who we mentioned in the previous chapter in relation to round and flat characters, we can amplify the idea. In his book *Aspects of the Novel* Forster gave a subsequently much used example to illustrate the difference between story and plot. He quoted this sentence: 'The King is Dead.' What sort of sentence is this – 'The King is Dead'?

It is something that has happened. It is an event or an action. It is an event that might happen in a story. Stories are full of such events or actions. Things happen in stories. Forster then gave another sentence; another event that could happen in a story. This was: 'The Queen died.' Forster then looked at the two events, 'The King died. And the Queen died' and said that this could be a story but it could not be a plot. Why was that? Look at the two sentences.

Snapshot

'The King died. And the Queen died.' According to E.M. Forster, this is a story but it is not a plot. What did Forster mean and what would make it a plot? Think about it, and then write down your thoughts in your notebook.

There is no right or wrong on this – just write whatever you come up with. If you wish you can start with 'It is not a plot because … ' and 'to make it a plot we would need to … '

These events, the death of the king and the death of the queen, are two events that might well have occurred independently of each other. It might be that the king died and then 40 years later the queen died. E.M. Forster said it was not a plot because there was not necessarily a *connection* between the two statements. To make it a plot we would need to connect them. The solution Forster gave was this: 'The King died and the Queen died *of grief*.'

What is different here is that you can see that this immediately connects the two events. One happened, the queen died, because the other had happened, the king had died.

Causality

Key idea

The small, inconspicuous word 'because' is at the heart of plotting. It tells us that the events in a plot are held together by a causal link. Remember: because, because, because.

In a plot, event D happens because of event C; C happens because of B, B happens because of A. Plot is like the skeleton of the living creature that is your story. It is the bones beneath the skin, the structural frame on which all the colour of character, setting and atmosphere hang. A story, like a vertebrate, will have a complicated skeleton full of joints and bones and cartilage holding it all together and allowing flexibility of movement. This is the role that the small word *'because'* plays, because it is crucial in all plotting.

Focus point

Think of plot as the skeleton of the living creature that is your story.

Workshop: examining causality

Make a list of 12 actions – six for a character named 'he', and six for a character named 'she'. For example:

1 He went to the shops.

2 She bought a new dress.

3 He lost money on the horses.

4 She went to the bank.

5 She got into the car.

6 He made a phone call.

7 She got a new job.

8 He felt sick.

9   She bought some flowers.

10   He got promoted.

11   She called the vet.

12   He made a cake.

Make *your* lists in your notebook.

Now, using the examples above or your own, connect these sentences into pairs by using the word 'because'. Put all 12 together in whichever way you like. For example:

- He made a phone call because he felt sick.
- He went to the shops because she got a new job.
- She got into the car because she went to the bank.
- She called the vet because he lost money on the horses.
- She bought a new dress because he bought some flowers.
- Because he got promoted he made a cake.

What have you come up with? We would have to confess that our first attempts are not very inspiring. Are any of yours really quite good or can you play about with them to make them more interesting?

🔑 Key idea

The events in a story are like the links on a chain. That is how you connect them.

Our examples are all a bit ordinary. Looking at just one of our sentences – 'He made a phone call because he felt sick.' It is rather an obvious statement. There is nothing startling in it. If you feel sick you would quite reasonably make a phone call to a doctor, husband, wife, partner or friend, would you not? There is no real surprise there. It is an ordinary and a, what we might call, closed situation. It doesn't raise any questions. It closes the situation off and is rather dull because of it. Given that, what if we changed it to, 'He felt sick because he called the vet.' This is potentially more interesting. Why? Because it raises questions; we want to know why he feels sick because he's called the vet. There are potential answers – the obvious one is that he got bad news about a loved pet, but the point is that the statement itself is more interesting and opens itself up to potential questions and answers. It is an open and not a closed situation. Are any of your sentences like that? Are there any closed sentences that you could open up? Have a look at them. See if you can move the parts of the sentences about in order to make a closed statement into an open one.

Let's try moving our sentences' parts around in a different order:

He felt sick because she called the vet.

She bought a new dress because he lost money on the horses.

She went to the bank because he made a phone call.

He made a cake because she got a new job.

218

She bought some flowers because he went to the shops.

He got promoted because she got into the car.

'He got promoted because she got into the car' is immediately potentially more interesting than either 'He went to the shops because she got a new job', or 'She got into the car because she went to the bank', both of which are closed and a little dull. Many of these refreshed examples are more interesting than the first ones we came up with because they are suggestive; they raise questions and are open rather than closed.

Building plots

Focus point

To build plots, connect different actions in your stories with the word 'because'.

Workshop: building the plot

How would we develop a quite ordinary statement into the plot of a short story? Choose one of your sentences; one that you like. We might choose 'He got promoted because she got into the car.' Can we develop this into a short story? How do we do that? Let us ask questions of it. First of all, the big question: how did her getting into the car win him promotion? Possible answers might be:

- She was a fantastic driver and she raced through traffic to get him to the interview on time.' (This is OK but maybe a bit ordinary, although you could have lots of thrills and spills on the way.)
- She delivered important documents on time. (This has possibilities.)
- He won promotion because she got into the car with his Lothario boss. (Does this have potential for development? Yes, it could be developed in many different ways rather than the obvious one.)

How do you choose which to go with? You could try developing them all; keep your mind open and let the ideas flow. That is a good approach, but in the end what you really want to do is to choose the answer that gives you the most possibilities for further complications and for consequences to flow for the characters in your story.

Ansen Dibell, *Plot*

'Plot is built of significant events in a given story – significant because they have important consequences. Taking a shower isn't necessarily plot, or braiding one's hair, or opening a door. Let's call them incidents. They happen, but they don't lead to anything much. No important consequences.'

We are going to see if we can develop a story from a simple ordinary sentence. The sentence we are going to work with is, 'He decided to make a phone call because he felt sick.' First of all we ask questions of it. Why was he feeling sick? We could make it stronger with the answer that he was feeling sick because he had taken poison. In which case we would have the sentence, 'He made a phone call because he had taken poison.' Already we have a character taking decisive action because of a desperate need: not to die. There is suspense too. Will he get through to whoever he is calling (presumably the doctor, the hospital or a friend or partner?). And will someone be able to help him in time?

By asking more questions we can develop this further. How did he come to take poison in the first place? Was it an accident or was it deliberate? Did he take it through his own fault or did someone feed it to him? An accident will take us down one route; if someone had given him the poison we will be heading down another. For the sake of this exercise, let's take the more dangerous route. What if his wife or business partner had given him the poison? If that was the case we would now have someone out to kill him and we would want to know why. You can see that we have come up with some answers but answers that have raised more questions.

 ## Key idea

Asking questions is the heart beat of plotting.

And, crucially, here we have unearthed some of the most important elements of story and plotting. These elements have big names. We have a central character that is called the protagonist. The protagonist is up against someone who wants to kill him, called the antagonist. And there is a degree of conflict between them (one is trying to kill the other and that person is trying to survive).

 ## Focus point

Protagonist, antagonist and conflict are three of the mainsprings of plotting stories.

Having taken the situation to this stage, if we want to firm this up into the plot for our story we would continue to ask questions:

- What was the poison?
- Was it fast-acting or slow?
- Who was he phoning: a doctor or a friend?
- Did he get through or not?
- Was the phone dead?
- If he got through, could they help him?

- Where is he? Is he in a house or cut off somewhere in the mountains?
- What time of day is it? Late at night when there is likely to be no one around, or in the middle of the day?
- Was his wife with him?
- If so, what was she doing?

Focus point

To develop plot ask questions about your character all the time. Who are they, what would they do in a certain situation?

Write

Write a short story based on the analysis in this book or the analysis of your own sentence statement. Make sure that you:

- have a protagonist
- have an antagonist
- have conflict
- make it concrete
- set it in a particular place
- set it at a particular time
- add sense perceptions – bodily reactions, choking, temperature changes
- add emotion – fear, anger
- add dialogue
- add a degree of heightened tension and suspense
- add a resolution – it either succeeds or fails.

(750 words)

Write

Write the story suggested by the following sentences. This is your plot, your skeleton. Write the story using this as the order of events. Stick to the order and get them all in.

- 'Because he felt sick she called the vet.'
- 'Because she bought a new dress he lost money on the horses.'
- 'Because she went to the bank he made a phone call.'
- 'Because he made a cake she got a new job.'
- 'Because she bought some flowers he went to the shops.'
- 'Because she got into the car he got promoted.'

(750 words)

Plot-driven stories pull at and against the credibility of character.

How many plots are there?

Comedy writers sometimes say there are two basic plots: 'The Odd Couple' and 'The Fish Out of Water' and, surprisingly, many stories do break down into those two situations. Sometimes a story combines both. Since George Polti wrote *The 36 Dramatic Situations* in 1945, some say people there are 36 plots. However many plots there are, the important thing to remember is that 'plot' is also a verb; a verb is a doing word, so in a plot something must be going on.

How do you find or create plots?

There are probably many ways to find or create a plot, and many different sorts of plots, but we will explore two different methods of plotting:

• **Method 1:** Take an existing plot, build your story around it and put characters into it.

• **Method 2:** Create your characters and develop the story and plot from them.

We will discuss them both here, first Method 1 and then Method 2.

METHOD 1

Method 1 can cover inventing a plot, coming up with a plot yourself, or taking an existing plot, someone else's invention, and making it your own. Shakespeare is not alone in finding his plots in the work of other writers. It is common practice and has an honourable history. Greek dramas were based largely on myth. The second method you can adopt is to let your characters suggest the story they want to be in. It can be harder to use an existing plot because different characters can almost take over the writing and suggest different things. But if not whole plots, then incidents and events can be found in a pre-existing form in other material: maybe in an historical account, maybe in a piece of reportage or a magazine article and developed by a writer into a short story or novel. An incident or incidents like this can be combined with a more developed interest in character.

In their most extreme forms the first method can give you a piece with great pace, something that is all plot and less formed with regard to character. On the other side, a character based piece can be all about character with little going on in the way of a plot. The trilogy of films involving the character Jason Bourne, *The Bourne Identity*, *The Bourne Conspiracy* and *The Bourne Ultimatum* are plot- and adrenalin-driven. The first of the three films has a little more interest in character, but not that much. The film sets the characters up briefly and then gets straight into the action. Thereafter this film, and arguably both following films, is an extended search for character. Bourne does not know who he is and goes in pursuit of his identity. But though in a sense he is in pursuit of his character, the nature of the film is plot-driven as he is thrust from one action sequence to another. The movies are akin to the 'Die Hard' sequence of films or the James Bond movie franchise. They have some interest in character but their main interest is in plot and the onward pace of the action. In these films the onward movement, the pace and the action are paramount. What plot-driven films do is pull at and against the credibility of character. They do not rest long enough to explore character in too much depth so characters in these types of stories have little or no development. They can have no development because that is sacrificed to the onward rushing pace of the tale.

The second method can give you stories which are really studies in character or relationships. Very little happens in plot terms but the reader learns a lot about the character and their lives. In contrast to the bulk of adrenalin-filled American films, many European films are like this. Henry James' short story 'The Beast in the Jungle' has hardly any plot but the effect of time on the two characters, John Marcher and Mary Bertram, is profound. Stories like this, particularly today with us all living faster lives, can be hard to read. We can get impatient for things to happen. In truth, the best writing is often a mix of both these approaches.

Write

Find a fairy story or a myth or fable that you know and like – for example, 'Red Riding Hood', 'Cinderella', 'Sleeping Beauty' and 'Beauty and the Beast'. Go through it and list the events. Write them down, one after the other. Summarize the events in 12–15 lines so that you have a firm grasp on what happens. Think of how you could rewrite it as a contemporary tale. Stick closely to the plot; try to use everything and find contemporary equivalents for the things in the story.

(750 words)

Focus point

If you feel you can't plot very well, try working from a fairy tale or a myth; they give you the essential framework of who, what and when.

Fairy tales and myths are good to work from because they give you the essential framework, the skeletal structure that a good plot can provide. Some of them are more tightly plotted than others; some of them remain more stories of events than plots, but they do have a structural shape upon which you can build a story. Many of the elements can also be translated in interesting ways into contemporary tales full of things that we recognize and understand and relate to. Many writers have used fairy tales as a structure on which to build their own work. Barbara Cartland, it is said, rewrote 'Cinderella' in most of her highly saleable books. Angela Carter made a considerable name for herself by taking fairy tales and rewriting them. This sort of work is in the same tradition as Hollywood turning Shakespeare's *Taming of the Shrew* into a high-school teen movie *Ten Things I Hate about You* and using the essential stories and plots that Shakespeare borrowed from somewhere else anyway.

Another helpful way of looking at existing story structures that we can borrow is to look at the types of stories that there are. Two useful story types that you can use to fashion your own plot are the Siege Story and the Quest Story.

The Siege Story is when characters are tied together, psychologically, emotionally or economically. Characters in these stories cannot leave; they have to stay. Situation comedies, commonly known as sitcoms like *Cheers, Frasier, Porridge, The Big Bang Theory* and *The Good Life* all have at their heart the idea of oddball characters yoked together. The fact that they are chained together this way racks up the tension which leads to the essential conflict. Sitcoms have to use this principle, else why would the characters stay in the situations in which they find themselves when sensible people would up and leave?

Your task in working with a siege plot is to think of reasons why they can't because if your characters up and leave, your story goes with them. Your characters have to stay and have to fight with each other. Stories built around this siege idea include disaster movies like *The Poseidon Adventure* and *The Towering Inferno*. All the various versions of 'Airplane' are siege movies as is the 'Die Hard' franchise of movies and, though it seems a crime to reduce it to such a level, so is Homer's Iliad. Albert Camus's novel *The Plague* is a siege story about a town cut off by sickness. The Ealing comedy *Passport to Pimlico* is a siege story about a part of London which, after being cut off by an unexploded bomb, severs all links with the rest of the UK. You can have psychological sieges as in novels like *The Go-Between* by L.P. Hartley. This is a story of illicit love in a country house between the wars. The social pressures on secret passion. The country-house murder mystery is a form of siege plot, with the closed circle of suspects and the house marooned and cut off from the rest of society. Agatha Christie's *And Then There Were None* uses this idea.

Quest Stories are driven by desire or need. The more powerful the desire, the more powerful the story. Homer's *The Odyssey, The Lord of the Rings, Star Wars* and *E.T.* are quest stories with central characters driven by a fundamental need to find something, or quite often, to get home. They have to overcome great odds and in the best stories a combination of both personal, internal and external problems. *Oedipus Rex*, the great play by Sophocles, is a quest story. Oedipus, the central character of this play, seeks to discover why sickness and famine have struck his people. Told by the Oracle that a great sin has been committed he determines to root out the cause. He is a fantastically strong willed character who overcomes every obstacle in his path to uncover the truth of the situation; even at the end of the play when he discovers that he is the cause of the problems he does not shirk from facing the consequences. This is a truly great quest story and it shows how old and how tested a convention it is.

METHOD 2

Method two involves creating a character and following that character wherever they go. You let the character dictate the direction, pace and goal. They may move swift as an arrow; they may meander and digress and, as they do so, they dictate story shape and tone. Forming a story around a character will be considered in the next chapter, under conflict and genre.

Structuring a story

The most common way we understand story structure is beginning, middle and end. We know and understand stories with a beginning, a middle and an end, stories that fall naturally into those three parts.

Workshop: the worst thing I ever did in my life – the consequences

This is a fun exercise which teaches some good things about story structure – beginning, middle and end.

Stage 1

Take three pieces of A4 paper.

Write at the top of each page these words and only these words: 'The worst thing I ever did in my life was … '

When you have prepared your three sheets of paper with the beginning words get ready to write what that worst thing was on each piece of paper. You might think that you have never done anything bad so have nothing to write. You may think you have done so many 'worst things' that you can't choose between them. Whatever your feelings, get ready to try to put something down on each of the three pieces of paper; and try to make each one different. Later, you will have to trick your mind and try to forget what you have written (and doing three will be hard) but don't dwell on it. Do you have to be truthful? Be truthful if you want to but you do not have to be truthful. You are doing an exercise. It doesn't really matter what you write so try to do it fairly quickly.

First, here are some rules to help you. As a rule, throughout this exercise:

- Avoid generalities such as 'The worst thing I ever did in my life was to get depressed'.
- Be concrete and specific rather than general.
- Keep it brief and write it in as few words as possible.
- Do not write a paragraph or two explaining everything.
- Just say what you did.
- Do not explain or say why you did this worst thing, or what the result was – that bit will come next – write only what you did.
- Use the active voice – this is something you did, not something that happened to you – for example, 'The worst thing I ever did was get married', 'wet my trousers on my second day at school', 'eat twelve pies', 'steal my best friend's husband'.

Now write the ending to the first sentence – one on each of the three pieces of paper.

Write.

Stage 2

Once you've written the first sentence, fold the paper over. Fold forward, just enough to cover the sentence you have written. Underneath the fold write these words and only these words – 'I did it because … ' Now mix the papers up so that you do not know which is which. Keep the paper folded.

Do not look at what has already been written.

Now write the ending to the second sentence, i.e. why you did it.

Do not say what the outcome was or what it led to, that will come next.

It is better to write 'I did it because drink makes me crazy' or 'because I failed double maths' than 'It seemed like a good idea at the time' or 'because I felt like it'. These last two examples are empty and vague.

Write.

Stage 3

Once you have written the second sentence fold the paper over, as before, to cover both sentences this time. Underneath the new fold write these words and only these words – 'The result was … '.

Keep the paper folded.

Mix up the papers again.

Do not look at what has already been written.

Now write the outcome on each sheet.

Keep it brief and concrete.

Remember to avoid abstract nouns such as 'the result was unhappiness, misery or bliss'.

Write.

Stage 4

Open the three papers and read what you have written on each.

You can tidy up any grammar or changes of gender ('he' for 'she', etc.), so that the sentences read fluently, but otherwise change nothing. How do they read? Are they funny? Do they work? Do any of them make stories as they stand? Read them out loud to yourself and as you do, read out every word in full as if you were reading a story to someone.

We will look at some examples produced in writing classes: some of these are as brief as jokes; others resemble short novels.

The worst thing I ever did in my life was to be shy.

I did it because I couldn't help it.

The result was confusion.

Overall this feels rather empty. 'To be shy' is a state not a deliberate act. The second line seems just to reinforce the character's passivity. The end is vague and unexpected. It could be developed, but there is a lot of work to do to fill it out and join up the gaps.

The worst thing I ever did in my life was to sacrifice what I believed in for the sake of monetary pleasure.

I did it because the man I loved didn't want me to leave.

The result was fame and fortune.

This has a good potential set-up: a writer could do something with it but the ending is vague.

The worst thing I ever did in my life was wet my trousers on my second day at school.

I did it because I wanted to see what happened next.

The result was I've hated beans on toast ever since.

This is very concrete. All these lines are good – the idea that wetting trousers was a character's deliberate act is interesting and sets up good expectations, somewhat satisfied with the amusing and unexpected ending.

The worst thing I ever did in my life was buy that jade necklace.

I did it because no one thought it was important.

The result was I chopped off my finger.

This has a nice concrete beginning. The second line seems to link well and set up a mystery – why was it important? There is quite a jump to the last line, but it's good and a writer could make that work. Gaps in these skeleton outlines can be fruitfully explored. What happened to lead to the loss of a finger?

The worst thing I ever did in my life was to eat twelve pies.

I did it because drink makes me crazy.

The result was I lost my job, but what a night.

This is simple and energetic, but not really surprising. It all holds together and suggests a strong character voice and a situation rather than a story. The character is strong – but for a story could there be more of a twist?

The worst thing I ever did in my life was to throw my bike in the canal and claim it was stolen.

I did it because I didn't want to tell the truth.

The result was I lived happily ever after.

This has a good beginning, a deliberate concrete act. The reason fits, but the end is weak, a hackneyed cop out and the story goes nowhere.

The worst thing I ever did in my life was to get married.

I did it because I failed double maths at school.

The result was I had to go to bed without any television for a week.

227

This is an odd story about school-age marriage with character and a hint of conflict.

> *The worst thing I ever did in my life was steal my best friend's husband.*
> *I did it because Parsifal bores the crap out of me.*
> *The result was the Pope looked me right in the eye and cursed me.*

A powerful and interesting story with questions of morals and behaviour, suggestions of a religious theme or context, and lots of conflict. It suggests a type and class of person and a distinctive social world.

The consequences stories you have produced may well be as mixed as these examples. Some will work well, some won't work; some will be banal, and others will be quirky and odd. Compare and reflect on your results. As you do so, keep these questions in mind:

- Why do some work and some not?
- Why do some seem to 'fit' quite well, and is that a good thing?
- What is the definition of something working and something not working?
- How important are the gaps in the narrative?
- Is it better that the pieces fit together neatly and perhaps dully, or is it better if there are gaps and surprises, things that don't connect?
- Which outlines have potential for a better story?
- Where does the humour come from?
- How important is surprise?
- How important is the juxtaposition of events that don't normally belong?
- How important is being concrete and specific as against being general?
- If you were to write the 'story', how would you make the leap between the three parts and make your story work?

 Write

Write a 100- to 200-word story from the outline you think works best. Open the story with sentence one, use sentence two in the middle and make sentence three the last sentence.

(100–200 words)

As further development you could extend any of your outlines that work into longer pieces. As a variation, you could try doing the exercise using 'The best thing I did' as the first sentence and then compare the stories where 'good' things happen and the stories where 'bad' things happen. Which are 'better'?

 Focus point

Use the Siege Story or the Quest Story to help you plot.

Summary

In this chapter you have studied the difference between story and plot, examined causality in plotting, practised building a plot, written a short story from a skeletal outline, understood that stories are made up of surprise, gaps and incongruities as well as ideas, characters, situations and events that 'fit'.

In the last few chapters we have been concerned with telling stories. The exercises we have done have thrown up elements most important in a story – those of character, setting and plot. We have already spent some time on character, setting and plot. But now we need to spend some time looking at conflict.

Next step

What is conflict? Think about this question. We will be considering it in the next chapter as we look at genre fiction.

16

Conflict and genre

Read any reasonable book on creative writing or any notes from publishers or a broadcaster like the BBC and they will all stress the need for 'conflict' in a story. But what do they mean by conflict? We are used to hearing the word used in the context of a news bulletin about a war zone. But what do we mean in creative writing? Think about this question and write down your answer in your notebook.

Conflict

WHO WANTS WHAT AND WHY CAN'T THEY GET IT?

In creative writing it is opposition and the clash of wills that causes conflict. There is an old question that American 'B' movies were apparently built around, 'Who wants what and why can't they get it?' This is a very handy question to ask at the start of a story you're writing because it highlights and focuses the conflict. 'Who wants what and why can't they get it?' If we break this down, you will see that it gives you the various key elements important to a story:

Who? – This gives us a protagonist, a who, the person who will drive the story. This who

Wants – has a desire for something; this is the goal that they must achieve. Whatever it is they want gives us the next essential ingredient, the

What? – What is the protagonist's need or desire?

The entire thing is succinctly put together in the one sentence:

'Who wants what?'

But to get a good story you need something on the other side. Because if we said our story was 'Angela wants a new car' and she went out and got a new car there would be no story. The story comes from the difficulties she has in getting the new car. So, on the other side, we need opposition. Opposition provides an obstacle to the main character's need or want:

'Why can't they get it?'

This part of the sentence balances out the first part because it gives us our opposition.

Why can't they get it? Because we have something or someone bent on stopping them from getting it. How do they stop them? They block their path. They put obstacles in their way. What is the result of two opposing forces clashing over something? The result is trouble, or conflict. Hence the handy sentence 'Who wants what and why can't they get it?'

If you were to split this up and write it down as two sentences you would have:

- **Sentence 1: Who wants what?** This gives you the elements of main character, want or need and goal.

- **Sentence 2: Why can't they get it?** This gives us the equally essential elements of Opposition/obstacle and the end of the story or the resolution.

THE 'CONFLICT EQUATION'

We already have a term for the main character, the who in our story. That term is the protagonist. The person who opposes them also has a name, he or she is called the antagonist and they also have a goal: to prevent the protagonist from getting what they want. Our equation therefore is protagonist, desire goal and, on the other side, antagonist desire goal. The antagonist then is an *obstacle* to the protagonist.

We can lay another equation out:

Protagonist + desire versus Antagonist + opposing desire = conflict

The obstacle could be the antagonist or there could be a series of obstacles caused by the antagonist. Facing and overcoming these obstacles causes conflict. Overcoming the obstacles and facing up to the conflict all lead to a resolution, an outcome of success or failure as the goal is either achieved or not. This is how the story unfolds.

The degree of desire with which your protagonist wants something is important. If he or she, as it is sometimes written, 'aches with desire' then he or she is going to move heaven and earth to achieve it. Therefore your protagonist has to want what they want very badly and it has to matter whether they get it or not. It almost always has to be a matter of life or death, and if not literally life or death, then it has to seem life or death to the protagonist in that situation as you present it. And of course he or she mustn't get it until the end of the story because the clash between the desire and the opponent *is* the story.

In a sense stories are all middles. They have a beginning which is a set-up that establishes a situation, say a person in a predicament, and it has an end where this predicament is resolved one way or another, but the main bulk of the story is the middle and the middle comprises all sorts of complicating thrills and spills, misunderstandings, wrong turnings, dead ends, and clashes between the desire and the obstacle(s) until the final resolution: The End. The middle is, in fact, all CONFLICT.

You could lay it out a story plan as GOAL OBSTACLE RESOLUTION. So, to plot a story you need to set out with someone, an individual or a group that wants something very badly; it is vital to their lives etc. Then you need to see how long you can prevent them from obtaining it; the longer the better too. It's a formula, but an old and a tried and tested formula. Not everyone uses it now; some people write stories now in a way that seems as if they use Einsteinian laws, and you need to be an Einstein to piece them together. Our formula is perhaps a bit closer to Newtonian physics. It works like Newtonian physics does, quite adequately enough for us in our daily lives on earth. A lot of genre fiction – detective books, thrillers, romance, historical novels, fantasy and science fiction are all written around this formula. So is Shakespeare: Macbeth wants to be King of Scotland; how does he achieve his end and what prevents him staying king? Think of the obstacles to Elizabeth, Jane and Mr Darcy in *Pride and Prejudice* before happiness and the end of the book is obtained. Raymond Chandler used it. Spy story writers like John Le Carré used it. Story editors know the formula and publishers recognize and know its value to a well-constructed story so you are better off learning it.

Focus point

To develop a story from character ask, 'Who wants what and why can't they get it?'

Key idea (once more)

Protagonist + desire versus Antagonist + opposing desire = conflict

Write

Find one of the characters you've written about in one of the earlier exercises, perhaps someone from the previous chapter, and take them to a point of change in their life. Think about this person and make sure that they are in a dilemma over something that is about to happen that will change their life forever. It might be someone faced with taking the bandages off, having had plastic surgery or having been in a nasty accident. Write this point of change down in 25 words and try to make it a physical and emotional change – something that deeply affects that person. Decide the opening scene of your story and write two pages of it, only that amount, keeping in mind that the first two pages of any story are vitally important.

In these first two pages you must:

- present the main character(s)
- set the scene
- introduce the important element of conflict
- state the character's problem
- set the mood.

(400 words)

UNDER PRESSURE

Key idea

How to plot from character – think of the worst possible thing that could happen to your character, and then make sure it happens.

When you are planning a story you also need to think of the ending. It is like making a journey. You get some writers who say they just set off, put the bags in the car and drive wherever the road takes them. Other writers might plan the trip meticulously, using satellite navigation, maps and Internet journey planners. Most writing probably falls somewhere between these two extremes and the simple truth is that you may not be able to be absolutely definite about it until you get there but you need to have some idea of where you are heading when you start. You need to have some idea of where you're going and what will happen when you get there. Having quite a specific destination is a necessity for travelling. So try to frame up some sort of ending in the light of the questions you've asked about your character and what they want or need. With a beginning and an ending in mind you can begin to form some sense of what you want in the middle. One or two complications in a short story, some difficulties to overcome, some necessary degree of conflict will help you frame up quite a decent story plan. This is quite suitable for all the different genres of writing.

A good device is to put characters into a situation that demands a response; a situation that confronts him with something that makes them react. Put them under pressure; this will reveal their character.

Alfred Hitchcock does this in many of his films. In *North by Northwest* and in *The 39 Steps*, Roger Thornhill and Richard Hannay respectively are going about their daily business when an incident happens and they find themselves caught up in a tense thriller which involves murder and being chased by the police across America or Scotland. Both men have to react under extreme pressure. We learn more about their characters as we see them react and have to make decisions in the heat of the moment. This is better than if we were simply told that they were resourceful, courageous, and determined characters. This comes back to the idea of showing and telling which shows us how the elements of creative writing connect up with each other and make it somewhat artificial when we separate them out for the sake of understanding and study.

Write

Take the two pages you have just worked on and write the rest of the story. Make sure the character pursues his or her need and that that need is thwarted. Make sure the protagonist keeps in pursuit of their need and has obstacles to overcome. You need to have conflict coming from a goal that is blocked.

(750 words)

Write

Another way to develop conflict and characters in a story can be to take two characters, character A and character B, and set them arguing about something. The characters need not to be over defined for this exercise. They might be a pair of sisters arguing about a borrowed dress or a husband and wife arguing over map reading. You choose. What is character A's view of character B? What is character B's view of character A? Just write it; get them talking, get them arguing and get them to reveal things about themselves.

(200 words)

Focus point

Get your characters arguing with each other; you can learn a lot about them.

Genre writing

Snapshot

What is genre writing? What is a genre? Cover up what follows, think about this question and write your understanding of the term in your notebook.

Genre is a French word meaning 'kind', 'sort', 'type' or 'category'. We use it in English for a particular category or type of fiction. You can write short stories and novels in a particular genre. Look in any good, large bookshop and you will see shelves and shelves of book categories in different genres. There are too many to list, but here are a few of the main ones:

- crime
- fantasy
- gothic
- historical

- horror
- magic realism
- romance
- science fiction

- spy
- thrillers.

There are others, and there are subdivisions within these genres – for example, 'chick-lit', which is a relatively recent subdivision of romantic fiction – but these broad categories are enough for our concerns. Looking at the list, you can see how some of them overlap and share elements with other genres, but these main divisions are understood by writers, readers and publishers.

If you want to write a romantic, detective, spy, thriller or chick-lit story or novel you need to know some of the requirements. But lack of space prohibits us giving an exhaustive or exhausting list here of what particular concerns characterize one genre rather than another. Broadly, we can say that if you write a crime story you will expect a murder and a detective, at least some sort of crime to solve. If you write a romance you will expect two people to find each other irresistibly attractive and be kept apart right till the end of the book. But, remember what we said right at the start of this book; the best way to learn about writing is to read and read and read. To learn about a particular genre you are drawn to, read everything you can that has been written in that genre. This is what Raymond Chandler did when he was starting out to write crime thrillers. He got regular copies of the *Black Mask* magazine, read the stories, chose the ones he liked and rewrote them. By rewriting them he learned how to write his own original stories. If you want to write Gothic horror, read some of the early examples such as *The Castle of Otranto* by Horace Walpole, *The Monk* by Matthew Lewis and *The Mysteries of Udolpho* by Anne Radcliffe. For horror or vampire stories, read Bram Stoker's *Dracula*, Mary Shelley's *Frankenstein* and any of the more recent Anne Rice books as well as Stephen King. For romance, read romantic fiction. Whatever genre interests you, seek out the best examples of that genre and read and analyse them.

HOW DO YOU KNOW WHICH GENRE IS FOR YOU?

You might ask why you should bother writing within a genre. The answer is that it may be just the thing you want to write. Also, knowing the genres available, and the popular ones, will really help you place your work if you try to get it published. Publishers have a great need to pigeonhole work. It helps them both understand what it is you have written and also know whether they can sell it or not. It would help you enormously in your writing and save a lot of wasted time and effort if you were to establish clearly early on in which pigeon hole you thought your work belonged. It helps when starting out if you are clear on this. There is no reason why a romantic vampire novel should not be a good read or a hard-boiled science fiction detective not do well, but publishers get very uncertain if you write across genres. It might help when you are starting out to stay within the boundaries of an established genre and spread your wings later. The mass book-buying public do prefer clear divisions and publishers, in the main, know their markets.

Focus point

Analyse the market and see what is currently selling (but keep up to date and keep in mind that the market may well have moved on by the time you have actually written what you thought was in demand). That said, do not restrain or restrict yourself at the start; just let the writing flow and see what comes. Thinking too much about staying within certain parameters might contain your creativity and that is not what you should do. At the start, it might be best to write what you like and worry about selling it later.

Lisa Tuttle, *Writing Fantasy and Science Fiction*

'*Most of the skills you need for writing fantasy or science fiction are the same as for any other sort of fiction. A good story, believable characters and a fluent, readable style are absolutely vital to all saleable popular fiction – whether thriller, romance, fantasy or science fiction. Whatever your other strengths and interests as a writer, you must be strong in all the basics of good fiction in order to succeed.*'

Key idea

Most of the skills and techniques you need to write good genre fiction in whatever genre, depend on the same skills that you need to write good fiction, full stop.

You will certainly need to know how to plot for genre fiction. One of the reasons that genre fiction sells so well, out selling literary fiction, the sort of fiction that wins prizes, is that genre novels tell good, plotted stories with a beginning, middle and end. These can seem low grade and old hat to literary novelists but to write convincingly in any genre, (and we can include literary fiction as a genre, it is certainly a category of fiction) you need a good story, believable characters and a good style that people find easy to read. By saying the style of writing needs to be easy to read does not mean you cannot write complicated sentences about complicated things, just that the better your prose is to read, the better people will enjoy what you write. You may not in the end choose to write in any particular genre. Perhaps literary is for you, fiction that seeks to say something about people or the world we live in or seeks to approach some of the big (or small) questions of life. If it is, then good. You know what it is you want to write and you should pursue it. But whether you decide to write in a genre or in the field of literary fiction you will need to be strong on all the things central to good fiction in order to succeed.

Key idea

Why bother with genre writing? It sells!

Kate Walker, *Writing Romantic Fiction*

'Romantic fiction is one of the best selling forms of fiction throughout the world. It is read and enjoyed by millions of women of all ages and from all backgrounds in every country. Around between 40 or 50 per cent of all paperback novels sold in bookshops around the world are romantic fiction, and almost 12 per cent of books borrowed from public libraries are romantic novels.

'The authors of such books can become household names like Catherine Cookson and Barbara Taylor Bradford and they have fans who will buy each new book as soon as it appears. In America there are magazines and bookshops devoted specifically to romantic fiction. Unlike other genres whose popularity fluctuates up and down, the popularity of romances stays consistently high.'

Workshop: genre writing

Which genre should you write in? How do you know which genre is for you? It might help you to make up your mind if you take a clean sheet of paper and do the following:

- Write a list of the genres you have read and enjoyed previously.
- List books you have read that fall under these categories (list any film or television adaptations of books you have read too).
- Take your time; list all your early reading too, anything you can remember from childhood. When you've done it, see if there is any particular genre.
- Make a list of the genres you do not like reading (that will also help you decide what to write).

Once you've done this you will know where your interests lie. Whatever genres you choose to write in, you will need to know the main requirements of that genre. Because you will have read so many of them a lot of that detail will be stored in your brain somewhere. And really the best way to do this is to read and analyse stories in that genre.

Next, find a short story or novel that you like in a genre that you like and know well; it might be easier to do this with a short story because of the size factor. Once you have found one, read it and note the following things:

- story title
- approximate length in words*
- main character's name and brief description
- whether it is written in first or third person
- name of viewpoint character
- main characters and ages
- occupations/class/backgrounds
- location(s) of story
- main character's problem
- antagonist or opponent
- plot (in 60 words)
- tone of story (upbeat or down-beat).

When you have done this, read the story again and answer these questions:

- Where does the story begin?
- Does the story start at a high point to catch the reader's interest?
- Which characters are introduced in the first scene?
- When is the main character introduced?
- What problem faces the main character?
- When is it presented? In the first scene or later?
- How is it presented, i.e. is it told or shown?
- Does the main character have a character flaw which helps generate the story? If so, what is it?
- Does each scene grow logically from the preceding one or do they jump?
- Is any flashback used? If so, where does it start and end?
- Where does the story end?
- Is there any change in the story from beginning to end? If so, what sort of change? (Does a character or situation or place or atmosphere change?)
- What proportion of dialogue is there to narrative?

(These questions have been adapted from David Silwyn Williams' *How to Write for Teenagers* (Allison & Busby, 1989).)

Once you have done this you will have a thorough understanding of the story structure and why it works. You can also use some of those ideas in your own pieces. You should do this exercise several times with other stories to see how a range of genre material works and differs.

Focus point

If you want to write genre fiction, study the requirements and use them. But do not think because you are writing in a genre, it is easy.

Pamela Rochford, Preface to *Writing Erotic Fiction*

'Writing an erotic novel is easy, or so a lot of people would have you believe. But sustaining the few pages of erotic fantasy – which just about anyone can write – to the 80,000 words required by most publishers, involving interesting characters and a believable plot (or at least been well written and deliver Coleridge's 'willing suspension of disbelief' in the reader) is much harder.'

We have generally been stressing the accessibility of writing in this book. But it is wrong to believe that anyone can write anything. Writing genre fiction is not a soft option; it is as hard as writing any other form of fiction. There are the same issues of believability, self-belief and just plain stamina.

Write

Write the following story in a genre of your choice. Use these elements in any way that you wish to fulfil the requirements of the genre.

1   Young man, Rick, at his desk.
2   Young woman, Sara, enters.
3   They speak quietly at first, then loudly.
4   The phone rings, interrupting them.
5   Rick answers it, says something to Sara and leaves, taking a laptop with him.
6   Rick drives fast on a motorway and stops in a motorway service station. He gets a coffee. He is joined by another, older woman.
7   They kiss.
8   Rick shows her something on the laptop and the two study it intently.
9   The woman gives Rick money.
10 Rick checks his watch and drives fast back to a building and into a meeting with a large number of people.
11 Sara enters.

You continue and conclude the story.

(750 words)

Edit: checklist for genre fiction

Now you have the first draft of your story edit it using the checklist below. Ask yourself, honestly, whether you have:

- created believable, enjoyable main characters (for romantic fiction these should be sympathetic heroines, irresistible heroes)
- written effective dialogue
- invented a readable plot
- written from different viewpoints
- created the appropriate atmosphere and setting.

If your story is weak or unsatisfactory in any of these areas, then see what you can do about improving it. There are sufficient lessons already covered in this book to help you structure a consistent viewpoint, create atmosphere and setting, improve the plot and make your characters stronger and more believable. Look back over the previous chapters to get help in the area of your story that needs it.

WHICH SHOULD YOU START WITH – CHARACTER OR PLOT?

It is not only helpful to look at our own writing to help ourselves to learn but essential to look at what other writers have done and try to discover what their strengths and weaknesses are.

Key idea

Once you start writing you need to read as a writer not as a reader. Look at a writer you like to see how they do it. If you know some of their techniques you can emulate them.

Certain writers in certain genres start more with plot than with character. The James Bond films start with action, a dramatic, exciting action scene, after which they pull back to sketch in some character and some story. There are other writers for whom plot is the important thing and character is a part of the mechanics of telling the story. Characters in these stories are often two dimensional, 'flat; and not 'round'.

Agatha Christie was inspired to write her first detective story by a challenge from her sister who bet Agatha that she could not write something that her sister could not guess the end of before she got there. To that competitive sisterly exchange the world owes *The Mysterious Affair at Styles* and the entire Agatha Christie oeuvre that followed. Agatha Christie started and continued with plot; the mechanics of who did what to whom and when. She wanted to trick her reader and hold back the big secret, of whodunit, until the last possible moment. For her, writing detective fiction was to create a puzzle, pure and complex. The whole genre of the classical detective novel, in fact, is built around this puzzle element, the game, the competition between writer and reader. Certain readers love a clever, inventive writer who can outwit them;

the cleverer the better because this reflects on them as a reader. If they can't guess the ending then the writer is very smart; if it is a smart piece of writing but they do guess the ending of it, then the reader can take a pat on the back, it shows how clever they are. A good, well plotted crime, thriller or murder mystery is win, win for writer and reader and publisher.

In the genre of detective fiction or murder mystery, characters often come secondary to plot and are often twisted to fit the plot needs. If you have a strongly plotted story you need to be able to move people about and fit them in to suit your requirements and if your characters are strong and individual and capable of talking back to you and saying they don't want to be put in this or that scenario, then they can make the plotting difficult. You can end up either straining the plot or straining the character. If you have ever thought the characters in a golden-age detective novel remain somewhat pale and two dimensional, perhaps it is because they need to be. They need to serve the plot and don't need to have three-dimensional lives of their own. We might even say they should not have three-dimensional lives of their own for if they did they would resist being moved about in a way that serves the plot. They might talk back and say 'no'. The only characters with three-dimensional lives in crime and murder-mystery stories are the detective and his or her sidekick. The others are formed of various degrees of flatness.

Raymond Chandler once said that when he hit a problem in the story he would have a man come into the room with a gun in his hand. This is something of a throwaway remark, obviously, but as often with amusing remarks there is a truth at the heart of it. Having something dramatic like a man come into the room with a gun in his hand is a good way to increase tension in a story. A man with a gun in his hand immediately spells threat and danger and perks up a reader's interest. Such a plot device could also gloss over any amount of holes in a story and there can be big holes in these sorts of stories.

Among Chandler's novels, *The Big Sleep*, the first of his books about the private eye Philip Marlowe, is known for its convoluted plot. In it Marlowe is hired by a wealthy General Sternwood to get his daughter out of trouble. When the Sternwoods' chauffeur, Owen Taylor, is found dead in the harbour, apparently having driven off the pier and drowned, the doctor suspects the cause of death could be a blow to the back of the head. When the book was adapted for the screen it was necessarily pulled apart by the screenwriters, director and actors. This is a necessary part of the process of adaptation. In such dialogue with the original material, questions come up and inconsistencies spotted. In the filming of *The Big Sleep* no one apparently could work out who killed the chauffeur. Had he died by accident, killed himself or been murdered? The director, Howard Hawks, could not work it out. Three screenwriters are credited, including William Faulkner. They did not know. Someone contacted Chandler, he told a friend in a later letter: 'They sent me a wire … asking me, and dammit I didn't know either.' The plot was so convoluted that even the author could not unpick it! Does it matter, you might ask? It clearly did not stop *The Big Sleep* being published and selling. It is now recognized as a classic.

But if you are going to use a device such as 'Man enters with gun in hand' to raise the stakes, you need to consider what would happen if the character with the gun says: 'No, I am not coming in with a gun in my hand.' Or if he says, 'I don't carry a gun. I might come in with a bunch of flowers or the latest gardening magazine. That is more true to my character.' What Raymond Chandler would have done then presumably was to get another guy with a gun as he needed the device to ratchet up the tension, then looked at whether to keep the character with the flowers or whether he could bump him off. Character is definitely subservient to plot when it is used like this. You want a flat, one dimensional character coming through that door with a gun, someone expendable, not a fully rounded, three-dimensional character we can get to know and care about. This is character as plot device.

P.D. James claims to have known from a very early age that she wanted to be a crime writer because when she was read the nursery rhyme 'Humpty Dumpty' – 'Humpty Dumpty sat on a wall, Humpty Dumpty had a great fall …' – she wanted to know 'Did he fall or was he pushed?' It's a good story and Ms James uses it to good effect at talks to crime writers to make her audience laugh, but there is probably some truth in it too. Writers have an instinct for the sort of pieces they want to write and the area they want to work in. They know what feels right for them.

Stephen King, when he began to sit down and write, let his instinct as well as his talent and his imagination take him naturally down the path of horror and suspense. He belongs to these genres as much as they now belong to him.

Alfred Hitchcock worked in a genre, or, as great artists do, maybe he established a genre of his own. Something can now be labelled Hitchcockian and we know what that means. Such a piece of work will probably have a huge element of suspense in it; it could display a macabre wit. It could contain an icy blonde in peril and have a hero both ordinary and extraordinary.

The interrelationship of character and plot is fundamentally important to a Hitchcock movie. He likes to take a character and establish them in their ordinary world before he pitches them into an unusual or extraordinary world. He wants to see what happens to a character, to test them and see what it brings out of them. The film *North by Northwest* is a good example of this. The main character, Roger Thornhill, played by Cary Grant, is an advertising executive who gets thrown into the world of espionage. Hitchcock is saying that ordinary men can become heroes when they are pitched into extraordinary worlds.

It would be interesting to know whether Hitchcock started with character or plot. It is known that he spent a long time working with his writers planning and developing the stories he filmed so that the finished piece had both a tightly plotted story as well as good, believable characters. Hitchcock wanted that important balance. He did not want to make what he called 'ice-box movies'. These were films that he said worked in the cinema; they worked all the way home; they worked while you parked the car in the garage and walked into the house. They worked right up until the moment when you opened the fridge or 'ice-box' door and reached in for a glass of milk before going to bed and at that point you thought, 'Hang on a minute … why didn't the hero or heroine call the police or pick up the gun or shut the door, or …?' And this moment, the 'ice-box moment' Hitchcock said, was when the plot fell to pieces and the film stopped working. It had kept you on the edge of your seat in the cinema but after a short period of reflection when everything began to sink in, its flaws had become clear and it had come to be seen more as a guilty pleasure than a joy. The interaction of character and plot, that important balance and how we achieve that successfully in our work is the subject of our book. Hitchcock is an excellent example of how a great artist worked at achieving that.

A 'special world'

All genres have their own 'special world' that immediately characterizes the stories in the genre of science fiction, murder mystery or whatever. Keeping the thoughts about the special world and its unique characteristics in mind, try the following exercise and write it either as a ghost story, murder mystery, sci-fi or other genre of your choice.

Workshop: creating genre fiction

You are going to write a piece of genre fiction.

Study this list of jobs, professions and roles:

- alien
- astronaut
- coachman
- country squire
- detective
- doctor
- explorer
- ghost
- highwayman/woman
- housekeeper
- judge
- lover
- lord/lady of the manor
- murderer
- policeman
- prince/princess
- scientist
- soldier
- vampire
- victim.

Pick a genre and keeping your choice of genre in mind, be it ghost story, vampire story, murder mystery, etc., choose one of these occupations or professions and get ready to write from the point of view of that person in the special world of the genre. This exercise has a series of steps and surprise is important in this exercise so make sure you cover up what is below before you continue. The exercise will work best if you do not know what is coming in the next step. It may mean that you introduce something in one stage and have to do a complete turnaround in the next stage. Go with it; see whether you can make it connect and work. Test yourself and your powers of invention.

When you uncover each new request (labelled *a*, *b*, *c*, etc.) write quickly and under time pressure, say no more than 2–3 minutes each time (maximum 40–50 words at each stage), until you have reached the end.

(a) Think about the occupation/profession you have chosen from the above list. Imagine a person fulfilling this role and living in the special world of the genre. What is their name and what do they look like? Write a brief description in no more than 50 words.

(b) They eat something.

(c) They drink.

(d) They meet someone.

(e) They get dressed (or undressed).

(f) They travel somewhere.

(g) They witness something amazing.

(h) They have an accident, or witness one.

(i) They chase what appears to be a woman or a man.

(j) They make an excited phone call, or write a letter.

(k) They confront someone or something.

(l) They fall ill or nearly die.

(m) They are rescued by another character from the special world (choose one from the above).

(n) Bring the story to a conclusion.

(750 words)

Edit

Read over what you have written. Is there any basis in it for a story you can develop? It may not initially be coherent; maybe some of the connections are more like jumps, but do not dismiss them too easily. It can be a mistake to try and tie everything up neatly. Sometimes gaps and jumps in action can point the way to a more interesting storyline. Play around with it, see if you can make it work or if it feeds into anything you are already writing.

Summary

In this chapter we have looked at the essential need for conflict in a story, analysed genre stories, and written in different genres. If you already know which genre it is you want to write in, read two or three works in that field (enough to enable you to compare) and make a note of the relevant ingredients common to the stories. Is character paramount? Is it plot? How important is setting? Is technology an important component? (It may well be in science fiction, but also in murder mystery.) Use that list of ingredients as a model for your own genre writing.

Next step

In the next chapter we will consider another essential both of stories and characters; how your characters speak and the very next step will be to consider what dialogue is and how dialogue works.

17

Writing dialogue

Simply put, dialogue is the things that characters in novels, stories, plays and films say to one another.

Stuart Griffiths

'The primary purpose of good dramatic dialogue is to state clearly the facts which advance the action of the play. Its basic form is to be found in the Latin Mass or catechism – a simple statement and response, or a question and answer technique.

'The form has been, and is still, used to great effect by the commedia dell' arte, *Molière, courtroom dramas, detective stories, stand-up comedians.*

'Dialogue should grow out of a previous speech or action and lead into another. It is like a good scene sequence. Usually there is some momentary point of rest, a way-station that a particular passage of dialogue was making towards. Then kicks forward again.'

What is dialogue in fiction?

Irving Weinman

'Dialogue in fiction is the written representation of speech between two or more people. Dialogue in real life is the speech between two or more people, what they say to each other. Because most real-life conversation is full of pauses, broken thoughts, repetition and non-verbal sounds like "umm", "erm" and "aah" while thinking, writers would be crazy to put actual real-life dialogue into fiction. It would either bore readers or irritate them so much they'd stop reading.'

In our work on 'showing' we have already seen what a major part dialogue will play in writing fully rendered dramatic scenes. In Chapter 13 we saw how writing monologues can help you create characters but monologues can also form a large part of a short story or novel should a writer choose to use a monologue that way. Monologues are speech, they are a form of dialogue, albeit a dialogue a character has with themselves.

Dialogue in fiction appears in 'showing,' in scenes where characters talk to each other. It also appears, as we have said, in monologue form; dialogue appears in a character's thoughts, in what they are thinking. It appears in letters, diaries, in telephone conversations and even in emails and texts. Dialogue is at its most sparse in scripts. Indeed Tolstoy said that novels are plays with the stage directions written in. While this is obviously far from a sufficient definition of a novel, there is enough contained in the idea to make sense. Novelists will include dialogue in their novels and oftentimes pages of dialogue exchanges with little else on the page so that some pages do begin to resemble scripts.

Elmore Leonard

'All the information you need can be given in dialogue.'

But at other times novelists add other elements to dialogue, such as supporting narrative. This helps to create character as well as to keep the story moving along. A novelist will indicate the tone of voice in which a line of dialogue has been said (where a playwright or screenwriter does that sparingly if at all, preferring to leave it to actors and director to understand the tone from the context). A writer of fiction will also put across, with the dialogue, related and relevant facial expressions and body language, something again which scriptwriters will include sparingly, if at all. The supporting narrative to dialogue in a piece of fiction will help establish the atmosphere and setting as well as a character's unspoken thoughts and feelings.

It is important to be able to handle the aspects that fiction writers bring to support their use of dialogue because when considering dialogue which is just dialogue on a page, be it in a novel or a script, you can make the mistake of thinking that dialogue is only about what people say.

You must not forget that in life, when we speak, we communicate only partly by what we say. The majority of communication is also hidden beneath the surface and goes on with silence, tone of voice, and body language. Another thing that people forget with dialogue is that what people don't say is as important as what they do say. Inexperienced writers don't leave out nearly enough in their dialogue but put everything in. They do not pay enough attention to silence. Silence on the stage can be riveting if the dramatic moment is one of those highly charged situations. Silence if less riveting in a novel, partly because there is very little of it. The novelist has to write to create it, hence abnegating the silence, although silence well used can still be riveting.

Something else to remember when you're thinking of the silences beneath dialogue is that dialogue reveals emotion. People talk feelings as much as ideas. They are motivated to talk as much by what they are feeling than as by a desire to communicate an idea to someone. Like an iceberg, feeling is a very important part of the unseen seven-eighths under the water, often the most important part, in dialogue. Whatever the content of a character's words, beneath everything is how they feel and what they want: fear, anger, ambition, hatred, uncertainty, wanting to be liked or loved, wanting to impress someone or win someone over.

Focus point

So far as you can each line of dialogue should reveal the person's feelings. Lines that don't do that tend to be doing nothing.

Script editors can be good at spotting this. A good script editor will say, 'What are these two doing in this scene?' If the writer says, 'Just talking,' the script editor would say, 'They can't just talk.' What people say has to mean something to the character or to the story, and mostly it means what they feel, what their desires are, what they want or don't want. You also have to show the changes of feelings within a scene as information affects people.

Some functions of dialogue remain true for dialogue in prose fiction as well as in scripts. Among other things:

- Dialogue gives information. This is obvious, but the difficulty is to do it without it being obvious. Without a little bell going off 'bing' in the reader's or viewer's head as they think, 'I'm being told something here.'

- Dialogue gives us information about the person speaking, about the person spoken to and about the situation they are in.

- Dialogue reveals emotion. People talk feelings more than ideas. You also have to show the changes of feelings within a scene as information affects people.

- Dialogue advances the plot. It helps the story along. Again, it shouldn't be obvious that that's what dialogue is doing. But you need a plot to advance; dialogue can't exist with no relation to the 'story', to what the piece is about.

- Dialogue characterizes the speaker and the person to whom it is spoken. And again dialogue cannot exist without a character to speak it.

- Dialogue cannot exist with no relation to the characters, to who is saying what is said.

When you write dialogue in fiction or in scripts, try to establish the difference between each person's speech. There is often a clear difference of diction and tone, even of sentence construction.

> 'These scones are stale. Could you please change them for fresh ones, and may I have cake without cream?'

is said by a different character to:

> 'I'm tellin' you now, they'll dig it up and flog the lot, and bugger off to Florida.'

A fiction writer may or may not feel the need for supporting narrative to bring these differences out but these differences are what actors can bring out of a script very well. But the writer has to put them into the script (or story) in the first place, or there will be nothing to bring out. A good test when you write a script (and this can also be used for a dialogue exchange in a novel) is that you should be able to put a ruler over the names of the people speaking and be able to identify who is speaking from what they say. What they say is as much a function of who they are and how they say it as the words they use. And the words they use are as much a function of who they are and what they want as anything else.

A classic British sitcom like *Dad's Army* would pass this test easily:

> 'Stupid boy!'

could only be said by Captain Mainwaring.

> 'Don't panic! Don't panic!'

and again

> 'They don't like it up 'em, sir! They don't like it.'

could only be Corporal Jones.

> 'We're doomed. We're doomed.'

could only be Private Fraser. While Pike would regularly say:

'Mr Mainwaring, my mum says I shouldn't go out without my scarf ...'

This recognition works partly through the use of repeated phrases which have become associated so strongly with the characters. But this lays the template. Everything else each character says in those scripts comes directly from them being the sort of characters they are. Mainwaring is always fussing about his appearance and his rank. Pike wears his muffler in all weathers. Jones dodders about out of time with everyone else and panicking nine to the dozen while telling everyone else not to panic. Successful American sitcoms like *Cheers*, *Frazier* and *Friends* all have strong characters who say the things they say because of the characters they are. Dialogue is intimately related to character and characterization. In fact, dialogue is a characterizer.

Key idea

What they say and how they say it is one of the important elements that will characterize the people in your stories.

It is a little bit different in prose because as we have said you have all sorts of other things you can directly tell the readers. You can tell the reader who said what line – sometimes you need to or it can get very confusing. You can also say how the line was said, refer to body language, accent etc. You can fill it in for the reader, which is the job the actor does on stage. But, in spite of all the supplementary things you can supply it is still as important to make all your people speak differently from each other in prose as it is in scripts.

Focus point

Dialogue is intimately related to character and characterization. Characters say what they say because of the people they are: because of the people they are, they say what they say.

What is a script? The 'iceberg' metaphor

People sometimes think that a script *is* dialogue. On the surface a script may look as if it is all dialogue, with some stage directions, but a script is like a poem; what you see on the surface is not all that is there. Beneath the surface of all that white paper, like the proverbial swan swimming elegantly along on the surface of a lake, there is a huge amount of effort going on. Think of a script as an iceberg. A small amount of it is on top; the bulk of it is under the surface:

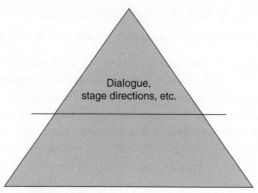

Figure 17.1 The 'script iceberg'

The script is not only what is visible; it is what is invisible too. As a scriptwriter you only leave on the surface what is visible but you do not only deal in the visible. In a script you can write the line, 'Perkins?' and this can be a good line depending on the intended meaning. This is communicated by nuance of tone and how it is said. As a writer, you are dependent on the actor; the way they say the lines, or lean forward, pick up a pencil and snap it; the way they smile, chew their lips and so on. The actor does all that but you have to create the vehicle for the actor. To a large degree, you have to know it all or at least the potential for it. You need to know your created world as well as the world you live in. But, unlike a piece of fiction, you do not put it all in the script. To write a script, you have to learn what to leave visible, what to bury beneath the surface and what to leave out altogether. The bit below the land or water line is massively important, maybe more important than the bit above the water line – as the captain of the *Titanic* discovered. To write a successful script, learn to write underwater.

Some psychologists say that in communication 30 per cent is conveyed by the words we use and 70 per cent is conveyed by body language: by the way we look, smile (or not), by the way we say things.

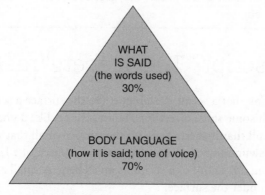

Figure 17.2 The communication iceberg

Both scripts and dialogue work in similar ways: as something like an iceberg.

See the language iceberg below.

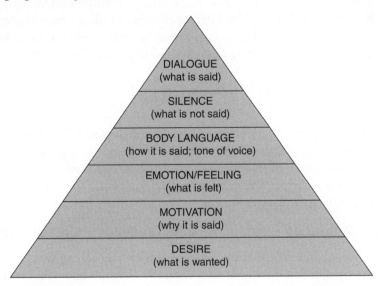

Figure 17.3 The language iceberg

Dialogue is what characters say. For example, 'I love you,' 'I would like to love you,' 'I hate you,' or 'I used to love you.' Of course, what they say may not be what they mean. Other factors come into play.

Underneath what characters say is what they do not say and this is sometimes more important and more powerful than what they choose to say. When you counterpoint what they say with what they don't say, their words can really mean something else. 'I love you' can mean: 'I would like to love you,' 'I hate you,' or 'I used to love you.' Silence itself can be a powerful tool in dialogue that is too easily overlooked.

As we have said, characters also communicate through the *way* they say something and their body language while they are saying it. 'I love you' can mean, 'I hate your guts' because of a look in the eye or a biting of the lip while saying it. 'You are awful' can mean you *are* awful. Or, when said with a flirtatious, comedian's smile, can mean just the opposite.

- Underneath what they choose to say or not say will be what the character feels: their emotion. Do they think the other character is awful or do they secretly fancy them?
- Underneath the words, the silence, the emotion and the body language is why characters choose to speak or not speak, their motivation for speaking in the first place.
- Underneath the motivation and intimately connected with it, is what they want or need, or feel they want or need.

Remember that the iceberg is meant to be helpful. It is a schematic way of presenting something that is not schematic. The interaction between these elements does not maintain a rigid, fixed and hierarchical order. Maybe the need creates the motivation, possibly the motivation and need are difficult to separate; perhaps a character speaks without thinking and the motivation for that only becomes clear later, but the iceberg is laid out in this way just to make the parts clear. In reality, in life and in stories and scripts, all these mix together and the different elements of silence/body language/motivation/desire are stronger and weaker depending on the circumstances. But it does show the many, complicated layers to dialogue and why it can be difficult to write.

How do you write dialogue?

Where does dialogue come from? Where do you find dialogue? It may help sometimes if you look at the iceberg when you are writing dialogue, just to remind yourself to consider the order in which things can occur. The *desire* or *need* for something motivates a character to express this desire in feelings, in body language, in choosing not to say certain things but saying others.

Desire – motivation – emotion – body language – silence – speech

Certainly this would underline that the dialogue is what you end up with, not what you start with. You need to find the words for a character to speak once you know who they are and what it is they want in a situation. But you do not write dialogue schematically to some rigid formula.

Workshop: elephants

This is a good exercise that playwright Bryony Lavery uses in workshops for theatre writers. It is good for testing both your ability to write dialogue for stage, and any other sort of dialogue. It is an exercise designed to help you test your mind and get it right for scriptwriting, and it shows some of the difficulties of writing dialogue. Because you will be doing this on your own you will need an ordinary kitchen timer.

Sit somewhere where you won't be disturbed. Set the timer to ring in two minutes, close your eyes, and think of a white elephant. Just concentrate on a white elephant; however it is you visualize it, just keep in mind a white elephant. If you lose focus and your mind wanders off, then bring it back to the white elephant; think of nothing else but a white elephant. Do this for a couple of minutes until the timer goes off. Have a pause for a few moments and let your mind clear.

Now reset the timer, sit where you are and do NOT think of a white elephant for two minutes.

When these two minutes are up just think about what happened. In what ways did the first attempt differ from the second? Was one harder than the other? If so, why?

Was it easier to think of the elephant or not think of it? Did you keep the thought of the white elephant out of your mind, or did it keep coming in however hard you tried to keep it out? What did you do to keep it out? Did you either banish it completely or concentrate on something else? Some people say they find it easy; others that they find it hard. What was your experience? Whatever the answers there is no right or wrong with this, we are all different. We are all different in our abilities to either hold two things in the mind or concentrate on one thing to the exclusion of another, but it is very useful to be able to split your mind like this. Splitting your concentration and your thoughts can help you in writing for separate people, which is one of the essential tenets of good fictional and stage dialogue.

Imagine you are writing a scene with two characters in it; you need to be able to concentrate on what is going on in the minds of both characters. You need to be able to think the thoughts going in the mind of character A to the exclusion of character B, and then do the same for character B, because people in life and characters in stories do not know what is going on in the heads of other people. They are necessarily excluded and to some degree groping in the dark. That is why they speak. If they did know without speaking what the other was going to say, that would be telepathy. Sometimes we do feel a telepathic communication with other people; we seem to know what they are going to say before they say it. But that is not common. Life in many ways would be simpler if we did know what people were going to say before they said it but probably more problematic too. Who wants people to know all our thoughts? That would be dangerous and in some ways more boring. Stories certainly would be more boring. Part of the essential interaction of life is trying to communicate; trying to unpick what is going on in any situation is part of that communication. Part of what goes wrong in life is that we don't understand each other and that is also part of the motivation for being with each other in the first place. An essential element of that is the attempt to unpick what lies behind what someone has said; we want to understand each other. It is central to the art of the dramatist that he or she creates characters who don't understand each other, and whose attempts may well be doomed or at least very complicated. The dramatist will write scenes in which people are trying to find out what exactly is going on, doomed to failure – at least until the final act – in both comedy and tragedy. That is what makes a play. Actors, when they are coming to a part, will spend a long time trying to find out why characters say what they say, what intention lies behind the dialogue they use. A character could say one thing but mean another. 'I love you' could mean 'I hate you.' 'I am very happy' could mean 'I am the unhappiest I have ever been in my life.' 'We hope you'll take this promotion' might mean 'We hope you will resign!'

A big thing that can go wrong when we are writing dialogue is that we can make it sound as if characters A and B did know what the other was thinking before they spoke. In fact, often the very act of speaking is how the characters find out what they are thinking. Capturing this lively spontaneity of thought and speech is one of the key things to writing dialogue that works, that is not stilted and that sounds real and convincing. It is what actors call 'being in the moment'. They want to be in the moment when they act; they want to say the speech as if it is newly minted in their brains in the moment that they are speaking it. As writers, your job is to create the dialogue exactly like that.

Write with a pen or pencil on paper and while you are doing it count to 100 out loud. Do not worry about what you are writing; just write. It will be nonsense, it could well be surreal, but your task is to write *and* to keep counting. Do not stop either writing or counting out loud. You *must* do both at the same time. If you get stuck, write a number or two until you get started again. But don't just write numbers down. You know you will have done it properly if you end up with a headache!

After your first go, pause for a moment, read through your writing, then do it again. Having had one go at it you may well do it better the second time.

This is similar to an exercise that actors sometimes do in order to get inside a speech. Something by a playwright like Shakespeare which might be both complicated and very familiar, can be helped by this sort of approach. It can be hard to give a speech that everybody knows well, for instance the famous 'To be or not be' soliloquy in *Hamlet,* a sense of freshness and newness. The actor wants to convey the sense that the character Hamlet is thinking and speaking those words for the first time in his life, not simply reciting a speech that he has heard many other actors do and which he has memorised. As a writer you want to write the speech as if it is fresh and new, each word leaping into his mind as he finds voice for his thoughts. In a rehearsal the voice coach or director might well ask an actor to do a motor activity like picking up bits of paper off the floor and putting them all into a waste paper basked while reading the speech in order to take their conscious mind off the process. Instead of reading the speech with a sort of laziness that comes from being too familiar with the words or from a received sense of performance, taking the conscious mind off the activity in this way, giving it something else to do, allows the mind to access another part of itself and can release creativity. It can and does release a new energy. The actor might be so concerned to get the paper in the bin that their consciousness is divided between text and work and the words can get a new energy and a new muscularity to them. This sort of activity can release nonsense but then some creativity can be nonsense or can certainly come out of nonsense.

Here is a piece of writing by a student doing the exercise of counting to a hundred.

> *Dogs can kill mobile phones if they get their teeth stuck into them. But they have to taste like gravy, especially when they are eating Brussels sprouts with them. Sugar and steak go well with mobile phones as far as dogs are concerned. But Collies are particularly fond of cottage pies with a covering of puff pastry. Dachshunds like sausages interlaced with small helpings of doughnuts.*

The theme of this piece was set with the first word, 'dogs' and the writer tried all he could to stay on that theme even with the various nonsense things that came in as he clutched at words in order to keep writing. Here is another one:

> *Cars park all night outside our house under the trees that shed little leaves and sticky things onto the windscreens drawing flies and bugs like insects which cohabit in the summer months. Spraying them gets them off the glass but that can leave their bodies encrusted and their wings flapping in what little breeze comes along between the months of July and September.*

It sounds almost plausible, doesn't it? Again the writer has tried to stick to a theme suggested by the first word and he does get across a picture of a car stuck under trees in the summer with an encrustation of sticky leaves and insects covering it. Did you take a similar approach? If not, in what ways did yours differ? What sort of result did you get? Was the piece vaguely coherent or very disjointed? Did you resort to writing numbers down? Whatever you managed, have another go and see what you come up with this time. You might just let your start dictate the theme and try to concentrate on that sufficiently so that you write something that tries to be consistent.

Here is another example:

Time goes so quickly in the summer months. All the butterflies and bees can be time keepers if you keep on them as they do their business in the garden dipping in and out of all the exotic flowers which are dripping their nectar which bees will turn into the most delicious honey by a process unknown to man in spite of how much the scientists try to find out what it is they do in their darkened honeycomb nests in the cool of the beehives at the bottom of the garden by the fish pond darkened with heron shadows.

And after that you need to take a big breath. It goes on without a break in that long sentence to the end because one thing you seem unable to do in this exercise is think in punctuated sentences. But that is OK.

Key idea

Punctuation is something you can always correct later. You can't always generate ideas.

As always in creativity, the secret is to get something down and tailor it later. It is always easier and better to work with marks already made on paper than it is to find inspiration from a blank piece.

Here are two more pieces written by students doing the previous exercise of counting out loud to 100 while writing.

Danger. Time is running out. They're here and there is nothing we can do to stop them. If they keep advancing, we will lose. Where did they come from? What do they want? Why won't they leave us alone? Oh sod it. Let's go down to the pub. They can't touch us there, surely. 80.

This disease had got worse and worse, he could no longer no longer function properly. He still wanted to move after the last treatment but the nurse insisted he stay still. He reflected on his past life, the best bit was when he went to London and met Zena; she was the love of his life and still had a place in his heart. It was a pity he had drunk so much at the time, now he had control but he hadn't been able to stop his addictive behaviour until the fatality occurred. This changed his life forever and he was never the same again.

Using no other words other than the ones in the examples, take one of the examples above and turn it into script for two or more people.

The best way would be to read them both through; decide which one you are going to use; decide where you think you could break the sentences to make a reasonably coherent dialogue. Do not add anything. Simply break the piece where you like. Have one-word sentences if you wish, but try to write it as a dialogue exchange in a play. It does not matter what sort of play, just make sure you differentiate the characters from each other and from any action(s) you want them to perform.

For example:

```
HELEN: Aren't you sick and tired of being a
fool?

Jack puts the gun down.

JACK: Love you, babe.
```

There is no right or wrong on this but here is a possible example:

```
MARY:    Danger?
HARRY:   Time is running out.
MARY:    They're here.
HARRY:   And there is nothing we can do to stop
         them.
MARY:    If they keep advancing we will lose.
HARRY:   Where did they come from?
MARY:    What do they want?
HARRY:   Why won't they leave us alone? Silence
MARY:    Oh sod it. Let's go down to the pub.
HARRY:   They can't touch us there, surely.
MARY:    80.
```

We don't know what it is they have sighted, but something is coming towards them. It might be something alien-like; maybe we are in the middle of a scene in a science fiction piece. Do not worry about the gaps in and around a piece of script like this. It does not have to tell us everything. It only needs to make sense in the story you are writing.

Here is a version of the second one:

MAN:	This disease
WOMAN:	Had got worse
MAN:	And worse
WOMAN:	He could no longer
MAN:	No longer
WOMAN:	Function properly.
MAN:	He still wanted to move
WOMAN:	After the last treatment
MAN:	But the nurse insisted he stay still.
WOMAN:	He reflected on…
MAN:	… his past life.
WOMAN:	The best bit was when he went …
MAN:	… to London
WOMAN:	And met
MAN:	Zena.
WOMAN:	She was the love of his life.
MAN:	And still had a place in his heart.
WOMAN:	It was a pity he had drunk so much
MAN:	At the time. Now he had control
WOMAN:	But he hadn't been able to stop
MAN:	His addictive behaviour
WOMAN:	Until
MAN:	The fatality occurred.
WOMAN:	This changed his life
MAN:	For ever
WOMAN:	And he was never the same again.

Without knowing why, this developed into one of those conversations between a couple who have been together a long time. They know the story and they can start and finish each other's sentences. It has the feel of one of those clips inserted at various stages in the film *When Harry Met Sally*, where different couples talk about their relationships and how they met. Two of the interesting questions throughout this were, where to break the sentences, and what to do with the repeat of 'no longer' right at the beginning. One character could have said both 'no longers'. Repeating like that could have signalled an emotion like upset or being unable to cope or some other sort of anxiety which manifested through it being hard to get the words out. It became perfectly natural for one of this couple to echo the words of the other. What did you do with your attempt?

Focus point

Write

Take either of the two dialogue examples we have just looked at and turn them into a piece of fiction. Add supporting narrative where you feel it needs it, add words to convey the tone of voice, facial expressions, atmosphere and setting and aim at a piece of fully rendered fiction in which the dialogue plays its part.

(750 words)

At the beginning of any piece you must carefully delineate your characters. Dialogue can help you differentiate characters and make them different. Conflict is often at the heart of this and it can be good to put your characters into conflict over something. The simplest way is to have them disagree. Put them into a situation in which character A wants x and character B wants y. Make them disagree and aim at getting two points of view. To do this you will need to go into character and ask why they are different, where they are coming from, but you must differentiate your characters not only through their wants and needs but also through the way they speak.

Write

Have a look at the piece you wrote while counting to 100 and use this as the basis of a piece of fiction that includes dialogue and conflict. Once again, add supporting narrative where you feel it needs it, add words to convey the tone of voice, facial expressions, atmosphere and setting and aim at a piece of fully rendered fiction in which the dialogue plays its part.

Edit

How well does it work? You can be surprised at how well it can fit. And if it mostly fits you can always tweak the bits that don't. But be sure that they don't fit. It may be that something that seems difficult actually will be the best part of it once you can find the right context. Cut any extraneous descriptions or supporting narrative; add writing in any areas that you think needs it.

Inspiration for dialogue

As well as producing dialogue yourself in conscious or unconscious ways, you can find usable dialogue all around you in the real world.

Irving Weinman

'Writers, even beginning writers, have been speaking dialogue all their lives. Your first and best source of dialogue is your own speech.'

Listening to and recording the speech of others is where you need your notebook, which should always be with you. Here is a snatch of dialogue overheard in the street and jotted down quickly there and then in a notebook by a writer:

A teenage boy runs after a teenage girl. He catches up with her and puts his arm around her back.

'What have I done?'

She looks at him witheringly. 'Just looking at you makes me sick.'

'Cheers babe,' he says, brightly, with a smile as he peels away.

Snapshot

What are the strengths and weaknesses of this snatch of dialogue? Think about it, *cover up* the following and write your thoughts down.

Note how they do not actually talk to each other, in that she does not answer his question. We know that he has done something or at least that he thinks she thinks he has done something, because he asks her, and he sounds all innocent about it; what has he done? We know that it 'makes her sick'. Though he asks her to tell him what he has done, she knows that he knows or thinks that he should know because she is so hurt and she does not deign to tell him. Using silence and body language, she expresses feelings and her answer gets her huge hurt and anger across. He, probably wisely, decides not to pursue it there and then; he takes his arm away and says with the brightest of smiles, as if he is thanking her for a birthday present, 'Cheers, babe.' A fond greeting to go with the fond smile. How many writers would write that line and that cheery smile? He also does use silence; he leaves the subject alone and says no more and he peels brightly away. Either this is an admission that he knows what he has done or that he thinks this is not the moment in which she is going to accept and forgive. Whatever he is thinking, he decides to leave it there.

Look at the questions this snatch raises:

• Who are they?

• What has he done?

- Why is she so angry with him?
- What hope is there that she will ever forgive him?
- Will he try again?
- What price will he have to pay to win her back?
- Will he want to?

 ## Key idea

Good dialogue leaves gaps and raises questions. Writers don't always have to fill the gaps or answer the questions.

An inexperienced writer making up this dialogue would possibly spoil it by making it all too connected and also by trying to fill in the gaps, the white paper that is there. The temptation would be to tell us, the reader/viewer, what it is that lies behind it. But it is the fact that we don't know what it is about and the disconnected nature of the dialogue that makes it so good. It is what we might call the gaps between the words that, working with the words, give it meaning. The words are the tip of the iceberg; the rest of it is all there below giving it a foundation of weight and meaning. The hard bit in writing dialogue is to find and write the bit below the words; the white paper wherein these gaps lie; it is so easy to fill them in with words, words that add density to the piece and which people in real life would not say.

If we were watching this scene in a play we would be intrigued and want to go on watching. Look for dialogue with gaps in it. There might be story wanting to come out.

 ## Key idea

Good dialogue is like a fishing net; it has holes in it through which you can catch things, and through which you can let things go.

 ## Snapshot

Write ten lines of dialogue on separate pieces of paper; don't think or plan to make them fit together; just write them one after the other. For example:

- 'The rain is hammering down.'
- 'Don't talk to me about Japanese cars.'
- 'I love your perfume.'
- 'Elephants are huge.'

Do yours now.

Fold each up, put them in a pile and then pull them out of the pile one at a time until you have five exchanges of dialogue. Can you find a scene or a story around them?

For example, here is an exchange written from the examples above:

- 'The rain is hammering down.'
- 'Don't talk to me about Japanese cars.'
- 'I love your perfume.'
- 'Elephants are huge.'

It may seem like nonsense but all that first appears nonsense is not so. You would be surprised at how much of a story you could weave around these snatches of dialogue. Have a go with the ones you wrote …

Take your notebook out with you next time you are out and about and jot down anything that strikes you as potentially intriguing or usable.

When you use it, don't close it off. Remember that good dialogue does not close a situation off. That is what happens with dialogue that we call leaden or dull. It does not keep things open. It is rather like a heavy boot coming down with a thud, whereas good dialogue should float and sing. The snatches of dialogue we looked at before have gaps in them and our conscious, ordering mind might not like that but it is in the gaps that the potential story lies.

Good dialogue keeps a situation open.

Workshop: dialogue and scene

This exercise is good practice for dialogue.

Get a video or a DVD and watch a short film or TV clip with the sound off – a conflict scene if possible (and not one that you know the words of, for example, the famous dialogue in *Casablanca*), then:

1 Write the dialogue as you think it is.

2 Run the scene again and this time write it as you think it might be or want it to be.

3 Run the scene again, this time with the sound on, and listen to the actual dialogue and compare it with yours.

Note any similarities and any differences.

Summary

In this chapter you have explored what dialogue is in fiction and in scripts; looked at where dialogue comes from and explored ways of writing dialogue and the subtext. Read some books, or scripts, that are full of dialogue. See how the writers have used what the characters say to achieve characterizations, plot movement, etc. Is there anything you can learn from this?

Next step

In the next chapter we will examine what makes good and bad dialogue and also look more closely at writing scripts.

18

Writing for radio

In this chapter we will look at good and bad dialogue; how to write dialogue in scripts; writing subtext; and script layout. As our focus here, we will be using radio drama.

Dialogue in scripts vs dialogue in fiction

 Snapshot

Writing dialogue in scripts is different from writing dialogue in fiction. What do we mean by scriptwriting? Or rather, what do *you* mean by scriptwriting as opposed to fiction writing?

Cover up what is below and write your answer in your notebook.

Scriptwriting is writing, usually narrative in form (writing that tells a story), for live performance on stage, or for recorded performance on radio, television and film. It is writing for other people to perform and that brings with it special excitements and problems.

 Snapshot

Why is writing a script different from writing a story or a novel? Come up with three differences and write your answer in your notebook. When you have done that, continued with this book.

Here are some thoughts on how a novel is different from a script:

- In a book, readers can stop and start when they like and return to a specific scene or page to check details or read something again.

- In a play, the story carries on even if the listener or viewer is not sure about something or even what is going on. This means that in writing scripts, for whatever medium, you have to be very clear about the story so your audience won't get lost. Therefore you have to be clear who the characters are and how they are different from each other, what each wants, and also about plot twists and turns. You can use twists and keep information back to intrigue and surprise your audience, indeed for the most effective play you must, but you should not confuse your audience.

- Scripts are different from novels, poems and stories in another important way. In all of the latter fields, you create the work alone; scriptwriting is a collaborative process. You need others to help you realize your vision.

- You have to like white paper and collaboration if you want to write successful scripts. In writing a script you are writing a blueprint for other people to work on to bring to life. You need to put on the page only enough for them to erect the construction you have in mind. Depending on the medium you are writing for you will need actors, director, designers and technicians to realize your vision. If the collaborative process does not excite you, you would do better to stick with writing stories, novels and poems, material that in some real sense only needs to engage with the reader. Once you have written your prose or poetry, in theory all you need is a publisher and a reader. Once you have written a script, you need a lot more help and people-involvement before your words can reach an audience.

All that said, you can't group all the script media together in one lump. They each have different natures and different requirements. Writing for radio is not the same as writing for stage or screen. If you want to write a script in any of the main genres of radio, stage or film, what do you do? You do what we have said throughout this course with regard to other forms of writing. You research the field.

Key idea

Research the field and know your market.

First of all, why write for radio? As well as for the enjoyment it brings to writer and audience, there are good solid professional reasons for writing for radio.

Vincent McInerney, *Writing for Radio*

'Radio is always seeking fresh material. It is a dragon that must be fed ... more and more food must be found. The chances of a new writer breaking into radio are good.'

But, of course, as with anything, it has to be done well.

Good and bad dialogue

Workshop: script assessment

Read the following excerpt from a script:

JACK: I'm sorry but I have to go.

MARY: But I don't understand — you've always liked it here.

JACK: I know but I don't like it now.

MARY: Why?

JACK: I don't know why — I just don't.

MARY: You can't go just like that. Don't you think you ought to tell me why?

JACK: I don't know why. I don't know my own feelings.

MARY: It's her, isn't it?

JACK: I don't want to talk about it.

Think about what might be wrong with this script. Cover up what is below and write down your answers in your notebook. Look at every word and every line. When you have decided what is wrong with it, rewrite the dialogue in a way that improves it; make it better according to what you think is wrong with it. You may use stage directions, you may even rewrite it as prose if you wish, though for the sake of the exercise and the commentary that follows it would be better to keep it in script form. Edit this piece now, without looking at the version that follows below.

(200 words maximum)

What did you come up with?

From the work we have done you should be able to say that the original dialogue is all too obvious and that Jack explains himself too much. The writer has left no gaps. There are no gaps in this dialogue that could keep the situation open for us. There are no gaps that also raise questions. This is all less likely to engage our minds than a piece of dialogue doing the opposite.

Rib Davis, *Writing dialogue for scripts*

'In poor dialogue the audience is invited to take everything at face value.'

Here is the example again in another version:

MARY: *(stunned)* But — why?

JACK: *(quietly, trying to get away)* I don't … know.

MARY: *(very hurt)* You must know!

(HE MOVES TO THE DOOR, BUT SHE REACHES IT BEFORE HIM, AND SLAMS IT SHUT)

MARY: No! You can't go. I want to know, Jack — you owe it to me.

JACK: I'm sorry.

MARY: Sorry? *(hurt and angry)* After 13 years all I get is 'sorry'? *(No response)* This is our wedding anniversary. *(Beaten)* Won't you even tell me her name?

There are gaps in this dialogue that keep the situation open for us. These gaps also raise questions. They engage our minds. There is a desperate meaning underneath the exchange. The characters are speaking emotion, and we, the listeners, are feeling and hearing it. Yet the emotion is expressed through what they say combined with what they don't say and what they do, and not actually by anything explicitly stated by either character in the words they used. This is the complicated, subtle and sophisticated nature of good dialogue.

268

Note also in the above dialogue sample the use of 'stage directions' giving action, characters' names and, because this is radio, *sound*. All of these elements are clearly separated. We have use of sound in the slamming of the door. The script also gives the actor an idea of how to say the lines – for example 'quietly', 'trying to get away'.

Write

Try this exercise developed from *Writing for Radio* by Colin Haydn Evans.

Write two short scenes for one of the following two situations, conveying the bracketed meaning *without revealing the same in the words used in the dialogue*. Write it as a script with the characters' names on the left, using dialogue and stage directions.

1   A young man is telling his doting, widowed mother that he intends to emigrate to Australia. (**MEANING:** He can no longer live with her suffocating love and devotion.)
2   Jack and Jill are seen as not only the ideal married couple but the life and soul of every party. (**MEANING:** They have nothing to say to one another when alone.)

(200 words)

Edit

Take the dialogue example above between Mary and Jack, and novelize it; using all the details given, turn it into a piece of fiction. You should write the dialogue as speech and turn the other elements such as 'Mary (stunned)' into supporting narrative and description, of the kind you find in prose.

(200 words)

Script layout

How do you lay out a script? It depends what kind of script you are writing, what medium it is for.

One of the biggest worries beginning writers have with scripts is that they don't know how to lay them out correctly. When you are writing anything the best thing is to try to get it down on paper and worry about the layout later, to be creative. But if you want to submit your work to anyone then you must make it look professional. This holds true for prose and script work. In film it is particularly so. Producers and editors like a film script to be laid out in standard format because they are familiar with that format. It means they can read it easily and can estimate its running time. Both of those things are crucial.

Key idea

If you submit a script laid out in the accepted way you will be treated as a professional.

We will be able to give only the basic requirements for script layout here, but if you are serious about scriptwriting you should follow up other sources. The good news is that there are plenty of books and websites geared to showing you the correct script layout for the medium you want to write in. Some are listed at the end of the book. A really good way to learn about script layout is to read scripts. But be warned that published scripts are not always correctly laid out. They are often condensed and squashed together to save on paper. A real script has a lot more white paper. Good radio scripts are available to be downloaded on the Internet at the BBC Writersroom website – http://www.bbc.co.uk/writersroom.

What is the standard layout for a script? As we have said, it depends what medium you are writing in; they are all different. But any script, whether it is for radio, stage, film or television, can be broken up into the basic elements we have seen in the last example:

- action
- dialogue
- speakers' names.

The abiding rule is that you must type and lay out all three of these elements distinctively from each other so that it is easy to tell them apart. You must also write actions in the present tense ('Jack kisses Jill', not 'Jill was kissed by Jack').

Focus point

In scripts you must use the present, active form, not past and passive. Your script is an active ongoing story with a goal and a direction and needs to read that way.

For our purposes here we will look at the typical layout for a radio drama. Radio has its own particular needs and the best way to find out what is required is to go the BBC Writersroom site mentioned above.

Remember:

- Keep to the format.

- Lay out your script so that what you write on the page lasts for a minute of broadcast time. This will enable anyone looking at it to make a rough guess as to how long it will take to run.

Read the script example in Figure 18.1.

THE BICYCLE SURGEON

A play for radio

by

Bill Bogs

Tel: Bill Bogs
Email: info@billbogs.com
Street
Town
Postcode

Broadcast length: 30 mins

Figure 18.1 Sample radio script

Cast

SIMON HARDING	West London accent, 20 years old
CLAIRE COX	Birmingham accent, 19
KAREN COX	Midlands accent, 40s
Prison guard	Scots, 40s
Prison visitors	

MAIN ROLES in capitals; subsidiary parts/possible doubles in lower case.

SCENE 1	**EXT: BICYCLE RACK OUTSIDE UNIVERSITY STUDENTS UNION**
FX:	SOUND OF SOMEONE TRYING TO PUMP UP THE TYRES OF A BICYCLE WITH A BICYCLE PUMP. AFTER EACH SHORT BURST THEY STOP, PUFFING HARD.
CLAIRE:	Oh!
FX:	SOUND OF CLAIRE STARTING TO PUMP AGAIN.
SIMON:	What are you doing?
FX:	SOUND OF PUMPING CONTINUES.
SIMON:	Quite right, it's obvious. You're frying an egg.
FX:	CLAIRE STOPS PUMPING AND PUFFS LOUDLY.
CLAIRE:	Not now not now not now.
FX:	SOUND OF PUMPING RESUMES – ANOTHER SHORT BURST BEFORE CLAIRE STOPS PUMPING AND PUFFS LOUDLY.
CLAIRE:	(SCREAMS) Ah!
SIMON:	You got a problem?
FX:	SOUND OF CLAIRE PUMPING AGAIN.
CLAIRE:	Today of all days.
SIMON:	What's wrong with Fridays?
CLAIRE:	Will you go away?
SIMON:	I can't. My bike's beneath yours. The one with your handlebars through the spokes.
FX:	SOUND OF CLAIRE PUMPING AGAIN.
SIMON:	As fast as you pump air in this end it's coming out the other.
CLAIRE:	I can see that.
SIMON:	I might be able to help.
CLARE:	Oh, all right.

Figure 18.1 (*cont.*)

FX:	EFFORT AS HE KNEELS DOWN BESIDE THE BICYCLE.
SIMON:	Ah ha. Aha ha.
CLAIRE:	What?
SIMON:	Forceps.
CLARE:	What?
SIMON:	Hand me my bag.
CLARE:	(EFFORT) Here.
FX:	SOUND OF SIMON UNZIPPING HIS BAG.
SIMON:	Ah ha. Thought so.
CLAIRE:	What?
SIMON:	Contusions and abrasions. You've been hitting the kerb a lot.
CLARE:	What?
SIMON:	Lots of scar tissue on this wheel rim.
CLAIRE:	What are you – some kind of doctor or something?
SIMON:	I will be. In 20 years' time I shall be a famous surgeon.
CLAIRE:	Great, but I haven't got 20 years.
SIMON:	Well, here's your problem … this beauty.
FX:	SOUND OF SIMON PULLING A NAIL OUT OF THE TYRE.
SIMON:	A carpet tack.
CLAIRE:	Oh bloody hell. Useless piece of junk.
FX:	SOUND OF CLAIRE HURLING THE BICYCLE AGAINST THE BIKE RACK.
SIMON:	Temper, temper.
CLAIRE:	Why me? Why now? Why today, of all days?
SIMON:	Take my bike, if you want.

CLAIRE:	What?
SIMON:	Anyone ever told you you say what a lot?
CLAIRE:	What?
SIMON:	I said, take my bike, if you want.
CLARE:	What? Can I?
SIMON:	Sure. If it's still rideable after you just wrecked it.
CLAIRE:	Oh, I'm sorry. Did I do that? Sorry.
SIMON:	(EFFORT) The spokes are only a little twisted. A minor operation will separate them.
FX:	SOUND OF SIMON PULLING THE BICYCLES APART.
SIMON:	(THE VOICE OF A TV SOAP DOCTOR AND A CONCERNED PATIENT) 'The operation was successful. Both children are doing well.' 'Oh doctor, how can we thank you?' 'Don't thank me, Mrs Spiztburgen. I'm just doing my job. This bike will live.'
CLAIRE:	(GETTING ABOARD HIS BIKE) Thank you. Thank you.

You're an angel, (FADING) whoever you are.

FX:	SOUND OF CLAIRE CYCLING OFF AT SPEED.
SIMON:	(TO HIMSELF, WISTFULLY) Simon. The name's Simon, Claire.

SCENE 2 INT: UNDERGROUND STATION

FX:	TUBE TRAIN SCREAMS INTO THE STATION. DOORS OPEN. RUSH HOUR CROWDS DISEMBARK.
CLAIRE:	'Scuse me, 'scuse me. Let me on. Out of the way. Out of the way.
FX:	DOORS CLOSE. TRAIN PULLS AWAY.
CLAIRE:	Phew!

WE GO INTO INTERIOR MONOLOGUE AS CLAIRE HANGS ON A STRAP.

FX:	SOUND OF THE TUBE CONTINUES UNDER IN BACKGROUND.

Figure 18.1 (*cont.*)

CLAIRE:	(INTERIOR MONOLOGUE) Come on, come on. God I hope this goes well …
FX:	FADE UP TRAIN SLOWING DOWN
CLAIRE:	Oh don't slow down, slow down. Don't stop. Not today of all days … please go on, go on, go on, go on …
FX:	TRAIN PICKS UP SPEED AGAIN
CLAIRE:	Thank God …
FX:	TUBE SCREAMS INTO STATION. DOORS OPEN.

SCENE 3 HOLLOWAY PRISON RECEPTION AREA

FX:	NOISY RECPETION AREA. SOLID GATES, ELECTRIC DOORS SLAM SHUT. HUBBUB OF VOICES. WE HEAR KNOCK ON OFFICE DOOR. DOOR OPENING. THEN ALL RECEPTION AREA SOUNDS SUDDENLY STOP AS THE DOOR CLOSES.
CLAIRE:	Excuse me. Excuse me, I'm here to visit someone.
GUARD:	Name?
CLAIRE:	Mrs Cox. She's my mum.
GUARD:	Your name. Sign in. Here. Your name and who you're visiting.
CLAIRE:	Oh, I see, right, sorry.
CLAIRE:	Now where do I go?
GUARD:	Down the corridor, third on the left. Wait till you're called. Next.

The big thing to note from this script is the absolute essential for radio to *think in sound* and therefore to write in sound.

Claire Grove and Stephen Wyatt

'When you are writing something, you have to keep asking yourself the question – what are the listeners going to hear? What will they understand from what I give them?

'Radio listeners are smart. They don't need everything spelled out. They can understand nuance and they use their imagination to see and understand in their minds what your characters are about. What they cannot do is grasp information that can only be grasped visually. Or pick up details that exist only in stage directions not in sound.'

Look at the script example again while we just go over some of the details about it. It starts with the title page. This has the important details of the title of the play and your name, centred and high up the page.

Towards the bottom of the page it will bear other relevant information. Your name again with your contact details, including phone and email address.

Also, very importantly, it includes the broadcast length. You can check this pretty accurately if you follow the standard layout because that should give you a timing of a minute per page. Doing that helps you and anyone you send it to look at and get an accurate idea of the running length.

Page 2 has the cast list. List everyone who speaks, in order of speaking, with the main roles in capitals and subsidiary roles, or roles that might be doubled, in lower case. This will help a producer know how many actors they are likely to need, what age, gender and with what range of accents.

Things to note on the actual script include:

- Use one-and-a-half lines of space between all lines of dialogue.

- Double space between dialogue speeches and between dialogue and sound effects. Use FX or SFX on left-hand side of page for sound effects. Put all sound effects in capitals.

- The speeches will be numbered in the final draft, consecutively and the numbering will start again on each new page, but you do not need to number them. Numbering is to allow anyone reading and discussing the script to quickly and accurately refer to speech 1, 2, 3 or 8 on page whatever when they want to query, discuss or alter a line.

- The series of dots … ellipses they are called, indicate that the speaker has either stopped speaking or been interrupted.

The actual script begins with the caption 'Scene 1'. You should use scene headings to separate the scenes in a radio play. A simple Scene 1, Scene 2, Scene 3, etc., will do. You then need to state where the scene is opening. In this case the setting is 'the bicycle rack outside the university students union.' It is an exterior acoustic so the sound will need to reflect that. Listeners can tell just from the quality of sound whether a scene is set inside or outside. You need to tell the producer and sound engineer that. For a sound effect, use FX or SFX. This tells the producer and engineer that you want a sound effect and what it is. We open with the sound of 'someone trying to pump up the tyres of a bicycle with a bicycle pump. After each short burst they stop, puffing hard.' The listeners will hear this play open with the sound of someone pumping up a bicycle tyre in an outside space.

We then hear Claire exclaim and start pumping again. Note that the lines of dialogue are separated from each other clearly; we know clearly when Claire speaks and when Simon speaks.

The first scene introduces the characters. Claire is trying to go somewhere but has a problem with her bicycle. Simon offers to help and confirms the puncture. He then offers her his bicycle and she accepts it readily and pedals off. She does not even know his name but he knows hers; he says it wistfully to himself as she cycles away.

This should signal to the listeners that he has seen her before and is keen on her. She does not appear to have noticed him before. The potential tenor of their relationship has been set up. Note that the actor direction, 'wistfully' is the only suggestion to an actor of how to say a line. It is not necessary to put things in like 'eagerly', or 'angrily', or 'sadly' when you write a line. You do not need to tell an actor how to say it, in the main. The temptation to do so when you are starting out is very strong because you are not confident enough in your own writing or confident that other people will see what you are trying to say. Therefore you lack the confidence in the actors that they will find the way to say the line. They may not find the way you wanted but they will almost always find a way that works. It was felt important to put in 'wistfully' here, to signal to the listeners that he knew her name, even though she did not know his and that he was a least a little interested in her.

We then move rapidly from the exterior acoustic of the bicycle rack to Scene 2, and the interior acoustic of the underground station with the noise of train and doors and Claire trying to get on the train. Once aboard we go into Claire's interior monologue – again something that will be done with sound. Signalling this to the sound engineer will be enough for them to get the right acoustic. Finally, in this extract, we change location again by sound, cutting to the Holloway Prison reception area for Scene 3.

Looking at this scene raises a point to consider. We know we have changed location from the train; the hubbub and noises of clanging doors tells us that, but do we know where? Sound effects can be used to signal scene changes but they are not enough on their own. They can be ambiguous. The script tells us this is the reception area of the prison, but would the sounds tell us that? Might it not be a hospital? Dialogue is needed to point up the exact location. Look at the dialogue in this scene. Does it point up where we are? From it we learn that Claire is visiting her Mum but is there anything about it that tells us this is a prison and not a hospital? The answer is no, but the writer here is deliberately delaying this revelation until the next scene where Claire sits opposite her mum and discusses what it is like being locked away. But in general the point holds; use sound and dialogue to confirm a scene change. Radio writers get very skilled at this. Lines like, 'see you down the pub' *Fade out* allied to the sound of (*fade up*) bar chatter, clinking glasses and a barman pulling pints 'what'll you have, Dave?' tell us immediately that we have switched from a tranquil place to a noisy pub. Those obvious sorts of lines become almost unheard by the listeners too. They are just grateful to be led from place to place and not left in a confused sound world limbo.

By this stage, the play *The Bicycle Surgeon* is well on the move and hopefully any listeners who tune in regularly to the slot in which the play is being broadcast will be sufficiently interested and intrigued enough to stay with it.

Focus point

One of the easiest things to do with radio is to turn it off or change station; you do not want them to do that in the middle of your play. If you intrigue and interest them you have a chance of keeping them with you.

How do you get the listener's attention? And how do you hold it?

Much of the advice already given in other fields about character and plot and dialogue applies equally in radio, though there are some special considerations with regard to radio. If you are writing a radio play, make sure that you:

- **Tell a good story.** As with the other areas of writing that we have stressed in this book, radio drama needs a good narrative. Whether you are writing something serious, something funny, or a deeply personal piece, it is the strong storyline that will keep your audience listening. But don't make the story too complicated with too many themes, characters and plotlines.

- **Really get to know your characters.** Each will have their own individual ways of speaking, full of mannerisms of phrasing and vocabulary. The danger is to have all your characters speaking like you.

- **Avoid your characters telling each other information they already know.** You have to find other ways of furthering the plot rather than having characters tell each other things.

- **Use the four elements of radio drama:** speech, sound, music and silence, but keep it simple. If your storyline is strong and your characters interesting and lively then you will not need to bolster it with music or hundreds of sound effects cues.

- **Vary your scenes:** have a quick scene followed by a slow scene, short by long, interior acoustic by exterior. Don't have all your scenes the same length taking place in the one location or have too many exterior scenes one after the other as it is hard on radio to make them all sound different. Vary the scenes themselves and where you set them.

Key idea

For radio, you must read radio plays but you must also listen, listen, listen. If you want to write for radio, listen to it. Tune in to 'Play of the Week' on BBC World Service or listen via their website.

Likewise, make sure that you **don't**:

- use scene headings like 'Act 1 scene i'. They belong in stage plays. Radio plays have sequences which might be one line long or 20 lines long. You can't say things like 'Bill, Carol, Pete and Jake all gathered round a roaring fire in the local pub.' The only way to establish the presence of characters on radio is to have them speak.

- have too many characters in a scene either or the listener loses the ability to tell who is who.

- give the characters names that are too similar. Jake and Jack, Jill and Janet get hard to keep apart in the mind.

- put in too many stage directions telling the actor how to say a line.

- fail to get the intention or emotion in the line of dialogue.

- overcrowd the piece with sound effects; use them sparingly and well.

Key idea

Think in sound.

Snapshot

Take this simple exchange of dialogue:

```
MEL: What time do you call this?

CAL: Not late.

MEL: Too late.
```

What sounds would you, could you, add to this to create the setting – inside a football stadium? A swimming baths? On an aeroplane or a train? Try a range of different sounds with the dialogue and see how it changes or works with the dialogue. Try the most clichéd you can imagine and then try and go off the wall. What is the most surprising and/or effective setting you can create?

A good deal of writing for radio, as for television and film, is adapted from other, existing material. We will now try a simplified form of adaptation here using material you are already familiar with.

Write

Look again at the extract in Chapter 11 about Madge and Molly and the horse trial. In that chapter you were asked to make a scene or two of the material, to dramatize it and add dialogue. Take either the original or the scene you developed from it and adapt it for a simplified radio play. Concentrate on the dialogue and the element of sound, on what we need to hear in order to realize the setting, characters and story. Lay it out correctly and write as if it was the beginning of a radio play. Don't worry about where it is going. Just use the material you have and adapt it for the medium.

(200 words)

You could follow this up by taking a favourite short story and seeking to adapt that too.

Write

Continue the story of Claire and Simon and, to practise layout, make sure that you lay it out in the correct way. You might want to take the story to a conclusion or just write another five or six scenes of a similar length to the example, developing it further. Ask yourself what questions the extract raises and see what clues there are for further development.

Ideas might be:

- Simon is clearly attracted to Claire. Will she ever notice him?
- How will Claire explain the fact that her mother is in prison?

Why is her mother in prison? Before you begin writing, remind yourself to think in sound; this is radio.

(750 words)

Workshop: write a short radio play

Take any of the characters and ideas you have developed in this course and write a short script for radio, in two or three scenes. Think about three of the four basic elements – speech, sound effects, and silence. We will ignore the fourth element, music, for this exercise but be clear how you will mix the other three elements to create a 'sound picture' in each scene. And remember that in radio you do not just need sound – you need *significant* sound. Sound that is specific and has a point; that tells us something about place or character.

Try to have at least two locations that are different from the other; perhaps one interior location and one exterior. Think about the different 'sound worlds' in those locations.

Have two characters in conflict.

Here are some ideas:

- a couple washing up after a party
- a boss and employee
- a head teacher and pupil
- policeman and suspect.

Ask yourself if a scene will be enhanced by having a pause between speeches to add to the dramatic effect.

(750 words)

Edit: test your story

When you have finished, cover up the character names on the left-hand side of the page and read the dialogue. Can you tell who they are from what they say? If not, if they sound alike, revise the dialogue so that you can.

Summary

In this chapter you have looked at good and bad dialogue, writing scripts, writing subtext and writing for radio. Building on this foundation we will go on to explore writing scripts in other fields. But if you are interested in seriously writing for radio, there is much more to be said and learned than in this brief introduction. Get yourself a book that specializes in the field; there are some suggestions in the back of this book.

Next step

In the next chapter we will consider the joys and challenges of writing for the stage.

19

Writing for the stage

In this chapter you will look at writing for the stage, including the stage as a physical space; stage script layout; entrances and exits; how to frame an entrance; set description; conflict.

Stage play format – basics

There is no accepted way of laying out stage plays so you are free to take your choice on that, but remember the previous advice:

- Keep the characters' names apart, and separate what people say from what they do. Separate characters, dialogue and action so that anyone reading it can follow what is happening.
- Make clear and separate the different characters – who is speaking when and who is performing an action.

 Key idea

Theatre is both a visual and a language-based medium. What the audience sees and hears are vital and so is the space. For theatre. think visual, think language and think action in physical space.

When you write for the stage it can help to think of a stage area you know, preferably in which you have worked or on which you have seen plays performed. If you have not seen plays in a theatre and want to write for the stage, go and see some. The more strongly you visualize the physical nature of that space the more chance your writing has of working in a theatre space.

You will find that the space will be one of these three basic forms:

- proscenium
- thrust
- arena.

Traverse is also used, but is less common.

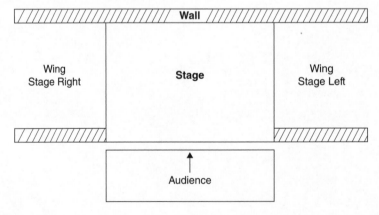

Figure 19.1

Proscenium – commonly found in large commercial theatres and probably most people's experience of a theatre space. It is characterized by a large rectangular arch that frames the front of the stage, like a 'picture frame'. The scenery surrounds the acting area on all sides except the side facing the audience. They watch the play through this open frame. Entrances and exits are usually made from the sides of the stage, the wings.

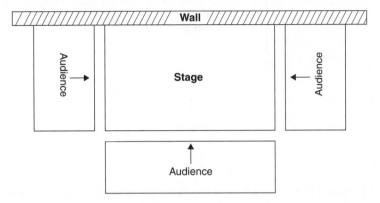

Figure 19.2

Thrust – this thrusts out into the audience with the audience on three sides. Entrances are made from the back or through aisles up to the front or sides. It can make for dramatic and involving theatre with the audience feeling they are right there in the action. It also limits the amount of set that can be used because any set put on the sides would block the audience's view. Designers tend to go for low couches and benches.

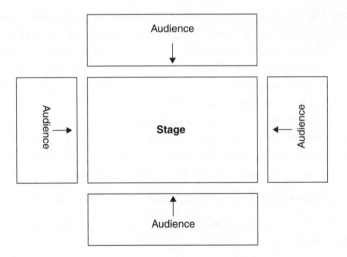

Figure 19.3

Arena (or theatre in the round) – the stage is usually in the centre of the theatre space and entrances made from any aisle or corner. This is a popular form of staging when a play is put on in a space not specifically designed for theatre; for example, a school hall, sports hall, church hall or a barn.

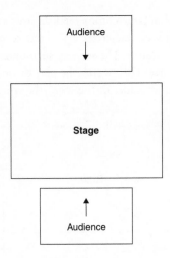

Figure 19.4

Traverse – a bit like a tennis match with the audience on the two longest sides, leaving some room for a set either end but nothing that can block entrances and exits which have to be at those ends. This can make staging difficult, which is possibly why it is not used as much, but for variety the actors can generally go off at one end, run around the back to come on at the other end.

Setting the play

George Bernard Shaw has the most elaborate scene and set descriptions. They border on the novelistic. Shaw wasn't the only one. A contemporary of his, Arthur Wing Pinero opens his wonderful affectionate play about actors and the theatre, *Trelawney of the Wells*, with a detailed description of 'a sitting room on the first floor of a respectable lodging house.' He tells us the room has two sash-windows with Venetian blinds that give 'a view of houses on the other side of the street'. He tells us that 'over the fireplace is a mirror: on each side there is a sideboard-cupboard. On the left is a door, and a landing is seen outside. Between the windows stand a cottage piano and a piano stool'. And so on in great detail, culminating with 'The furniture, curtains, and carpets are worn, but everything is clean and well-kept. The light is that of an afternoon early in summer.'

Many, but not all plays of that period had similarly detailed set descriptions.

Oscar Wilde's *The Importance of Being Earnest*, published in the same year as *Trelawney of the Wells*, opens a little more sparsely:

```
FIRST ACT

SCENE — Morning room in Algernon's flat in
Half Moon Street. The room is luxuriously and
artistically furnished. The sound of a piano is
heard in the adjoining room.
```

Fashions have changed now and though you do still get detailed set descriptions the style is often for something sparer and less detailed.

In what must have been quite novel and striking at the time, Thornton Wilder in his 1938 play *Our Town* has a set described thus:

```
No curtain. No scenery. The audience, arriving,
sees an empty stage in half-light.
```

Samuel Beckett's *Waiting for Godot* from 1955 is famous for many things including its pared down, minimalist style which includes the set description:

```
A country road. A tree. Evening.
```

Almost one hundred years after Pinero, compare Caryl Churchill's description of a table set for a meal in her play *Top Girls* of 1982:

```
Restaurant. Table set for dinner with tablecloth.
Six places.
```

There are contemporary writers of plays who write in more detail. In many respects it depends on the play but clearly things have changed since the elaborate, detailed, naturalistic descriptions of the Victorian period. Whatever style you adopt, you need a set description to make clear your intentions to the director and designer. They may choose to do something entirely different but you need to tell them what you want because this will help inform them of your vision for the piece. They, like the actors, will be looking at the text you give them for clues as to how you have shaped and formed the piece in your imagination. They need these clues to form the piece in their imaginations and in the imaginations of the audiences.

Key idea

Theatre is an imagination business. It takes place in the mind.

Write

Think of three different characters. Use some of the characters you have created in previous exercises if you wish. Think about the characters in terms of the place in which they most characteristically belong and write this place as a setting for a play. Write *three* 200-word descriptions and make each one different. Write one as if for a nineteenth-century play and two for a more contemporary play. Be economical with the description and only put into it things that will be used in the drama.

(3 x 200 words)

Don't bump into the furniture

Alan Ayckbourn

'Don't bring them on without a reason.'

An often quoted actor's line about the actor's job in theatre is that they have to learn the lines and not bump into the furniture. It was said by a deprecating actor as an ironic comment on their craft but, if it is in some way true for actors, then a large part of the playwright's job is to find reasons to get people on and off the stage successfully, which means plausibly.

 ## Key idea

If you want to write for the stage you must know what a stage is like and how it works for actors, director and audience.

Britain's greatest playwright, Shakespeare, knew how a theatre worked. He was an actor himself and he knew what actors needed in terms of a script: good characters, fine speeches that also left room for 'business' and good practical reasons (as well as lines of dialogue) to get them on and off stage. Characters are always entering and leaving scenes in a play and one of the fundamentally practical things a writer needs to do is to write believable reasons and lines that will get them into a scene and take them off again. Shakespeare's plays are full of entrance and exit lines. In Act 1, Scene i of *As You Like It*, Oliver, hoping to see an end to his young brother Orlando, arranges with the wrestler, Charles, that in the upcoming wrestling bout, Charles will break his 'neck as his finger'. When Charles has gone, Oliver confesses to the audience,

OLIVER: 'I hope I shall see an end of him, for my
           soul — yet I know not why — hates nothing
           more than he.'

He then tells the audience that his next task is to bring the gentle, noble Orlando up to a state of mind where he will fight Charles and he has an exit line to take him off stage which is –

OLIVER: 'Nothing remains but that I kindle the boy
           hither, which now I'll go about.'

'Which now I'll go about.' He tells us the audience what he has to do and that he is going off to do it. In this way he keeps the audience in the picture, keeps the story moving and gives himself a way of getting off stage successfully and plausibly.

Immediately after his exit Rosalind and Celia enter.

CELIA: I pray thee, Rosalind, sweet my coz, be
           merry.

ROSALIND: Dear Celia, I show more mirth than I
          am mistress of, and would yet you were
          merrier.

Note their entrance lines. They come on talking; actors like to do this. A line of dialogue helps to get them from the side of the stage to the middle of the stage more easily than silence. We also learn who both these women are because they use each other's names. This may seem an artificial device if you look at it coldly because we don't use the names of people we know so much when we are talking to them. We don't say, 'Harry, you know

I hate Parma ham.' But in theatre it is so necessary to use names, certainly the first time a character comes on. It is essential to do this for an audience because they need to know who has just come on and what their relationship is to the story. Why have the audience sitting there puzzling about such matters and getting annoyed when you want them to be getting into the characters and the story? Using characters' names like this becomes invisible. It is useful information that the audience registers; they then settle down to take in the rest of it.

At the end of the act, Act 1, Scene iii, after Celia and Rosalind have decided to run away to the forest to join Rosalind's banished father, Celia says,

```
CELIA: Now go in we content
       To liberty, and not to banishment.
```

There is their exit line. Contemporary plays are more naturalistic and perhaps don't signpost as obviously as this, but one of the dramatist's main jobs remains to get characters and off the stage successfully.

Though theatre has changed since the time of Shakespeare, you still need to visualize a stage when writing because this will help you construct your script with plausible entrances and exits for the characters and the actors playing those characters. If you do not get this into your script, should you be lucky enough to get your script into the hands of actors and director, these things will soon be found out. Actors and director pour over your script because that is what you are giving them to perform. They have to pour over it; it is the tool you are giving them to bring your brainchild to life. They look at it for clues and answers to find out what it is you intended. Actors are very concerned about entrances and exits. Among things they want to know when grappling with a part are:

- Where have I come from and what have I been doing there?

- Where am I going when I come on stage, or when I leave it?

- Why am I going there?

- What exactly do I want to achieve?

You, as the writer, need to help them find answers to this in the script. You may not explicitly state all of it but there need to be clues that can be followed and fleshed out. Actors are hungry for reasons; give them a plausible reason and they will make it work.

Other questions actors ask are:

- What is preventing me from achieving what I want?

- How do I have to change other characters in order to achieve this?

- What shall I do to make them change?

These again are important elements that you must get into your script; perhaps not always explicitly, but present in such a way that actors and director can mine them in the rehearsal room.

Alan Ayckbourn

'Don't let them go off without a reason.'

Snapshot

Get hold of some stage play scripts. You can buy published plays from a good bookshop; Nick Heron Books, Josef Weinberger and Samuel French specialize in publishing plays. Your local library should have a good stock too. It does not have to be the latest play. It is better if you look at a selection, from the Greeks to Shakespeare and up to the present day. Get a selection, half a dozen and read them not for the story of character, but simply for clues as to how writers have handled entrances and exits. Find sections in the play when characters enter and exit and try and see what preparation has been done in the script to get a character either on or off the stage. The beginnings of plays are always a good place to start because people have to enter, or the play will not begin, and these characters usually introduce other characters to us, but characters come and go throughout a play so dip into a script where there are significant entrances and exits and focus your attention there. Make notes and keep a record of the plays you read and the entrances and exits you spot and any techniques that are common.

Key idea

One of the basics in playwriting is getting characters on and off stage. Actors need to 'frame' their entrances; they need to make them important or noticeable; you need to help them by putting this in your script.

You can help actors 'frame' their entrances in several ways – have a character enter doing something significant; have them do something that is characteristic of them or that will be significant for the story as it unfolds.

They may be eating, singing, running, arguing with someone, kicking a football. The more energy they come on with the more they will engage the audience and ask questions in the audience's minds.

Sound can prepare an entrance – the sound of a car pulling up, keys in a lock, off-stage voices or singing. The audience know someone is about to come on and their anticipation rises.

If you have characters already on stage, they can prepare for the arrival of a new character by doing something such as hiding; or putting something away that they do not want to be found.

The person on stage may be busy and preoccupied and not see the entrance of another character; the arrival surprises them and there is a moment of recognition. The audience wonder what the relationship is between these characters. The new character has to do something to attract their attention.

The characters on stage would talk about the impending arrival of another character. A good deal of nineteenth-century plays do this. Just keep in mind that an entrance is an important moment for an actor and you should build it into your script.

Immediately following the set description of *Trelawney of the Wells*, the first characters are introduced this way –

> MRS MOSSOP — a portly middle-aged Jewish lady,
> elaborately attired — is laying the tablecloth.
>
> ABLETT enters hastily, divesting himself of his
> coat as he does so. He is dressed in rusty black
> for 'waiting'.

We see Mrs Mossop doing something significant – laying the table. From this we would guess that she lives there and is preparing to entertain.

Ablett's entrance is hasty; he is in a rush because he is late. He has rushed there from another job and he is doing something significant; taking his coat off so that we see underneath he is wearing 'rusty black' for 'waiting.' Ablett is not a professional waiter, he is 'filling in'. This tells us something about the pretensions of the people we are about to meet and of the event which is about to take place. Character and story are already beginning to work their magic.

Questions are raised about both of these characters who are in the middle of doing something and answered almost immediately when we discover Mrs Mossop is laying the table for a farewell 'cold collation' for one of her actor lodgers and Ablett is a grocer hired for the occasion to add a little poshness and wait at table. Ablett and Mrs Mossop then proceed to use another of the traditional framing device; they set us up for both story and the rest of the characters by discussing them and their situation so that when they arrive, we are prepared for them.

Write

Take one of the exercises we have looked at so far in this book, perhaps the last exercise in Chapter 18. To remind you, the suggestion there was for you to write about:

- a couple washing up after a party
- a boss and employee
- a head teacher and pupil
- policeman and suspect.

Reread the scene as you wrote it and, using one or two of the techniques you have observed other writers use in their plays, prepare by the introduction of new dialogue and action into the scene for a new character or characters to enter and then introduce this character or characters into the scene. Think long and hard about why they need to come on. And this need has to be their need as a character not your need as a writer, i.e. because you need a new character to

pep a scene up. Remember too, to have the new characters doing something significant as they enter. Remember that the scene is no longer for radio, but for the stage.

(200 words)

Now take the same characters and write whatever additional dialogue or action is needed to allow one character to exit plausibly. Again give them good motivation, a good reason for going.

(200 words)

Conflict

Conflict is one of the staples of theatre writing (as it is of much other creative writing, as we have already said).

 Lajos Egri

'All competitive sports are conflict. A saloon brawl is conflict. A fight for supremacy among men or nations is conflict. Every manifestation of life, from birth to death, is conflict. There are more complex forms of conflict, but they all rise on this simple basis: attack and counter attack. We see real, rising conflict when the antagonists are evenly matched.'

In the following exercise, keep in mind any stage space you know well and write a scene for a stage play. Remember that you are writing for a physical and visual medium. All good plays have a strong visual life as well as good dialogue. Remember that you can do a lot with characters without them necessarily speaking; think of the way they move, what they look like, think of the objects they relate to. Ask whether and how they touch other characters. Keep 'show not tell' in mind.

Workshop: direct two-party conflict

Put the characters of MAX and NANCY in a conflict situation and, using dialogue and stage directions, try to get them from the first line of dialogue to the last line. Each character should have 36 lines. Try to keep both characters strong, and the speeches short. Use stage directions but keep them simple and to the point. Do not change location. Keep them in the same physical space.

Decide who your characters are (this would be important normally as it is good to write with a name, even if it is a 'working name'; but you have been given the names in this case).

Consider:

- age
- background
- relationship to each other
- motivation (what they want)
- what they are in conflict over.

Describe the set (briefly):

- where they are

- what the audience sees on stage.

Anything mentioned in the set should be used in the play.

Start with the following line of dialogue:

`MAX:  Did I ever tell you about Sioux?`

Then continue with the dialogue between Nancy and Max until they have had their 36 speeches, ending with:

`MAX:  Right now the Lido seems like one great idea.`

(750 words maximum)

Here is an example done from this exercise. Because this is for stage, it will include stage directions that would work on stage.

The play is entitled 'The Dinner Party'. The CAST is:

MAX BARKER – A department store manager, 40s

NANCY BARKER – His wife, a sports physiotherapist, 40s

Act 1 Scene 1

	Front room of the Barker house, a semi-detached house in Chiswick, West London. There is a sofa centre, heavily cushioned armchairs and a window upstage centre masked by floor length nets. A door left leads to the hall, another door right leads to the kitchen.
	MAX discovered on, sitting on the sofa.
	Enter NANCY, wearing an apron, from the kitchen. She goes and peers through the window.
MAX:	Did I ever tell you about Sioux?
NANCY:	I hope they're not late.
	NANCY moves about the room adjusting the position of things like cushions and nick- knacks a minuscule amount.
MAX:	You'll wear the carpet out.
NANCY:	You did remember to give them directions?
MAX:	He's got sat nav.
NANCY:	Why are they so late?
MAX:	He's got sat nav.
NANCY:	It's fashionable, I suppose.
MAX:	Did I ever tell you?
NANCY:	What time did you say?

MAX:	7.30 for eight.
NANCY:	7.30 for eight? Why not say 7.30 for 7.30? You told me 7.30.
MAX:	I meant 7.30.
NANCY:	So why say 7.30 for eight?
MAX:	I didn't. I said that you'd said 7.30 for 7.30 and he said, right then, 7.30 for eight.
NANCY:	You're hopeless.
MAX:	You're wonderful.
NANCY:	Feet!
	As if scalded, MAX immediately takes his feet off the sofa.
MAX:	Sit down a minute? I want …
NANCY:	Nuts!
MAX:	What?
NANCY:	Where are the nuts?
	NANCY speeds out to the kitchen.
NANCY:	The one thing I asked you to do.
MAX:	(*to himself*) Want anything doing, do it yourself.
NANCY:	(*off*) Want anything doing, do it yourself.
	MAX automatically slips his feet back up on the sofa.
MAX:	I started to do it and then you asked me to polish the TV.
NANCY:	(*returning*) They're your guests.
	NANCY returns with a bowl of nuts
	MAX quickly takes his feet off the cushions.
NANCY:	She is, anyway.
MAX:	Listen, I never told you …
NANCY:	He's a pervert.
MAX:	What?
NANCY:	He is.
MAX:	A pervert? Why do you say that? You don't know him.
NANCY:	He rang up.
MAX:	And?
NANCY:	He breathed.
MAX:	Well, of course he did. We all breathe.
NANCY:	Not like that.
MAX:	Like what?
NANCY:	(*Does heavy breathing*) Mr Cox doesn't breathe like that.
MAX:	I don't know anybody who breathes like that. Except your uncle Gerald and he smokes 40 a day.

NANCY:	He knows better.
MAX:	Your uncle Gerald?
NANCY:	Mr Cox.
MAX:	Isn't Mr Cox dead?
NANCY:	Nor the vicar.
MAX:	You don't know the vicar. Unless he calls when I'm out.
NANCY:	Obscene caller in your own home.
MAX:	The vicar?
NANCY:	Why she married him, I don't know.
MAX:	The vicar?
NANCY:	Ha-ha!
MAX:	You can't say these things. You don't know her either. You don't know anything about either of them. That's why I thought I'd invite them round. So we could both get to know them. Seemed a good idea, at the time.
NANCY:	The hors d'oeuvres are spoiling.
MAX:	I thought you were doing cold salmon for starters.
NANCY:	The lettuce is curling.
MAX:	I never told you, did I? About Sioux?
NANCY:	What kind of woman spells her name like that anyway? Is she a Red Indian?
MAX:	I think it is more politically correct to call them Native American Indians now. And you know she's not. But I didn't tell you about …
NANCY:	Venice.
MAX:	Venice.
NANCY:	You told me.
MAX:	Not about the Lido …
NANCY:	You never took me to Venice.
MAX:	I never took her. We went … to a conference.
NANCY:	You promised you'd take me.
MAX:	Did I?
NANCY:	You never take me anywhere anymore.
MAX:	You never want to go anywhere anymore.
NANCY:	How would you know anymore?
MAX:	Well do you? Where do you want to go?
NANCY:	Crisps! Crisps!
MAX:	Crisps?

NANCY:	Where are the crisps?

NANCY speeds out to the kitchen

NANCY:	The one thing I asked you.
MAX:	(*to himself*) Want anything doing, do it yourself.
NANCY:	(*off*) Want anything doing, do it yourself.

MAX automatically slips his feet back up on the sofa

MAX:	(*under his breath*) Right now the Lido seems like one great idea.

This is a fairly long scene, certainly longer than the average television or film scene. It can be this length because it is for the stage. It takes place in one place; uncommon for television or film but very common for stage, given the physical nature and special constraints of theatre writing. You can see that a relationship has developed quite nicely here. We learn a lot about the two of them from the way they speak to each other; from what they say and from what they don't say. There seems to be a subtext of conflict going on beneath the surface to do with the woman named Sioux. Max appears to want, or maybe he does not really want, to tell Nancy what happened in Venice. He never quite gets round to it. Nancy in some ways seems already to know and yet does not want to know any more from the way she deflects a lot of what he says. And from the way she brings the subject back to the expected guests. There is a quite a lot of 'business'; for her; this is what actors call the physical things they do in scenes. She moves about the room straightening things, checks the window and flies in and out of the kitchen with crisps and nuts. On top of all this we have the dialogue exchanges about nuts and crisps and obscene callers. Is this all helping the characters not to talk about the bigger issues? Somehow this dialogue seems right because characters do not talk in neat statements. Character B does not neatly answer the statement that character A has made or answer the question that A has posed. They talk across each other, tangentially like this, each driven by their own desires and motivations and each using their own combination of body language, silence and words to communicate.

- A good deal of stage conflict can be called direct two-party conflict. This is where two parties are directly in conflict with each other. The Max and Nancy scene is such a scene. But if a third party is introduced it can develop the conflict considerably. The adversarial court system is based on this two and three-party conflict. Defence versus prosecution are in direct two-party conflict; the third force of the judge changes this from direct two-party conflict to three-party modulated conflict. The judge's role is to hold the balance between the two warring parties and to *modulate* their conflict. This is a device that has been used in many plays and films of the courtroom drama genre. It is a structure that can provide conflict and tension; the staples of drama. The judge in Bertolt Brecht's *The Caucasian Chalk Circle* is a stage embodiment of this mediating force in a three-party conflict.

In two-handers (plays with two parts) the relations between characters and the options for scenes are limited to:

- A – B on stage
- A on stage
- B on stage.

If you introduce a third party you increase the options a good deal to:

- A – B on stage
- A – C on stage
- B – C on stage
- A – B – C on stage
- A on stage
- B on stage
- C on stage.

Much of Greek drama functions within those limitations very successfully. In terms of conflict you can have:

a two-party direct conflict A vs B

b three-party modulated conflict A vs B, appealing to C (courtroom trial model)

c two-party direct conflict A/B vs C

d three-party modulated conflict A vs C, appealing to B

e two-party direct conflict B/C vs A

f three-party modulated conflict C vs B, appealing to A

g two-party direct conflict A/C vs B

h the scene can either be resolved or left open.

You can see that the permutations are increased and this increases the potential for variety in the drama.

Write

Introduce a third party into the scene with Max and Nancy – either Sioux or her partner. Try to follow the pattern above and develop the scene.

(750 words)

Edit

When you have done a draft read it over and edit it. Cut out anything extraneous either in the dialogue or the scene setting or the 'business' you have created for the actors to do. Make the script as condensed and concise as you can get it.

Summary

In this chapter you have explored writing for stage, how to describe a set, how to frame a character's entrance, two-party direct conflict and three-party modulated conflict. There is so much more to play writing than this. This has been a necessary brief introduction. If this is an area in which you want to specialize, get a book or two devoted to the subject and see how they tackle the entire process. Above all, go to the theatre and read plays.

Next step

The next step will be to look at the most dominant, populated and lucrative mode of writing today, that of screenwriting.

20

Screenwriting – the visual language of film

In this chapter you will look at: writing for the screen; basic terminology, format and layout of a screenplay.

What is a script? What is a screenplay?

Robert Edgar-Hunt, John Marland and James Richards

'A screenplay is an unusual document. Typically, it comprises around 120 pages – wide-margined and sparsely typed. There isn't a great deal to show for all the effort the writer has poured into it, and few (if any) people will read it for its own sake. A script really exists to enable something else to happen. It is a blueprint from which something bigger and more spectacular is made.'

Screenwriting is such a technical industry that it is worth clarifying a few terms at the outset:

- 'Screenplay' means a script of any length.
- If the film is short, it might be abbreviated to 'horror short' or 'sci-fi short'.
- 'Script' and not 'screenplay' is likely to be used to refer to most television pieces, for example sitcoms, soaps and series.
- 'Teleplay' can be used to differentiate a screenplay from a script for television, but this is mainly in the United States.

There can be a tendency in teaching screenwriting to dwell on the technical aspects, such as terminology and layout. This is because it is in some ways easier to teach these. You can lay down clear guidelines as to what a screenplay should look like because there are industry standard practices. It is something that is easy to get wrong but it is also easy to correct and to teach. It is not so easy to teach whatever it is that makes one screenplay lift off the page where so many others sink. It is easy to teach the idea of writing good dialogue and some of the techniques involved, but not easy to teach someone to write the crackling dialogue of a great theatre piece or a terrific screenplay. But then we are talking about inspiration and talent here.

Key idea

A teacher cannot teach inspiration: but a teacher can hope to inspire. It is the same as planting a garden. You can only plant the seeds in the best possible place, and water and tend them; you cannot make them grow.

Format and layout

Technical things are important in screen writing. Format and layout are arguably far more important here than in writing fiction and we ought not to go any further without looking at formatting and layout.

Without going over a few basics and looking at an example of a screenplay page or two, it will be hard to ask you to take ideas and turn them into screenplay form. But you might ask: Why should I format my screenplay? Think about this, *cover up* what is below, and write your answer in your notebook.

Uncover what is below.

Submitting a screenplay to someone is like a job interview; you want to make a good first impression. A screenplay also needs to be formatted correctly so it is easy to read. You are not just writing for yourself and it is not just you who will be reading it. It needs to be easy to read for the cast and crew. It also gives you an idea of how long your script is in screen time.

Beyond the point of having fun or for education, of learning how to do it, there is little point in writing a film or television script. Whereas you don't need professional help to have a poem, story or novel read you do need professional input in order to get a script made. Also, film and television are such expensive and technical mediums that there is little point in trying to write scripts unless you want to get them made or to use them as calling cards to get future work. In either case you need to follow the rules. If you do not, you will not be taken seriously. It is very important in writing for the screen, whether it is film or television that attracts you that you find out what guidelines there are to follow and to follow them. We will cover some of the basic ones here but you can find detailed guidelines for both film and television in many published books on screenwriting and on various websites. If you are really serious about screenwriting then look them up. When it comes to formatting your scripts, the easiest way to do it is to write it using script formatting software. Programs like Final Draft which you can purchase from shops and online (http://www.finaldraft.com) and Celtx, which you can download free from the Internet (www.celtx.com) are both good. Rough Draft is another free option (http://www.softpedia.com).

But you can also do quite well with an ordinary computer and word processor, though it takes a bit more fussing over, by following the guidelines in the main books written on screenwriting.

The first thing to say is that a screenplay is no different from other scripts in some ways; in other ways, it is fundamentally different. The ways it is similar are that in a screenplay you must:

- differentiate the components
- use only one side of the paper
- leave wide borders around the script.

The ways it is different are that in a screenplay you must use:

- **Scene:** screenplays are divided into scenes. Individual scenes vary in length but are generally on the short side.
- **Slug line:** each scene is headed by what is called a slug line or scene heading. For example: EXT. HOSPITAL. DAY. This tells us whether the scene is inside (INT. for

interior) or out (EXT. for exterior). It is outside in this case. It tells us where it is (the hospital) and when it is (this time it is day). When we go inside the hospital the slug line will be INT. HOSPITAL. DAY.

- **Scene direction:** this contains descriptions of the character's actions, what he or she does, and events that occur in the story. Scene directions are always written in the present tense with active verbs, and characters' names are usually capitalized the first time you introduce them in scene direction, and after that in lower case. For example: 'SUSAN turns her head quickly. The ambulance speeds to a halt by the emergency doors. The orderly flings the doors open. Susan jumps in.'

- **Character cue:** this is the name of the character who speaks. It is always capitalized and always centred above their speech.

- **Actor direction:** this is put in brackets under the name of the character. It is used to describe the way a character speaks or to whom they speak. Actors don't like them, preferring to find their own meaning. But they can help if the real meaning intended goes against what appears to be the meaning on the surface.

- **Dialogue:** what the characters say. Dialogue in screenplays is short.

- **Avoid long speeches:** avoid characters talking in exposition, telling other characters things they should know already just because you want to get information across to the viewer. Think pictures, think 'show not tell'.

- **Camera shots, camera angles:** *do not* put these in your screenplay. Leave them to the director. If you want to get a particular shot across, get it into the scene with scene description. *Show* the director what you want in the way you write the scene; don't *tell* him/her how to shoot it. He/she will resent it.

Keeping to the above tips and following this layout can help you and anyone else time your script.

 Focus point

There is an industry accepted standard for film script layout and you *must* follow it if you want to be taken seriously.

Read through the screenplay format example in Figure 20.1. It is based on *The Bicycle Surgeon* radio script we met in an earlier chapter. Keep in mind the points we have just made.

One page of screenplay will equal one minute of screen time.

1.

EXT. STUDENTS UNION. BICYCLE RACK - DAY

CLAIRE pumps a bicycle pump furiously, then stops,

out of breath. She feels the tyre. It is still flat.

Gasping, she pumps furiously again.

EXT. STREET - DAY

SIMON sitting very upright in the saddle, cycles steadily down
the street properly attired in cycle helmet, face mask and high-
visibility day-glow jacket.

EXT. STUDENTS UNION. BICYCLE RACK - DAY

Claire stops, out of breath. She feels the tyre. It is still flat.

EXT. STREET - DAY

Simon is passed by several faster students heads down, without
helmets, cutting in and out of the traffic.

                    SIMON (v.o.)

          I remember the day she first

          spoke to me.

EXT. STUDENTS UNION. BICYCLE RACK - DAY

Claire hurls the bike away from her just as Simon comes round the
corner.

                    CLAIRE

          Agrh!

Simon goes flying. There is a CRASH of metal on bone and stone after
which Simon sits on the ground with both bicycles on top of him. He
spots something on her wheel rim. He examines it closely.

                    SIMON

          Contusions and abrasions.

          You've been hitting the kerb

          a lot.

Figure 20.1 Sample screenplay layout (page size reduced to scale)

                    CLARE

        What?

                    SIMON

        Lots of scar tissue. The wheel

        rim.

                    CLAIRE

        Medical student. Great.

                    SIMON

        Here's your problem…

Bringing a pair of tweezers from his top pocket,
forceps-like, Simon pulls a nail out of the tyre.

                    CLAIRE

        Why me? Why now? Why today, of all

        days?

                    SIMON

        Want a lift?

                    CLAIRE

        What?

                    SIMON

        I said, I can give you a lift, if

        you want.

                    CLARE

        What? Can you?

She helps him up.

                    CLAIRE (cont.)

        I didn't mean it. Sorry. I have

        a temper.

Together they try to pull the entangled bicycles off him. Simon
chatters, covering up his nervousness in the voices of a TV Soap
doctor and a concerned patient.

SIMON

'The operation was successful.

Both children are doing well.'

'Oh doctor, how can we thank you?'

'Don't thank me, Mrs Spiztburgen.

I'm just doing my job. This bike

will live.'

CLAIRE

(looking at him oddly)

A lift would be great … I think.

SIMON

Where to?

CLAIRE

To the station. Thank you. You're

an angel, whoever you are.

She gathers her bag up and hurtles out the gate at speed

SIMON

(to himself, wistfully)

Simon. The name's Simon, Claire.

EXT. STREET — DAY

CLAIRE

Where's your car?

SIMON

My car? Yes, er… my car.

He holds out his cycle helmet.

EXT. STREET - DAY

SIMON pedals hard, a big smile on his un-helmeted face. CLAIRE is on
the seat behind him, legs dangling, head in helmet, scowling.

CLAIRE

What? What? What? What?

SIMON

(shouting)

Anyone ever told you you say what

a lot?

Figure 20.1 (*cont.*)

                    CLAIRE

                  (shouting)

          What?

INT.UNDERGROUND STATION - DAY

Tube train SCREAMS into the station. Doors open. Rush hour crowd
disembark.

CLAIRE fights against the stream.

                    CLAIRE

          'Scuse me, 'scuse me. Out of the

          way. Out of the way.

DOORS CLOSE. TRAIN PULLS AWAY

INT.   TUBE TRAIN   -   DAY

Claire hangs on a strap under a man's armpit.

INT.UNDERGROUND STATION - DAY

Tube train SCREAMS into the empty platform. Doors open.

Claire is the only passenger to get off.

EXT. HOLLOWAY PRISON - DAY

A sign reads 'HM Prison Holloway'.

Claire reads the sign and frowns.

INT. HOLLOWAY PRISON. RECEPTION AREA - DAY

Claire walks along a stark corridor.

Gates SLAM shut behind her.

INT. HOLLOWAY PRISON. RECEPTION AREA - DAY

A queue of visitors. Claire waits in line.

INT. HOLLOWAY PRISON. RECEPTION AREA - DAY

Claire walks to the desk with a GUARD behind it.

>   CLAIRE
>
>   (voice low, embarrassed)
>
>   I'm here to visit someone.

>   GUARD
>
>   Name?

>   CLAIRE
>
>   Susan … Mrs Cox. She's my Mum.

>   GUARD
>
>   Your name.

>   CLAIRE
>
>   Oh. Claire Cox. I'm her daughter.

>   GUARD
>
>   Sign in. Your name and who you're visiting.

>   CLAIRE
>
>   Oh, I see, right, sorry.
>
>   Claire signs in on the pad

>   GUARD
>
>   Down the corridor, third on the left. Wait
>   till you're called. Next.

CLAIRE limps off, embarrassed and humiliated.

Figure 20.1 (*cont.*)

The first thing to notice is that the script is in Courier 12 point (12 point refers to the size of the font; Courier is the style – in the figure this is reduced to scale). This is the industry accepted font. Follow it.

Note also how the script starts with the direction FADE IN. This always comes at the very start of a script. FADE OUT comes at the end. To end a scene you can also use DISSOLVE TO: FADE TO BLACK: and FREEZE FRAME. Remember, if you FADE OUT or FADE TO BLACK at the end of a scene, you must always FADE IN again at the start at the next one. The convention is to use CUT TO between scenes, but there is really no need for this either. How else do you get from scene to scene? A script that left them out would be perfectly intelligible and save space and paper. Unless they really are necessary to the story, leave them out.

We then have the slug line:

```
EXT. STUDENTS UNION. BICYCLE RACK — DAY
```

You have a slug line at the start of each scene. This introduces the scene; it is always in capitals. You must start the slug line with INT. or EXT. then the PLACE. The last thing is the TIME OF DAY – use only DAY, NIGHT, DAWN or DUSK or very occasionally CONTINUOUS if there's no break. Do not use scene numbers. They go into a shooting script and you are not writing a shooting script. Not yet.

Next we have the scene direction:

```
CLAIRE pumps a bicycle pump furiously, then stops,
out of breath. She feels the tyre. It is still flat.
Gasping, she pumps furiously again.
```

Stage directions or business should be 1½ –2 inches from the left (in the United States: 2 inches).

The first words in the screenplay are from Simon.

```
            SIMON (v.o.)
      I remember the day she first
      spoke to me.
```

Dialogue is indented 2½ inches from the left and a little from the right. The character's name goes above the dialogue, in capitals and indented another 1½ inches. Everything is left aligned, not centred or justified. Except the page number which goes top right. Use A4 paper for European scripts, Quarto for US scripts Single-space scene descriptions and dialogue, double space between paragraphs, and three spaces above the slug line. Follow these specific rules and your script will be clear and easy to read.

There are a few more general rules to know about, too.

Put the stage directions in the present tense and make sure they describe only things we can see or hear. You can say that someone is 'sad' or 'happy' but you cannot write 'he sat silently remembering the scent of her perfume'. That is not easy to see on screen.

```
Claire stops, out of breath. She feels the tyre.
It is still flat.
```

That is observable.

You can put extra dialogue description in brackets, half an inch to the left of the character name, as in:

                              CLAIRE
                    (looking at him oddly)
                A lift would be great … I think.

But use this sparingly. As we said previously, actors and director dislike being told how to approach things.

Capitalize a character's name in the scene directions for the first appearance only, as in:

            CLAIRE pumps a bicycle pump furiously
            SIMON […] cycles steadily down the street

From now, neither Claire nor Simon will be in caps unless they are speaking.

You would use capital letters (caps) also for CAMERA directions, which should be used hardly at all or you will be trying to tell a director how to direct it. Use caps, too, for SOUND and MUSIC. Again, use sparingly.

        Simon goes flying. There is a CRASH of metal on bone

You can use the abbreviation CLAIRE (O.S.) to show that she is speaking out of shot, or (V.O.) if you wanted a voice-over – that is, narration over the action.

                              CLARE
                    What? Can you?
                    She helps him up
                         CLAIRE (cont.)
                I didn't mean it. Sorry. I have
                a temper.

Using continued (cont.) shows that dialogue has been interrupted by action or a new page. But don't use too much dialogue … As we have seen in previous lessons, dialogue should be brief and not state the obvious – it should give hints as to the characters' true feelings but not state them openly. Just as we said in other scriptwriting the characters should all be different from each other and speak differently. A quick way of assessing the amount of dialogue in a scene is to cover every speech with your thumb. If the dialogue continues below your thumb it is quite likely too long. Of course you will want to have some longer speeches in your screenplay; in which case, break them up with some piece of action so that they look more dramatic on the page.

Because this is film you should tell the story through visual images, through pictures. Try to make the pictures vivid and always related to the story and though you should not tell the director what to do, you can subtly get your vision across, in the way that Shakespeare does, by building it deeply into the scene. Setting a scene high up on a mountain or on top of a tall tower block and looking down at the world below; or setting it in the depths of the ocean and building the action around that will mean that you have more chance of your vision coming across than if you are less specific.

In the screenplay example, notice that the writer has also not been afraid to change the existing material. The Claire and Simon in this script are different characters to the ones on the radio play. The writer has not felt the need to stay exactly with the original material but has left things out, modified, added new material to make the writing work for the different medium. In many ways it is a new and different piece of work. That is all right. Let the writing develop, let the characters develop. You can change things in such a way that it sheds new light on them and their situation. Oh, at the end, do not forget to include:

```
FADE TO BLACK.
```

These Formatting exercises are good exercises to do because they get you into the mind set of thinking in pictures and thinking how professionals want the material presented. Using the formatting tools and style actually influences the way you think about the story. You could just write the story and worry about the formatting later. You could write the story, (which after all is the important bit) type it out and then get some screenwriting software program to format it for you. Such a program will format a radio or stage script into a screenplay in a few seconds and it will look like a professional piece of work. But just because it looks like a professional piece of work does not means it will read like a professional piece of work. It will still read like a radio or stage work. And solving the problems of exits and entrances, use of sound etc., will not solve the essential fact that the work has been written for the medium of radio or stage and not for the screen. To work on the screen a story needs to be conceived for the screen. Even when working with an adaptation and adapting original material for a screen, the screenwriter has to turn that material into a visual screenplay. The films from books, plays, and real life stories that work are the ones that successfully do this. Using the correct layout and formatting right from the start can help that creative process. Form and content will be working together and not against each other.

Workshop: introducing a character

To practise formatting and layout, we want you to introduce a character in a screenplay. Before you write, you need to have a strong visual picture of the character and the world they inhabit. Think of a character you have written about earlier in the book, perhaps in the sections on character, and ask the sorts of questions we asked earlier to help you develop them.

- Do they ever apologize if they've done something wrong? (Or even if they haven't.)
- Do they ever do anything wrong?
- Did they feel loved by their parents?
- Was their childhood happy?
- How do they cope in a crisis?
- Which do they put first: money, power, family, love, ambition, health, or something else?

- What are their virtues and vices?
- What are their motives in life?
- What big unfulfilled need do they have?
- What is their idea of perfect happiness?
- Which historical figure do they most identify with?
- Which trait do they most deplore in others (and themselves)?
- What do they most dislike about their appearance?

What is their favourite smell?

What is their greatest regret? (Do they regret anything?)

Which talent would they most like to have?

Not all of these things will make their appearance in your screenplay but it is good for you to know them as they help you get the character down on the page and know what they will be likely to want and need and do in your story.

Using a slug line and screen directions (but little or no dialogue), in no more than 200 words, create and introduce a character in a screenplay. Convey information about:

- the **impression** they create (what they look like, wear, etc.)
- their **attitude** (their temperament, personality, what they want)
- their **world** (where they live or come from, as well as how they live).

(200 words maximum)

Screenwriting as a visual medium

Screenwriting is a visual medium. In the following section – a kind of extended workshop – we are going to work on the visual nature of the craft of screenwriting. To do this, we are going to use the building blocks of work we have already done in previous chapters. We looked at the senses and show and tell in previous chapters. It would be a good idea for you to look over those chapters now, especially Chapters 6–10.

Focus point

Film scripts are visual. Think visual. For screenwriting think dramatic not narrative, think 'show not tell'.

Think, 'I need to make pictures for the viewer.' The viewer needs to see what you write. More importantly, anyone you try to sell it to needs to see what you write. You need to show them that you can write visually. As a writer you have to help anyone reading it to see the pictures in your written script. Screenplays rely on visual detail in every scene.

Consider the following story outline:

'Kate comes home one day, finds her dog in the kitchen choking. Unable to clear his throat she bundles the dog into the car and rushes him straight to the vet, who immediately calls the police.'

Snapshot

Read this over a couple of times, then *cover up* what follows and in your notebook or on your computer write down what you think are the various important elements in the piece. By this we mean:

the characters

the action – that is, what happens.

Now that you have done that, look at what follows:
- elements in the story
- characters:
    - the lead character, Kate
    - the dog
    - the vet
- action of the piece:
    - Kate coming home
    - finding the dog choking
    - trying to help
    - rushing him to the vet
    - the vet examining the dog
    - the vet immediately calling the police,

If you are a fiction writer, writing a short story or novel, you will approach this differently from someone writing a screenplay. You would have decided on your point of view, your viewpoint character, and would probably be inside Kate's mind. You would describe her arrival home in one state of mind, changing to anxiety as she discovers the choking dog, her sense of panic as she seems unable to stop the dog choking, the rising panic as she speeds him to the vet and her shock as the vet calls the police. In a stage play you would have the problem of how to show the choking dog. Do you have it happen off stage and get Kate to relate it to a friend, or the vet or the police? Do you have an actor portray the dog, or puppets? Actors can be excellent at conveying animals on stage, and so can puppeteers, think of the big stage hit *War-Horse*. However you do it, you would need dialogue and action to convey the story.

As this is to be a screenplay, a good approach is to break this down into a series of important scenes and then find the way to link them. What scenes are pivotal in this action sequence; and how do you link them?

Focus point

Remember: you are a screenwriter; think visually.

In your mind, you need to picture Kate's small car driving up to the house, her feet crossing the gravel. The door opens to show her face as she hears the noise of choking. Her eyes and mouth show immediate concern. She rushes into the kitchen. The choking dog is down on the floor. Kate drives fast, looking in the rear view mirror at the dog choking in the back of her car. The car skids to a halt outside the vet's. Kate struggles to get the choking dog out of the back. The vet's door opens and the receptionist sees Kate and dog come in. Kate brushes past her to the vet. He examines the dog. Looks at Kate with concern, reaches for the phone and asks for the police.

In a screenplay, the individual scenes on their own do not always make sense, but when they are put together in the right order they can build up to a story, like this, told in pictures. This story you will note is as yet a silent picture. We can add dialogue where we need it but note:

Key idea

A screenplay is not dialogue. The dialogue grows from the situation. You need to get the story situation down first and find the dialogue for your characters later.

Snapshot

Imagine you are going to write a screenplay of this story. List the scenes in the story as you think they would appear. Be brief, focus on the actions. Do not go into extraneous detail. When you have done that look at the example given below.

(200 words)

Listing the scenes in our screenplay we might see:
- Kate's small car drives sedately along the street, Kate at the wheel.
- She stops to wave a neighbour out of his drive.
- She pulls the car up at the house.
- Kate parks it very carefully.
- Her feet cross the gravel.
- The door opens to show her face as she hears the noise of choking.
- Her eyes and mouth show immediate concern.
- She rushes into the kitchen.

- The choking dog is down on the floor.
- Kate drives fast, looking in the rear view mirror at the dog choking in the back of her car.
- She cuts in front of other cars and is hooted at.
- The car skids to a halt at a crazy angle outside the vet's.
- Kate struggles to get the choking dog out of the back.
- The vet's door opens and the receptionist sees Kate and dog come in.
- Kate brushes past her protestations into the vet's room.
- A parrot the vet is holding flies loose.
- The vet examines the dog.
- The parrot hangs upside from the light fitting, watching and squawking.
- The vet looks at Kate with concern.
- He reaches for the phone and asks for the police.

To develop the full potential of this story as a sequence of pictures there are other things we need to consider. What are they? Do you remember the ideas we dealt with under the two chapters on the five senses? Do you also remember how we used them in the work we did on showing, telling and ignoring? Screenwriting is very much a matter of showing and ignoring. You cannot put everything into a screenplay so you must ignore. You must not tell in a screenplay; a screenplay is where you show. How do you show? You show in pictures.

 ## Snapshot

What elements do we need in a screenplay image to get it to come over to a viewer? Think about the work we did on the senses and on show and tell and write your answers down in your notebook.

 ## Key idea

We've mentioned it before but remember, film is a visual medium. Think *visually*.

Essential elements in a screenplay include:

- **Colour** – this is very important in the making of pictures. Film makers are like artists in that they are painting pictures for us. In fact, director Ridley Scott studied art before he developed a career in film. What he directs carries over a painterly feel to it. He is a director very much interested in the visual picture; as is director David Lean. Some directors work in an amazing palette of colours; others are more monochrome. When you are envisioning your images ask what colour springs from, bursts from, is suggested by, the scene you are considering? In the story we have been sketching, what colour of day is it when Kate arrives home? Is it bright and sunny? Is it grey and rainy? What colour is suggested by the scene in the vet's room? What if it contrasts to the opening scene and the bright, white, antiseptic light of a fluorescent tube casts a shadowless glow over everything? When next you look at some films, compare the use of colour in them.

- **Light** – light and colour are closely related. If it is grey and rainy in the first scene this will set up a mood and a tone and an expectation in the audience. The overall sense of some of the Hollywood film noir movies is of a monochrome world and that is not just because the films were shot in black and white. One suspects it would still be monochrome even if shot in colour. They inhabit a monochrome world. Light is related to time of day; sunrise and morning will have different lights and different mood possibilities than sunset, dusk and night. Contrasting the light of the opening of our film to the light in the vet's room can add contrast to the film.

- **Movement** – what kind of movement do you want to have both within and between the different images that make up the scenes you are writing? Do you want to cut at a dizzying fast pace; do you want a slow, languid movement between images? This will relate to the kind of story you want to tell and the way you want to tell it. For instance contrasting Kate's steady, sedate drive home in the opening shots with the crazy, fast-paced driving when she rushes the dog to the vet's will move the story on as well as show her concern and add detail to her character.

- **Order** – the order of details in an image is an important contributory element to the quality of the image itself. You need to put the images in the right order to tell the story and you need to put the details within the images in the best possible order to make the images work. When the vet examines the dog does he say anything to Kate to tell us why he is calling the police, or does he just call the police thereby leaving both Kate and the viewers in suspense? Which is best? It has to be leaving the viewers in suspense. One of the most important things you need to decide in a screenplay is what you reveal when. This relates to how you tell the story; how much you let the audience in on and when you do it.

- **Sound** – this is another of the senses important in screenwriting. Different times of day and night will have different sounds and different qualities of sound associated with them. As we discussed in the work we did on radio, writing different locations will have different sound qualities. Something that takes place in an interior location will have a different sound quality to something taking place in an exterior location. Something set in outer space will have a different sound quality to something set beneath the sea or in the deepest recesses of a cave or a gold mine. Think how the sound or lack of it fills out the image you are considering. The sound of the choking dog filling the house as Kate enters will have an immediate effect on her. The coughing in the car will increase her anxiety and make her drive faster and more erratically, giving us the sound of squealing tyres and honking horns from other drivers.

- **Location** – you need to choose your locations carefully to have the most impact in your story. The need to relate to the character's place in the world and the needs of the story. Kate's home is important in this story. The sort of house will say a lot about her: a house in the suburbs with a front lawn and a car port will tell us that this is a different Kate from the Kate that lives in an apartment in the city. Choice of location plays a similar sort of role that a bass line plays in a piece of music. It is present all the time, underneath everything else that is going on. Sometimes it is given prominence, but always it is there, pulsing away and holding the whole piece together.

- **Contrasting elements** – it is very effective to put contrasting moments in a story against each other. Shakespeare does this a great deal on stage; dark scenes are often followed by comic scenes. Macbeth's murder of Duncan is followed by the comic scene of the porter. You can contrast a character's mood in a scene with music that indicates a different emotion to the viewer. Contrast is an element much used in art, yet also much undervalued. Without contrast of location, mood, tempo, pieces can be all of one pace or colour. A good piece of work needs variety in all its elements.

Write

Write a piece in which you use all these different elements of colour, light, movement, order, sound, location and contrast. They will be the elements that readers will be looking for and which may well excite people enough to want to take it further. That is what you must aim at.

Using these elements develop a more detailed image for the start of the choking dog story but do not write as a screenplay, yet. Very often in screenwriting the preliminary is to produce a prose 'treatment' of the story which contains all these plus elements of colour, mood, setting, etc. The 'treatment' needs to get the story across in a visual way, as if it was a film but in script form. Use no dialogue.

(750 words maximum)

After you have done that, have a look at the example below:

Sunlight flashes on trees and windscreens illuminating a bright day. Kate drives her car slowly and steadily along a suburban road. She stops and courteously lets a driver reverse out of a drive. She arrives at her bungalow and parks the car by the lawn. Birds are singing; sprinklers are playing. Waving at her neighbour she walks to her front door. Immediately in the house a choking, coughing sound reaches Kate's ears. She dashes to the kitchen. Her dog is choking and coughing head down to the ground. Kate tries to relieve the dog but is unable to. She piles him into the back of her car and drives fast to the vet. She cuts through the honking, hooting traffic, cutting people up and screams up outside the vet's. Bundling the still choking dog inside she brushes aside the receptionist and crashes in on the vet who is trying to inject a parrot. The parrot seizes the moment to get loose and flies up onto the light shade where it hangs squawking. At Kate's protestations, the vet examines the choking dog and rings the police.

How did yours compare? Was it longer or shorter?

316

There is no agreed length for a treatment. Treatments come in many forms and many lengths. Use only as much as is needed to tell the story.

Edit

Is there anything in the example above that will help you look at your own piece with new eyes? Compare this example with your own and see if there is anything that can help you revise it? Ask yourself how filmic is your version? Is there anything you can do to make it more filmic, more visual, more active? Focus on the action. Have you made your piece active using active verbs? If not, rewrite; make the piece active. However well you have done it, rewrite anyway; look at every word and make it even more active and even more visual.

Film openings

Films open in many different ways. Some films open with the film title and credits; others open with a series of images or action sequence, with the title and credits coming in many minutes after the film has started. You do not have to worry about where the credits will come, but as a writer you do need to think about how your film is going to begin. You have several options for the sort of opening image you want. You can start with a person. If you do, this person should be doing something typical. If it is the woman with the dog, have her doing the sorts of things she does normally. This holds true for all film openings you might consider writing. If you intended to write about a person who is a gangster then have them doing something that gangsters do. If they are a policeman or a teacher; show them doing something normal for them. Show your characters in their ordinary worlds before they enter the extraordinary world of the screenplay story. If you start with a person we want to know who it is and what he or she is doing. Alfred Hitchcock knew the value of showing a person in their normal life before they were pitched into a story. He does this in *North by Northwest* where Roger Thornhill, played by Cary Grant, is seen going about his normal life, dictating memos to his secretary, meeting potential business contacts in a hotel bar for drinks and telephoning his mother, before he is plunged into a spy thriller with murderous foreign agents who turn his life upside down.

If you don't start with a person, you might start with a place. If you start with location you need to establish where it is and what it is. If you are going to write the story of the choking dog decide where that is set. You need to decide this for any film you conceive. Is it a busy city, is it a desert, is it a quiet, tranquil village in which murder will take place, or in which a murderer will take refuge – as happens in another great Hitchcock movie starring Joseph Cotton, *The Shadow of a Doubt*. Joseph Cotton's character, on the run from federal agents who suspect him of being the murderer of several wealthy women, takes refuge in the town of his sister. There he strikes up a close relationship with his niece, Charlie, whom he eventually has to try to kill to preserve his secret. If you want to open with place you also need to decide how the audience come upon it. A camera panning in from up on high is a common device which starts with a general view and focuses in on a specific city, town or village. But there are many other ways you could do it.

Alternatively films can start with a picture or an image – you might want to start with a picture of something significant for your story; a negligee on a bed, a pair of ballet shoes, an abandoned yacht drifting on the ocean, a dead body in a pool of blood, or a smoking gun. All of these could interest and hook an audience waiting to know what you are going to do with them. For the exercise here perhaps a sign saying 'Beware of the Dog' and a dog choking and unable to eat; perhaps for Venice an image of a painter's easel with some ladies underwear draped over it. Sound might also be important and should be established early on. *The Shadow of a Doubt* makes great play of the Merry Widow Waltz throughout the movie but it is established right at the start of the film before being used in several normal and more nightmarish contexts later.

Some movies are centred on a strong and important plot. You might like to start right in the middle of an action sequence rather in the style of the James Bond films or the movies about Jason Bourne. These high adrenalin action sequences hook the audience and tell them immediately what sort of film they are settling down to watch.

 ## Write

Using the work developed from the woman and the choking dog, decide on an opening image for a film you will write. Start with one of the following:

- **A person** – who is it and what is he or she doing? (it does not have to be dog owner).
- **A place** – if you start with location you need to establish where it is and also how the audience come upon it.
- **An image** – you might want to start with a picture of something significant for your story; a negligee on a bed, an abandoned yacht drifting on the ocean, a dead body in a pool of blood, or a smoking gun would all be good pictures but probably not relevant to *this* story.
- **A plot** – you might start right in the middle of an action sequence, rather in the style of the James Bond films or the movies about Jason Bourne.

Think visual; try to incorporate as many as possible of the elements we have discussed: colour, light, sound, movement, location, contrasting elements.

(750 words)

Read another version of this story:

A woman returned home from shopping to find her pet Doberman choking and gasping for breath. Unable to help him she bundled him into the car and raced him to the vet. The vet examined the dog but said he couldn't immediately find the reason for the dog's problems. He suggested the woman go home and leave the dog with him overnight while he performed a tracheotomy and inserted tubes down the animal's throat so he could breathe. He would call her in the morning with the results. But when the woman returned home, the phone was ringing. She answered it. It was the vet.

'Get out of the house. Now!' he said.

'Why? What's wrong?'

'... Do it! Now! Go next door, go to a neighbour's, anywhere.'

She did as she was told and went next door. Within minutes three police cars screeched to a halt outside her house. Police officers rushed out and into her house. Shocked, the woman raced outside to see what was happening. The vet arrived and told her that when he had performed the operation, he had found two human fingers in the dog's throat. Fearing the dog had surprised an intruder and that he might still be in the house, he had phoned to warn the woman.

Shortly afterwards an ambulance came and the paramedics carried out an unconscious man whom police had found lying in a closet, having lost two fingers and a lot of blood.

Sometimes in this story it is one finger, sometimes two fingers, sometimes three. Sometimes the town is unspecified, sometimes it is named; for instance one version on the Internet begins 'My cousin and his wife lived in Sydney with this huge Doberman in a little apartment off Maroubra Road.' This version is full of detail like 'they went out for dinner and a spot of clubbing'. But it is the same story. It is an urban myth.

One Internet source says that 'The Choking Doberman' 'has circulated in more or less this form for at least three decades, on as many continents. In his book of the same title, folklorist Jan Harold Brunvand cites a plethora of known variants, including a British version dating back to 1973. The story became hugely popular in the United States during the early 1980s. In 1981 it was published as an allegedly first-hand account in an American tabloid called *The Globe*, though subsequent research revealed that the pseudonymous author ('Gayla Crabtree') had actually heard the story second hand in a beauty parlour.

Folklorists believe 'The Choking Doberman' is a descendant of a much older (perhaps as old as the Renaissance) European folktale about a clumsy burglar who injures his own hand while breaking into a house. His intrusion is revealed by the homeowners' discovery of one or more severed fingers. More can be found about this and other urban myths in *Encyclopedia of Urban Legends* by Jan Harold Brunvand and *The Choking Doberman* by Jan Harold Brunvand.

Focus point

When you are writing a script for television or film think pictures.

Ronald B. Tobias uses the story of 'The Choking Doberman' in the opening chapter of his book *Twenty Master Plots (and how to build them)*. He calls this sort of story 'invisible fiction' because nobody knows where it came from. He says:

> *'The value of this legend is that it evolved with constant retelling until it became* plot perfect, *the same process that perfected the fable, the fairy tale, the riddle, the rhyme and the proverb. The story went through thousands of oral rewrites until it could evolve no further.'*

The fact that it is pure plot helps us to understand the various elements and stages of a plot, which is what we are going on to do next.

Write

Construct a screenplay based on the story of 'The Choking Doberman', making sure that you use the standard screenplay format. Introduce the main character in the way you have just done above. The screenplay should include:

- more than one scene
- scene directions
- dialogue.

(750 words)

Three movements

Snapshot

Having written a brief screenplay of 'The Choking Doberman', go back to the original story and try to break the story up into three movements or acts. Describe where each begins. You should find that it is a story that *can* be broken down into three movements; the essential three movements of a screenplay. *Cover up* what is below before you start.

1 The set-up

2 Confrontation

3 Resolution

Uncover what is below.

Did you get something like this, either in your screenplay or in the break down exercise?

1 **The set-up** – 'A woman returned home from shopping to find her pet Doberman choking and gasping for breath.'

   After that we are into the confrontation stage of the story:

2 Confrontation – this goes from 'Unable to help him she bundled him into the car and raced him to the vet.' right up to 'Police officers rushed out and into her house. Shocked, the woman raced outside to see what was happening.'

3 Resolution – this begins with the vet's arrival and explanation and ends firmly with 'Shortly afterwards an ambulance came and the paramedics carried out an unconscious man who police had found lying in a closet, having lost two fingers and a lot of blood.'

In this story we have many of the elements needed for a screenplay:

- The **beginning, middle and end** stages correspond to the three movements of the standard three-act film.

- We have a **protagonist** (the woman).

- We have an **antagonist** (the intruder).

- We have **tension.**

- We have **conflict.**

- We have – in the choking dog – an exciting **hook** to draw in the audience.

- We have the **complications** of the woman being unable to help the dog and rushing him to the vet; and then the vet calling her up and shocking her with his instructions for her to leave the house.

- We have a **climax,** when the police arrive and discover the intruder,

- We have a **resolution** where the vet explains that he found the fingers and the bleeding man is taken away.

There are many urban myths we could use to do similar exercises; urban myths that in the retelling have become plots that work for their audience. 'The Vanishing Hitchhiker' is another one.

Ernest W. Baughman in *Type- and Motif-Index of the Folk Tales of England and North America* (1966) outlines the basic elements of the vanishing hitchhiker:

> *'Ghost of young woman asks for ride in automobile, disappears from closed car without the driver's knowledge, after giving him an address to which she wishes to be taken. The driver asks person at the address about the rider, finds she has been dead for some time. (Often the driver finds that the ghost has made similar attempts to return, usually on the anniversary of death in automobile accident. Often, too, the ghost leaves some item such as a scarf or travelling bag in the car.)'*

This is another story that has been told and retold in different ways. Maybe it does not give as much plot and structure as 'The Choking Doberman', but there are enough stages to construct a story and it does give an intriguing mystery element; something which can be gold for a screenplay.

A father and his young daughter were driving along a country road one night when the father was suddenly startled by something up ahead. It was a figure, dressed all in white, caught in the flash of the headlights. She stepped out into the road and he nearly lost control as he strove not to run into her. He stopped the car and ran back to the figure. The young woman was pale and cold. He asked her if she was all right. Did she need a lift? It was not good to be out there all alone late at night, miles from anywhere. She said nothing but nodded and he led her to the car. She got into the back seat and the man's daughter turned to talk to the young woman. She immediately admired her clothes and scarf which were from another period and asked if she had been to a fancy dress party. The young woman gave no responses as the young girl chattered away to her but sat in the back of the car, her white scarf draped around her neck. When she spoke at all it was to direct the father to a farm, three miles down the road. The father headed there. It was hard to find in the dark but he found the drive and drove the length of it to the farm house. It was all in darkness and he turned to the young woman to ask if anyone was home when he was startled to see that the young woman was not there. Both he and his daughter gasped. Had she got out of the car as soon as they had arrived? How had she done it? Neither had heard her. They began to doubt if she had ever been there but her scarf lay on the back seat.

The father told his daughter to stay in the car but she would not. Getting out with him she accompanied him to the farmhouse door. They knocked several times and eventually heard the sounds of someone coming from within. An old woman's face peered out at them. They explained why they had come and who they had brought and the man handed her the scarf through the crack in the door. The woman let them into the house and told them that the scarf had belonged to her daughter. She had disappeared on that road many, many years before. Today was the anniversary of her disappearance. There had been many sightings of her trying to find her way home. Father and daughter fled.

Remember the work we did on causality earlier in the book?

'Because *he felt sick she called the vet.* Because *she bought a new dress he lost money on the horses.* Because *she went to the bank he made a phone call.* Because *he made a cake she got a new job.* Because *she bought some flowers he went to the shops.* Because *she got into the car he got promoted.*

Films are built around this same element of causality. One thing happens because another has happened. One thing occurring triggers other things off. This is an important thing to keep in mind.

Key idea

Keep the principle of causality in mind because it is central to building a screenplay plot.

William Goldman

'Storytellers tell lies ... We must. Story ideas surround us, but they need shading, shaping, climaxes, beginnings; that's our job. What we must try and learn is which are the best lies ...'

Summary

In this chapter you have written for the screen. You have looked at basic terminology; screenwriting as a visual medium; format and layout of screenplays in detail; introducing a character into a screenplay; and the three-act structure in screenplays. This is really all that could be done in the space available. From this point, if you are serious about screenwriting, get one of the specialist books on the subject and keep developing your writing. Watch films and try and think critically about them. How do they work? What special ingredients do they have?

Next step

In the next chapter we will look at how you stop writing; also at preparing manuscripts and at the business of being a writer.

21

How to stop writing and start selling

Writing, if it is not solely done for your own pleasure, is a highly commercial undertaking and not only, as we have shown in this book, do you need to be your own creative inspiration, your own editor and your own best critic but to a large degree you have to be your own agent and business manager too. These days with the opportunities the Internet offers and the ability to self-publish, in many cases, you have to be your own marketing and sales person and retailer as well. A writer needs an abundance of skills.

Going to market

The majority of this book so far has been on the most important aspect, the writing; to help you get words down on the page in whatever form or genre you have chosen to write. Not only, to paraphrase Coleridge, getting words down, but the best possible words in the best possible order. If you were a farmer you would want to get your animals into the best possible shape before you took them to market; you would want them to be in prime condition so that they commanded the best price. Before you even consider 'the market' for your writing you obviously need your manuscript to be in the best possible shape. Before you offer a piece of writing to the world you need to know that it is finished and the best that you can get it. It is a very good idea to read it out loud to yourself.

Snapshot

Take a piece of work you believe is finished; read it out loud to yourself from beginning to end. If you stumble over anything, pause, ask is it you, is it the writing? If you have stumbled, would a reader stumble? Is there a glitch that needs smoothing out? As you read, make notes. Are you confused or bored by a passage? If you are bored, it is very likely a reader will be bored too. When you have finished, revise the piece using your notes to guide you.

Key idea

Before sending your work out, get a second opinion. One you can trust.

Criticism and encouragement

Who should you show your work to for a second opinion? It seems natural to show your writing to husbands, wives, partners, family members and friends. It has to be said that these are not always the best people to let see your work.

If you are lucky, friends and family can be very helpful and supportive. They often mean well and have the best intentions for you, but having good intentions and wanting the best for you does not necessarily translate into being the best critic of your work. We all read, or at least most people read, and most people watch television and see films, but none of this qualifies us to be genuine critics of someone else's creative writing. There are so many things that come into play when commenting on a piece of writing that we writers need to be careful and selective about whom we share it with. It is an acquired skill to judge a piece of writing and, while it is natural to ask, we often expect far too much of those closest to us to imagine that they can do it. While sharing what we have written with those closest to us comes from a good motive, to ask them to criticize it as well puts both them and yourself in a difficult position. You can expect loyal support from husbands, wives, partners and friends; that is what they do. Don't ask them to be your critic as well.

What all writers aim at is an ideal reader; someone who will read their work with intelligence and sympathy. But that is more when the work is finished. When you are writing a piece or when you are not certain whether it is finished or not you want someone who knows about the writing process and who can spot where something is not working. When you show a piece of work to another person for advice or comment it is because *you* are not sure of it yet. You have worked on it and got so far but you have got to the point where you would welcome an outside eye on it in the hope that that person will confirm any doubts you have or spot any weaknesses you have missed. Someone to say, 'It's great; except for that bit.' Or, 'I got confused there, or lost it, or something went wrong there. Can you run it by me again?' This simple putting their finger on something is what you need. An intelligent, sympathetic reader will pick up on where the work has gone wonky or off the rails or not quite delivered, or is just a little bit confusing, or plain boring. It will sometimes be a feeling that they have and they may not be able to put into words, but your job is to look at what they have highlighted and see if they are right. If they are, then they have been helpful. If you think they are not right, then again they have been useful and confirmed you in your view of what you have written.

Sue Grafton

'One of the most difficult decisions an unpublished writer makes is when to take advice and when to ignore all your well-meaning critics and do it your way.'

If you can find a reader who will do that for you, they are worth their weight in gold. You cannot expect more than that from them, or even from a writing tutor in a class. Reading groups and writing classes can help a budding writer. A class led by a tutor who is skilled and experienced in reading and hearing work and in giving comments on work is a good place to start. It rarely works if the facilitator is someone involved in the group and certainly not if the criticism is savage. Writers groups are there for writers to help each other. But, again, it is no one else's job to tell you how to write a piece. Someone else may sometimes help you spot where something goes wrong and even know what it is that has gone wrong. Maybe it's the dialogue; maybe a character is not quite believable. It is your job to put it right. No one can do that but you. To then expect the same person who spots it to know how to put it right is not the way it works.

Leo Tolstoy

'In a writer there must always be two people – the writer and the critic.'

A critic is not a writer, but a writer has to be a critic and sometimes their own worst critic. But you can also be blind to your faults, hence the value of showing your work to others. But what you don't want when you show your work to someone is for them to say nice things to you out of loyalty. Your writing, in the end, benefits from unflinching encouragement and fair but unflinching criticism.

 Focus point

If you have someone you trust; they may be a partner, friends, colleague or, if you are lucky, someone who works in the business, then get them to look at your work and give you their honest opinion. If the comments make sense to you and you wish to take them on board then revise your work, get it into the best possible shape before you send it to anyone. And when you get good advice from someone you trust, use it. If revision is suggested, do it. Do not fear revision; revision is at the heart of all good creative writing. It is in many ways where the real writing goes on.

Revision

 John Irving

'Half my life is an act of revision.'

When revising your work, it pays to pay attention not only to your characters and your story, but to your use of research. It is key in creative writing to be able to marry up what is researched and what is created *so that the reader is not aware of any join.* We cannot possibly experience everything in life. We cannot write everything as if it lived within us and flowed out from within a core of knowledge and experience like a river from its secret source. This is where the advice to 'write about what you know,' good in so many respects, falls short. We cannot know everything; therefore if we only 'write about what we know,' there are going to be some things we cannot write about. If we can only write about what we know and what we have experienced then there will be huge areas of human endeavour that fall off the edge of our creative maps.

 Focus point

What we don't know about we must research. We must use that research in our writing in such a way that it does not stand out as research.

One of the things that stands out in some people's writing is the fact that they have done a lot of research and they are determined that this research will not be wasted. It all goes in the book; whether it helps the book or not. Yes, we need to research but we need to use our research in such a way that it helps what we are writing about; the story, place or character. We must use it in such a way that it fundamentally helps the story. We must not use it in a way that works against the story. And great tracts of research stuck in anywhere do work against a story.

If on second or third reading an over-reliance on research stands out, then cut it out.

Focus point

A simple edit can transform a piece of writing. The trick is to know what to leave in and what to take out.

How to stop writing

Another aspect not commonly touched on in writing books, which are all geared to getting you to *start* writing, is of how to *stop* writing; how to know when enough is enough and of how to let a piece of work go. A commissioned writer has deadlines that have to be met. The play will not be produced, the book not published if those deadlines are not met (though they sometimes can be renegotiated). This can provide a firm end to a piece. The writer has to stop writing and deliver it. Someone writing on 'spec' without a commission has no deadline and could continue writing the piece for ever. How does this person know when enough is enough? Knowing when to stop can be a difficulty for a writer, although exhaustion usually tells you!

The advice given to writers is always to write and rewrite, over several drafts. The danger is that you can simply write too much and keep on writing when you should have stopped so that in the end you actually spoil a story. If you don't know when to stop you can overwrite. Knowing when to stop is a skill that comes with time. As with so much of writing you have to practise and learn through making mistakes. You have to mar a few pieces of work before you get the correct sense of when to stop and when to let go.

How to let a piece of work go

We have spent a lot of time in this book offering exercises and advice to help you get started and in trying to get a piece of work to come to life. And stories, if we are lucky, *do* take on lives of their own. It is what writers want to happen most of all, but the other side of it is that at some point we have to accept that they *are* alive and that we have to say goodbye to them. Writers and readers both have to say goodbye to characters and their worlds and when they have come vividly to life it is not always easy. A reader can pick up another book by the same author and maintain the contact, but for a writer being able to put the work down and move away from it can be more difficult, both from an emotional and a technical aspect.

Bringing a character and a world to life is the most wonderful achievement for a writer; you can come to love the lives of these characters, and enjoy spending time in their company. Creating character is breathing fire into them, fire and life; breathing air into their months and nostrils, feeling it in their lungs, sensing it energizing their arms, legs, brains and thoughts. When your characters begin to think and feel and breathe and want and desire and need and cry and love like a real person, they are truly alive. As a writer, you have done your job But how do you, the writer, say goodbye to a character with such life and love and drive and energy, someone who has come alive through your hands? Why would you want to? And why would you want start the journey of creating characters and worlds out of blank paper and lifeless computer screens anew?

Writers are faced with letting their work go in so many ways. In the professional world we have to let a 'finished' manuscript go to agents or publishers and editors. If writing scripts we have to let it go and get into the hands of producers, directors and actors. If you are in a writers group you have to present it for the criticism of your peers, although this is still work in progress so you can always do more on it. To permanently let go of your writing, to give it up to others, can be as hard for a writer as letting go of a part they have invested deep intelligence and emotion in can be for an actor.

Bringing a character and a world to life can be magical. As a writer, or an actor, you put so much energy and life into it that you can reach the stage where you don't want to say goodbye to the world at all, that you want to keep writing for or being these characters. When you create a world and the characters in that world come to life, it can be fun to go there every day and write for them or be them with their clever, funny, insightful sayings. It can be such fun that you do not want to stop. You love them and their world so much that saying goodbye can seem almost impossible, like a grief.

It can also seem easier to stay in this familiar world you have created than to create a new world with all is attendant pains of creating and giving birth. It is a comfortable place; somewhere good to stay. This feeling for a writer is mirrored by the actor who inhabits the role so much that he or she becomes that character on and off stage or set.

 ## Key idea

Being a writer you can live many lives in your head, far more exciting than your own. That is one of the reasons why writing can be addictive.

When a writer finishes a piece he can grieve because he realizes he will no longer be engaged on that project, spending time in the company of the people he has brought to life; living in their world, knowing their lives as his own (knowing their lives better than his own sometimes.) To live your life with characters in a magical, imaginary world you have created can be such a wonderful thing that leaving it can give you a feeling of betrayal. To have a play in production means it is written and is being rehearsed by actors and director. As a writer you can do no more to it except make small changes, often suggested by actors or director and, of course, approved by you. You may, it's true, go the theatre and watch the characters as realized by the actors, but by then they are living their lives as the director and actors have conceived of them, probably in ways you did not dream of, but hopefully that you like. Where the characters in your script go on to a rich, fulfilling and rounded existence is, for you, a form of goodbye akin to parents watching their children grow up and leave home.

Whether it is a play, novel or film script, you as the writer are faced with loss; with an empty desk, an empty page, and empty world because those characters that you have come to love are no longer in it and you are no longer in their world. You can miss these characters even as you try to go through the process again; picking up the reins of another set of characters in another play or story you want to write. Losing the characters from the energized world in your head and heart can feel like a sort of grief and taking up with other characters even feel like a betrayal. You can feel that you don't want to start again with these new people who are uncommunicative strangers. You can feel frustrated, even resentful and at a loss to know how to begin. These emotions can surely feed into you not knowing what to write next and contribute to what is known as 'writer's block'.

Fear of finishing

Whether it can be recognised as a psychological syndrome or not, it is important to recognise the part the fear of finishing plays in the creative writing field. Nearly all of the teaching about writing is geared to helping writers produce work; in the first place to get writers started. The topics covered are often how to start, where to get ideas from, how to overcome writer's block, how to keep on writing through the arduous middle period of the work, and so on, but there is also the question of how you finish, what constitutes 'finished' and what you do with the piece when you think it is finished. This is not the issue of how you get it published or performed; that is something different and has been regularly covered in many books on creative writing.

As we have said, it is not easy when you have invested time, energy, imagination, hard work and money and brought your book or script to life to be faced with the fact of no longer writing it. You spend so much time with a piece of work, you breathe life into it, which itself is some sort of miracle, you set it up on its legs, see it take its first few steps, then get stronger and stronger till in the end it runs vigorously away from you into the waiting arms of the world, (to suffer acclaim or bitter rejection) that you can be lost without it.

Letting go is hard and letting go of your work without it being perfect can be a trap that we fall into out of fear of letting it go. The first thing to accept is that we never get a piece of work perfect. There are always flaws. We have to accept that and let it be so. Do not hold on to the idea of achieving perfection; it is simply a way of holding on to the work.

'Poems are not finished; they are abandoned.'

The only advice is to let the work go; let it have its life. Rejoice in that. Bask in the reflected glow of your child's glories. However hard it seems you must start again on something else; begin a new piece of work. Though it is hard you will begin to feel the pulse of new lives as they come too, and you can work with hope that life will burn as brightly in them as with the other characters in the world that you have left behind.

A sensible approach can be to have two or three things 'on the go' at the same time. If you are always writing something you have to worry less both about what you are leaving behind and how to start something new. If you get stuck with a piece of writing, or tired of it, or need to give it a rest, or say goodbye to it, you can switch to another project or begin writing another part of the same project. If you only have one thing on the go and are stuck on chapter three, then start writing chapter four, or five or six. Don't *allow* yourself to get stuck. But if you can have two or three ideas coming along at the same time you can avoid the questions 'how do I start? And how do I stop writing this piece?' These are the sorts of questions that can lead to a devil of procrastination.

 Key idea

Do not worry about finishing or starting. If you are always writing something, even if it is in your notebook, then you do not have that terrible thought of how to begin or how to end and let something go hanging over you.

Finding your voice

Finding your voice is about developing skills, experience and confidence. Ultimately, through practice, trial and error, and perhaps some imitation of others you will write the way you write and say the things you want to say. In the end your voice will not be like anybody else's voice, it will be like you. Your work will bear *your* fingerprints, the fingerprints of *your* particular interests, *your* particular approach, *your* particular slant on the world. Through writing your writing will get better and better and become recognisably *you*.

One of the biggest decisions you can take on the road to being a writer is to what field or genre you are going to write in. To a degree that dictates much else of what follows for you in your writing and in your career and also helps you 'find your voice'.

If you are going to write fiction then you need to study fiction publishing. You need to know that publishers like books in genres. Publishers need to know when they publish something if it is horror, romance, science fiction, literary fiction or whatever. It is the same in all the other areas. Film companies feel the same. It helps a film company to market the product to the right audience.

It is reasonable advice when you are starting out not to write across genres or mix genres, because such a book or film, though perhaps incredibly inventive and even ground-breaking might find it hard to find a publisher or producer. It is reasonable advice, but not absolute. The fact that publishers say they are always looking for the next new thing does not mean that they will be able to recognise it when it turns up.

Focus point

Deciding what field to write in is one of the major decisions of the writer. You might want to work in many fields; that is fine. But you need to be aware that different fields and genres have different demands and working within those fields means you must take on those demands because they shape and inform the work you will produce. Therefore study the field in which you want to write.

Snapshot

Check out some publishers, magazines, film companies, television production companies to see the kind of work they are making. If your work would not seem out of place on their lists, then this could be a place for you to try. It will take some commitment and detective work but is essential ground work for finding out who to send your work too. How to do it? Look at books, films, television shows you like; not this time for the story, the characters or the plot, but to see who produced them. The end credits of a film or television drama will always tell you, as will a programme accompanying a theatre performance. *The Radio Times* is still the best source for information about radio production and writing. When you have found the name of a producer or production company, use the Internet to locate their websites and see what they say about themselves. You can learn a lot that is useful to you the writer in such trawling.

Each field or genre has a special world with rules and characteristics; study them, learn them. Learn from what is produced and published. Learn, also, from other writers, from what writers say and from what they do; look at other writers' work. It is not only helpful to look at your own writing to help yourself to learn but essential to look at what other writers have done.

Writing for television, film or radio

How could you possibly conceive of writing for radio, film or television if you did not listen to the radio or watch TV or go to or rent movies? But it is not just listening and watching. We have all watched a lot of television, but that does not mean that we would write for television. If you want to write for television, film or radio you have to begin to watch and listen with a critical, writer's eye and ear. You have to start trying to work out what is going on and how it works.

 ## Key idea

If you want to know how something works, study it, unpick it; look at its nuts and bolts and then put it back together again. Writing in the style of others has a long history. It is an opportunity that can help you find your field and your own voice.

 ## Write

Take a drama, soap, sitcom or film you like and write an episode or series of scenes for the characters in that work. Write for them as you know them to be, with their foibles and weaknesses, using all their characteristics. Write as if you were writing a sequel or a spec script for the producers. Mimic the style of the original. Have fun.

(750 words)

 ## Edit

Lay out the first ten pages of a script for film, television, stage or radio, or the first 20 pages of a piece of fiction. Prepare it for publication following industry guidelines. Don't make your script fancy – make it clear and simple, following what is required.

If you want to write for all the script mediums, television, radio, stage or film, listen to the radio, watch television, go to the theatre, see television plays. But, do not only see: read. Read play scripts. Read film scripts. Read the script of a play then go and see it, and then, when you come home, read it again. That way you will begin to see how a play has been lifted off the page by actors and directors. You will see what a writer has had to leave in their script and what to leave out in order for the actors to bring it out. Do the same with a film script. Read the script; see the film, read the script again. We are back at what we said at the beginning of this book: *Read, Read, Read.* As we also stressed in the early chapters: keep a notebook. Write down ideas for films, snatches of dialogue; the lovely, amazing things that people say that may suggest a scene or an exchange, or even provide you with the core idea for a story.

Incidentally, if you are writing for production or publication you should not write anything for which there is not a market, or in radio or television terms, a slot. Specifically for radio, aside from listening to the radio and doing market research yourself, which of course you should do, you can find out what is being broadcast, the time, length and requirements of the different slots from the BBC. They have guidelines and commissioning details and the BBC writer's room website. Or you could write to the BBC and ask them for their guidelines and commissioning details. This applies to all the other fields too. Publishers have guidelines for the material they want and don't want. Contact the publisher or producer, or production company you are interested in; ask them for their guidelines or at least for what it is they are looking for and in what form they will accept a submission. If you can, and you are at the stage where you have something ready that you are completely satisfied with, try to find out who exactly to send it to.

Key idea

Research your market carefully, choose your target carefully. You only get one shot at it. Inundated as they are with the work of other experienced and inexperienced writers, agents, readers, editors, publishers and producers don't, *cannot*, give you a second chance.

Submitting your work

So, you have your manuscript written and ready to send. You have read it out loud, showed it to someone you trust, and prepared it properly. What do you do next? You *pause*.

Even if you think it is finished do not rush to press 'send' on your computer or to put your manuscript into an envelope. Instead, put the work aside and look at it again after a gap of time. This gap might be a few weeks it might be a couple of months, or even longer; the important thing is to let the writing settle and to give yourself enough time to come back to it with more distance and the chance to be objective about it; this helps you to see if you have got the best words down in the best order.

Even with a piece of work you are satisfied with, there is always something you can look at again and try to improve and there is no substitute to separating yourself from a piece of creative work and going back to it later with a clearer, fresher eye. At that time you will see new possibilities, and faults will stand out more clearly. The passing of time also allows you to be more emotionally distanced from it and therefore less prone to want to keep every word. You can see the faults and you also have the desire to do something about them.

Focus point

Don't rush something off because you are sick of it and cannot see how to do anymore work on it. Leave it and come back to it later.

Only when you are completely happy with it, get it ready to send to a publisher, agent or producer. But remember, even when you have something good to sell there is no guarantee anyone will buy, so be prepared for disappointment.

 Catherine Ryan

'There is an element of good fortune involved in getting your story to the right editor on the right day. Learn your market well, and accept that your odds are better here than in the lottery – but not by much.'

You can help your odds by preparing properly. Prepare your manuscript. Follow the guidelines for the area you want to work in. Contact publishers, producers, check out industry accepted standards, follow the rules of presentation.

Also, buy some essential books. One book cannot possibly give you everything. *This* book has been about your writing. It has hopefully been of value but you should also get the most recent copy of the *Writers' & Artists' Yearbook*. It is the indispensable guide to publishing in all fields; a *must* for the professional and budding writer. Get it and dip into it. You will be astonished at the variety of fields in which you can write and the variety of advice on differing fields. Read and take note of the excellent advice on how to prepare your manuscript, how to write a synopsis, how to find the right agent or publisher and how to approach them. There is also a list of other books at the end of this book which will help you study and understand the world of production and publication further.

 Snapshot

Take a piece of work you believe is finished. Find an agent you hope will be interested in it by studying the *Writers' and Artists' Yearbook* or searching online. If you become interested in an agent or publisher, read their website and pay attention to what *they* say about their requirements, their authors and how they like to be approached. Write a query letter to the agent. Make it short, concise and to the point. Make it professional.

A typical letter will open with a greeting – not Dear Sir or Madam, but to a named individual. (You will have done your research.)

When writing your letter, use the following guidelines:

• Begin the body of the letter with a line or two introducing your short story, script or novel, explaining why you have contacted this particular agent, publisher or production company. Perhaps you have been referred by a friend or perhaps they handle work similar to your own. (Show that you have thought about your approach and done your research.)

• Make a brief pitch for your manuscript; a short, intriguing paragraph is quite enough. (And difficult to write.)

- Add a little about yourself; include relevant writing credits, or experience or expertise relevant to the work. (Don't worry if you don't have any of these.)
- Finish your query letter by stating you are enclosing a stamped addressed envelope either for return of the manuscript, or for a reply. If you don't want the manuscript back say so, but provide a small envelope with postage for a reply. Even in these days of electronic mail it is sensible to do so.)

And when they answer positively, asking to see your work, when you come to sending work off, don't over-seal the envelope. Be polite in your entire approach. Make it *all* easy for the person you are sending it to.

Snapshot

Revise your CV if you have one. If you don't have one, try putting one together. If you have written and published many works, obviously include them, together with extracts from any reviews. If you are just starting out and have nothing for a writer's CV, then say so. Do not lie to an agent or publisher; save that for your creative writing.

Finally, here are a few other things you should do:
- It is essential to talk to other writers you know or can get to meet. Find out what they do about publishing or production.
- Talk to other people in the industry, make contacts, network. You can do this by finding a way to join the writing community.
- Investigate your local as well as national links. It is better not to rush to join writers organizations such as the Society of Authors (SOA) or the Writer's Guild of Great Britain at first but by all means check their membership requirements.
- The Writer's Guild and SOA organize events, if you are a member you can attend and they are a great way to meet other writers and talk to people in the industry.
- You might be better, initially, to join a writers' group in your area.
- Your local library, which will have lists of local societies, will help you find one.

Summary

In spite of the warnings and difficulties, work does break through; whether you are writing in an accepted conventional, new or unusual way, don't give up. Keep trying; work hard and you will find your voice and your market.

William Styron

'The writer's duty is to keep on writing.'

Creative writing is a mix of the technical and the imaginative; inspiration in the cradle of technique and technique infused with inspiration. Do not forget either; keep practising both and enjoy the process. Ultimately you must write for the pleasure it gives you.

 ## Cyril Connolly

'Better to write for yourself and have no public, than to write for the public and have no self.'

Truly, the only secret to writing is to write as well as you can, commit yourself to it and be lucky. No one can teach you that.

Useful contacts

The Alliance of Independent Authors

(A professional association of self-publishing writers and advisors)
Free Word Centre
60 Farringdon Road
London EC1R 3GA
Email: info@allianceindependentauthors.org
Website: http://allianceindependentauthors.org

Arts Council England

There are nine regional offices each with a Literature Officer. Find the one for your area. Phone for details.
Tel: 0161 934 4317
Website: www.artscouncil.org.uk

Arts Council of Wales

Bute Place
Cardiff CF10 5AL
Tel: 03301 242733
Website: www.arts.wales

Arts Council of Northern Ireland

1 The Sidings
Antrim Road
Lisburn BT28 3AJ
Tel: +44 (28) 92623555
Website: info@artscouncil-ni.org

Creative Scotland

Waverley Gate
2 - 4 Waterloo Place
Edinburgh
EH1 3EG
Tel: 0345 603 6000
Email: enquiries@creativescotland.com

The Arvon Foundation

Free Word Centre
60 Farringdon Road
London
EC1R 3GA
Tel: 020 7324 2554
Website: https://www.arvon.org

BBC Writersroom

Advice and contacts for potential script writers
Website: http://www.bbc.co.uk/writersroom

Euroscript

London based and offers a range of courses on all aspects of writing screenplays.
Email: enquiries@euroscript.co.uk

The Literary Consultancy Ltd

Free Word Centre
60 Farringdon Road
London EC1R 3GA
Tel: 020 7324 2563
Email: info@literaryconsultancy.co.uk
Website: www.literaryconsultancy.co.uk

The Poetry Society

22 Betterton Street
London WC2H 9BX
Tel: 0207 420 9880
Email: info@poetrysociety.org.uk
Website: www.poetrysociety.org.uk

Society of Authors

24 Bedford Row
Holborn
London WC1R 4EH
0207 373 6642
Email: info@societyofauthors.org
Website: www.societyofauthors.org

The Future Bookshelf

Website: https://thefuturebookshelf.co.uk/

Writer's Guild of Great Britain

134 Tooley Street
London SE1 2TU
Tel: 020 7833 0777
Email: admin@writersguild.org.uk
Website: www.writersguild.org.uk

Further reading

Writing and reference

Hoffmann, A. *Research for Writers* (London: Writing Handbooks, 1999) – a standard work on research

Roget's Thesaurus (Penguin 2003) – indispensable

Stillman, F. *The Poet's Manual* (Thames & Hudson, 2000) – essential for any poet. Contains examples of poetic forms as well as a rhyming dictionary

Brande, D. *Becoming a Writer* (Macmillan, 1996) – deals with technical matters but focuses on the way to become a writer, developing writing habits and discipline, etc.

Sykes, C. *The Writer's Source Book* (Teach Yourself, 2011) – full of exercises for finding characters

Sykes, C. *How to Craft a Great Story* (Teach Yourself, 2013) – concentrates on story structure and contains many exercises on building plots and crafting stories

Poetry

Baldwin, M. *The Way to Write Poetry* (Elm Tree Books, 1982) – out of print, but well worth trying to get hold of. Probably aimed more at someone on the way than just starting out, but contains a lot of clear guidance to writing poems

Chisholm, A. *The Craft of Writing Poetry* (Allison & Busby, 1998) – treats poetry as a craft and takes you through the process of writing step by step

Sansom, P. *Writing Poems* (Bloodaxe Books, 1994) – based on the belief that close reading comes before writing, this book examines the work of many established poets before discussing the why and how of writing poems.

Fiction

Dibell, A., Scott Card, O., and Turco, L. *How to Write a Million* (Robinson, 1995) – this book and its companion volume, *More about …*, is basically six books in one. Put together, they cover all the main aspects of fiction writing

Doubtfire, D. *The Craft of Novel-Writing* (Allison and Busby, 1998) – a classic, more recently updated

Frey, J.N. *How to Write a Damn Good Novel* (Papermac, 1987) – contains good ideas on character and story development

Wood, M., Reed, K., and Bickham, J.M. *More about How to Write a Million* (Robinson, 1996) – companion to the one listed above

Scriptwriting

Field, S. *The Definitive Guide to Screenwriting* (Ebury Press 2003) – contains three books that cover Field's work on the importance of plot points in film story structure

Goldman, W. *Adventures in the Screen Trade* (Abacus, 1996) – contains much anecdotal material about writing in Hollywood and industry insights

Mackendrick, A. *On Film Making* (Faber & Faber, 2004) – an excellent book by a director who became a screenwriting tutor. Very practical and insightful

McKee, R. *Story* (Methuen, 1997) – an important and thorough book on story from a screenwriting guru. Needs close reading

Parker, P. *The Art & Science of Screenwriting* (Intellect Books, 2006) – comprehensive and accessible; good for the basics as it takes you through the process of writing screenplays

Vogler, C. *The Writer's Journey* (Michael Wiese, 1992) – excellent on showing the influence of archetypes and mythology on shape, structure and content in Hollywood films

Getting published

Blake, C. *From Pitch to Publication* (Macmillan, 1999) – written by a top agent, full of useful advice and insights about what an agent and publisher are looking for. Probably most useful to you if you are very serious about being published

Curran, S. *Get Your Book Published* (Thorsons, 1999) – a good guide, with practical advice and strategies to help you approach the right people in the right way

Lapworth, K. *Get Your Book Published* (Teach Yourself, 2014) – takes you through the pitfalls of publishing, both by others and by yourself

Legat, M. *Writing for Pleasure and Profit* (Hale, 1993) – Michael Legat has a lot of good things to say on the subject of writing and selling it. It is still relevant today. There are two more books listed below.

Legat, M. *The Nuts and Bolts of Writing* (Hale, 1989)

Legat, M. *An Author's Guide to Publishing* (Hale, 1991)

Writers' & Artists' Yearbook (London: A & C Black, 2014) – an essential recourse; a must for all serious writers

References

Ackerman, D. *A Natural History of the Senses* (Phoenix, 1996)

Ayckbourn, A. *The Crafty Art of Playmaking* (Faber & Faber, 2002)

Braine, J. *How to Write a Novel* (Methuen, 1974)

Browne, R. and King, D. *Self-editing for Fiction Writers* (Quill, 2001)

Davis, R. *Writing Dialogue for Scripts* (A & C Black, 2000)

Edgar-Hunt, R. et al. *Screenwriting* (AVA Publishing, SA, 2009)

Egri, L. *The Art of Dramatic Writing* (Touchstone, 1960)

Fairfax, J., and Moat, J. *The Way to Write* (Elm Tree Books, 1981)

Forster, E.M. *Aspects of the Novel* (Penguin Books, 2000)

King, S. *On Writing* (Hodder Paperbacks, 2012)

Goldman, W. *Which Lie Did I Tell?* (Bloomsbury, 2001)

Griffiths, S. *How Plays Are Made* (Heinemann, 1982)

Grove, C., and Wyatt, S. *So You Want to Write Radio Drama?* (Nick Hern Books, 2013)

Haydn Evans, C. *Writing for Radio* (Allison & Busby, 1991)

McInerney, V. *Writing for Radio* (Manchester University Press, 2001)

McClanahan, R. *Word Painting* (Writer's Digest Books,1999)

Newman, J., et al. *The Writer's Workbook* (Bloomsbury, 2004)

Singleton, J., and Luckhurst, M. *The Creative Writing Handbook* (Macmillan, 1996)

Stein, S. *Solutions for Writers* (Souvenir Press, 1995)

Strunk, W., and White, E.B. *The Elements of Style* (Allyn and Bacon, 1999)

Tobias, R.B. *20 Master Plots* (Writer's Digest Books, 1993)

Tuttle, L. *Writing Fantasy & Science Fiction* (A & C Black, 2005)

Walker, K. *Writing Romantic Fiction* (Straightforward Guides, 2002)

Weinman, I. *How to Write Great Dialogue* (Teach Yourself Books, 2012)

Wood, M. *Description* (Writer's Digest Books, 1995)

Writers' and Artists' Yearbook (A & C Black, 2014)

Index